Business and Dynamic Change

The Arrival of *Business Architecture*

BPM Handbook Series

Published in association with the
Workflow Management Coalition

Workflow Management Coalition

21 Years of Thought-Process Leadership

Future Strategies Inc., Book Division
Lighthouse Point, Florida

Business and Dynamic Change:
The Arrival of Business Architecture

Published by Future Strategies Inc., Book Division

3640 North Federal Highway B3
Lighthouse Point FL 33064 USA
+1 954.782.3376 fax +1 954.719.3746
www.FutStrat.com; books@FutStrat.com

Publisher's Cataloging-in-Publication Data

ISBN: 9780986321429

Library of Congress Control Number: 2015942112

Business and Dynamic Change: The Arrival of Business Architecture

p. cm.

Includes bibliographical references, appendices and index.

1. Business Architecture. 2. Intelligent Systems. 3. Enterprise Architecture. 4. Business Intelligence. 5. Business Process Technology. 6. Adaptive Case Management. 7. Business Capability. 8. Business Transformation 10. Business Reengineering

/Frank Kowalkowski, Gilbert Laware, Brian Seitz, William Ulrich, Michael Poulin, Michael Blaha *et al* (authors)

/Layna Fischer (editor)

/Keith D. Swenson (foreword)

Foreword

"Things work better when they work together, on purpose." - Tom Graves[1]

In his book "A Timeless Way of Building,"[2] Christopher Alexander reminds us that architecture should be much more than a static set of blueprints telling us how to build something. Good architectures leverage principles that allow a space to define itself, like the way that a town forms by itself. The world does not stand still, so your vision of the business must not be static.

One might be tempted to ask why we don't simply aim to get it right the first time. The reality is that what is right *today*, may not be right *tomorrow*, and that is why this book is about business and dynamic change. A blueprint tells you how something is arranged now, but does not guide you in responding to future stresses.

The chapters in this book are from visionaries who see the need for business leaders to define their organizations to be agile and robust in the face of external changes. The goal is to build something knowing that it will be changed; so that you have no need to go back to the metaphorical drawing board for every market condition change.

Consider what it means to say that the business will adapt in the face of external changes. The business architecture is not simply a model that specifies how to run the business for now and the next few years. The people making the architecture cannot know the pressures that will be faced. Instead, it must support leaders and executives within the organization to make consistently good decisions on how to adapt their practices. The architecture is not a plan that anticipates all the decisions; instead it embodies a set of core guiding principles that enable decision making.

Understand that the term "business" used this way is not limited to for-profit enterprises but includes all forms of organizations that have a strategic need to accomplish goals. Pragmatically speaking, business architecture is the conceptual understanding that people have on *why* particular choices were made in forming the organization in a particular way.

"Business architecture guides future changes to the business. Architecture is a proximate answer to the question: 'Why is our organization structured this way?' Knowledge of those choices will guide the organization in how it responds to external pressures."[3] More than a simple description of the organization at a high level, it is an understanding of the choices that were made, and the reasons that an organization was structured in a particular way.

As you explore these points of view, be mindful of the relationship between information systems and human systems. Should we design the business around the constraints of information systems, or should the design remain free of information systems at this level, and introduce them only as needed

---

[1] Tom Graves, Tetradian

[2] Christopher Alexander, "The timeless way of building," volume 1, Oxford University Press, 1979.

[3] From Chapter 5 of Keith D Swenson, Jim Farris, "When Thinking Matters in the Workplace: How Executives and Leaders of Knowledge Work Teams can Innovate with Case Management," Purple Hills Books, Feb 2015

in the operational model. There is no doubt that information technology is important in any organization today, but is it really the starting point for strategic design? Some feel that information architecture done too well results in something that loses the most important audience: the actual workers in the organization. Do workers exist to support the information infrastructure of the business, or does the information infrastructure exist to support the workers of the business?

Another topic to pay close attention to is that of *level*. The entire business must work together in some sense to be successful, and so the business architecture must, in that same sense, encompass the entire organization. At the same time, it must not be so voluminous that decision-makers are too overwhelmed to leverage it effectively. Several chapters here grapple with how to precisely define the boundary between business architecture and executional or operational architecture.

There has been a sharp rise in interest in this deep and rich subject in recent months. The Workflow Management Coalitions (WfMC) has put together the *Business Architecture Working Group* with participation by a number of the luminaries represented in this book. The Business Architecture Guild and some other groups are represented as well. It is a topic that is both very important, and at the same time very hard to characterize precisely.

New terminology is being invented so that a broader conversation can be carried into the public without misinterpretation. There is no question that this is the defining moment for Business Architecture and these contributions are from the self-same people who are bringing about this very important development.

Keith D. Swenson
WfMC Chair and Vice President, Fujitsu America

Table of Contents

Part 3: Appendices

Introduction

Frank F. Kowalkowski, Knowledge Consultants, Inc., and Gil Laware, Information By Design, USA

The key question is straight-forward; "What do I need in order to put together an organization to do something?"

Related to that is; "How can I change an existing organization to do something new or different?"

This important book presents a complete approach to **business architecture** and the *how-to* and *why-to* of architecting an enterprise. Top industry practitioners, inventors and thought-leaders gather here to present valuable insights into the emerging understanding of the importance of business architecture as a critical component of enterprise architecture.

Some Background

Simply stated, architecture is a structure that exists for some purpose that is represented by a set of components and their relationships to each other. In this case, we are interested in how this idea applies to structure of organizations of all types: governments, non-profits, for profit, educational and others.

Architecture as applied to organizations already has a long and substantial history. Much of it appears after World War II and is based on developments in conducting the war. Techniques for architecture have come from many disciplines especially business modeling and were applied individually to organizations. Each of these techniques was a response to different requirements in managing organizations.

To respond to these needs and requirement, frameworks, methodologies and bodies of knowledge emerged. Each of these approaches had specific outputs and outcomes that solved a problem or group of problems in an organization. This actually created an issue; many approaches and focal points had little or no integration of views.

The first seriously-organized approach to architecture dealt with reliably constructing buildings. These ideas and methods are several thousand years old. They have been refined over many generations of use with the evolutionary development of new technologies and materials. The good news is that they provide a template of sorts for doing *business architecture*.

In the last 30 years or so, the architecture approach within organizations has been applied to constructing reliable information systems. Challenges included projects were out of control, over budget, lacking in key functionality and more such as promised delivery schedules. To a large degree, the construction of information systems (a business need) has been met through the use of the enterprise architecture concept and related methodologies.

The current situation

Now we are at the point of applying these ideas to architecting organizations as a whole. Many parallel efforts have evolved and are currently in use. As a result, there is a need to make some sense out of the jungle of ideas, concepts and approaches to architecture applied to organizations.

This book will help you understand your options and how to relate them to your own organization.

Architecture of an organization can be divided into different aspects that focus on particular needs or purpose, for example:

- Strategic needs or operational needs.
- Important external content with specific time horizon where change is the issue and dynamics of the organization play a critical role.

This is much like a normal building architecture that differs if the building is a house, industrial structure or an office structure. The purpose determines what components, relationships and dynamics are in effect at certain points in time.

The book addresses these issues in two main sections:

Part One – The Big Picture of Architecture

Getting your arms (and your head) around the whole architecture space is not an easy task. These chapters introduce several variations with a lot of commonality on how to look at business architecture. Each of these has been used with success. With over 65 management models today and as many methodologies and analytical approaches, the big picture is really a work in progress. As the ideas are sorted out and worked into viable frameworks for representing an organization the value of business architecture efforts will greatly increase.

Part Two – Where the Rubber Meets the Road

Sometimes you need to get into the gritty details of the architecture work. This section introduces some specific uses and applications of business architecture concepts. Some are enterprise-wide and some are specific to certain aspects of the architecture. In each case there is value in applying the architecture concepts described, supported by the writers' rationale and drivers behind the efforts.

Who should read this book?

This book will stimulate thinking about a more complete approach to business architecture. As such, it is imperative reading for executives, managers, business analysts, and IT professionals that require an understanding of the structural relationships of the components of an enterprise.

Acknowledgements:

The publishers acknowledge with thanks the concepts and guidance for this book provided by Frank Kowalkowski and Gilbert Laware.

Formed under the auspices of WfMC.org, the members of the newly-formed **Business Architecture Working Group** chaired by Keith Swenson are also active contributors.

Business and Dynamic Change
The Arrival of Business Architecture

Part One – The Big Picture of Architecture

Getting your arms (and your head) around the whole architecture space is not an easy task. These chapters introduce several variations with a lot of commonality on how to look at business architecture. Each of these has been used with success. With over 65 management models today and as many methodologies and analytical approaches, the big picture is really a work in progress. As the ideas are sorted out and worked into viable frameworks for representing an organization the value of business architecture efforts will greatly increase.

BUSINESS ARCHITECTURE – INFORMATION NECESSITY

Michael G. Miller, HSBC Global United States

Architecture as described by Mr. Miller covers the utility of a structure collectively to all interested parties by showing the relationships among all its component parts. The intent of architecture is and was to provide utility to people and parties with a collective understanding of the utility being provided to the customer *today* and for the foreseeable *future* from each individual builder's perspective. By ensuring that the objects of interest to business show up in both the business architecture (which describes a business's *behavior*) and the information architecture (which describes a business's *structure*), we can better assure the completeness and accuracy of both models. When business architecture is explicitly linked to the information architecture, we can better serve the enterprise in a timely manner against the data tsunami which is occurring as a result of all the new technologies (i.e. Big Data, Cloud, Mobile, etc.) coming into play.

BUSINESS ARCHITECTURE: SETTING THE RECORD STRAIGHT

William Ulrich, TSG, Inc., USA, Whynde Kuehn, S2E Consulting Inc., USA

Mr. Ulrich and Ms. Kuehn describe a number of fundamental business architecture concepts. They include an overview, beneficiaries, common myths, core and extended perspectives, interdisciplinary alignment, governance, getting started, and a vision for the future Architecture. The Future Architecture is used to describe transitioning from a current environment to a future. Business Architecture covers a number of core "domain" categories that a business does (capability); the vocabulary it uses (information); how a business is organized (organization); and how a business delivers value to key stakeholders (value stream). As such, they believe that business architecture will become a critical, indispensable discipline in the business community.

MAKING SENSE OUT OF THE ARCHITECTURE JUNGLE

Frank F. Kowalkowski, Knowledge Consultants, Inc., USA

Mr. Kowalkowski maintains that a useful way to partition the architecture space is to have four perspectives. Starting with the external landscape that drives change in an enterprise, the strategic view that is the response to that change, the operational view that structures the enterprise and the execution view that carries out the strategy. Using these 4 perspectives, architectures are linked and related using quantitative and qualitative analytics to assess responses to external influences that cascade across the architectures and impact realization. The focus in this paper is on the first two architecture perspectives with some detail on how they are represented. This approach provides value at the strategy level for change such as merger, acquisition, consolidation, divestiture and disposal of enterprise parts.

Converting Decision-to-Action

Gil Laware, Information By Design, USA

Mr. Laware relates how architecture in general is used to describe transitioning from a current environment to a future environment by examining four architecture-based areas. Each are seemingly independent but are mapped to each other to enable the transformational change. These mappings help to dynamically assess and evaluate the solution alternatives available. Mr. Laware proposes these managed architectures become a new management tool as they influence the decisions about the desired future organizational / enterprise environment.

Design and Reengineering of Business: An Engineering Approach

Brian K Seitz, Intellectual Arbitrage Group, USA

Mr. Seitz has an approach that enables business leaders and IT professionals to work as a common group to design the business with common and popular management discipline methods such as Business Model Canvas, BPMN, and others to yield models which visualize the needed attributes of a business that affect its capabilities and performance. He is using this approach to re-engineer his employer's internal value stream with linkages between management disciplines and tools.

Building a Foundation for Business Architecture

Martin Klubeck, Michael Langthorne, Donald Padgett

Messrs. Klubeck, Langthorne and Padgett describe the underlying models that are interlinked: Business Architecture (What), Business Model (How), and Key Influencers (Why). They postulate that organizations need to embrace these models and methods for exploring and understanding the critical parts of the functioning organization. They state that "what a business does, how it does it and how it generates value" cannot be understood without an inclusive examination of all of the interrelationships of all of its parts.

How Business Architecture Enables Agility in a Dynamic Market

Dr Michael Poulin, Clingstone Ltd., UK

Business Architecture as described by Dr. Poulin arms an organization with models, services, and solutions that reflect external changes in the most flexible manner, which allows an organization to reach agility with the dynamics and even form competitive advantages in the market. He outlines 10 major principles that a successful Business Architecture should follow. It is a mechanism that links changes in the dynamic market with corporate strategy and a means of realization of this strategy. Nowadays, the ability to change quickly is the key to success.

Business Architecture: Information Necessity

Michael G. Miller, HSBC Global United States

ABSTRACT

Business Architecture is emerging from its origin as a component of Information Technology (IT) Enterprise Architecture to a necessity for the business to rapidly respond to change. This chapter discusses how one can combine business architecture and information architecture efforts to provide seamless alignment of the business and IT. This chapter will identify an approach to concurrently produce your business architecture and information architecture. This approach will explain how business and IT alignment can be assured through the synchronization of the business and information architectures and maintained over time through information audits. It will demonstrate how the *business architecture* can ensure *information architecture* accuracy and completeness. It will likewise demonstrate how the *information architecture* can assure *business architecture* accuracy and completeness.

INTRODUCTION

"Todd Gross, TV Meteorologist: Look, look at this. We got Hurricane Grace moving north off the Atlantic seaboard. Huge... getting massive. Two, this low south of Sable Island, ready to explode. Look at this. Three, a fresh cold front swooping down from Canada. But it's caught a ride on the jet stream... and is motoring hell-bent towards the Atlantic. What if Hurricane Grace runs smack into it? Add to the scenario this baby off Sable Island, scrounging for energy. She'll start feeding off both the Canadian cold front... and Hurricane Grace. You could be a meteorologist all your life... and never see something like this. It would be a disaster of epic proportions. It would be... the perfect storm."[1]

To paraphrase the movie *The Perfect Storm*, "Look, look at this. We got Big Data moving into businesses. Huge...getting massive. Two, the emergence of Mobile Technology, ready to explode. Three Cloud Computing is swooping into the picture, along with Social Computing and the Internet of Things as well as the Digitization of everything. You could be a technologist all your life...and never see something like this. It could be a disaster of epic proportions. It could be... the perfect data storm."

This is the digital universe. It is growing 40 percent a year into the next decade, expanding to include not only the increasing number of people and enterprises doing everything online, but also all the "things" – smart devices – connected to the Internet, unleashing a new wave of opportunities for businesses and people around the world.

Like the physical universe, the digital universe is large; by 2020 containing nearly as many digital bits as there are stars in the universe. It is doubling in size every two years, and by 2020 the digital universe – the data we create and copy annually – will reach 44 zettabytes, or 44 trillion gigabytes.[2]

The digital universe will continue to expand at a rapid clip and flood already saturated infrastructures and the people that manage them. The Internet of Things will add new levels of complexity – and opportunity – on top of what Big Data has offered in just the last three years. The bright stars of the digital universe of tomorrow will be the enterprises that will ride the data flood to new heights of productivity and prosperity.[3]

However the digital universe may actually be an obstacle for companies trying to become data-driven. There is too much information, it is too diverse, and it is too effervescent.[4]

Many companies are trying to wrestle with, from the business side, unprecedented volumes, variety and velocity of data, entering the business externally as well as emerging internally from new sources, such as signaling devices and social media. At the same time, new data requirements are arising for even more data for better decision-making. IT is struggling to employ new technologies, such as Big Data, Cloud Technology and Mobile devices, while maintaining data privacy and security in this increasingly complex technology environment.

First, business leaders must deploy new technologies and then prepare for a potential revolution in the collection and measurement of information. More important, the entire organization must adapt a new philosophy about how decisions are made, if the real value of big data is to be realized.[5]

The technologies are new and in some cases exotic... The cultural challenges are enormous, and, of course, privacy concerns are only going to become more significant. But the underlying trends, both in the technology and in the business payoff, are unmistakable.

The evidence is clear: Data-driven decisions tend to be better decisions. Leaders will either embrace this fact or be replaced by others who do.[6]

While there is much talk of businesses becoming data-centric going forward; there is also a call for businesses to streamline existing business processes simultaneously to lower costs, reduce complexity and to speed products and services delivery to the customer. These seems, at first glance, to be conflicting missions for the enterprise and if undertaken separately, as often is the case, missions that would compete for resources and clash. But that need not be the case. Rather than attempt to do the initiatives to separately and many times sequentially, these efforts can both be accomplished if done simultaneously. In this case, it will speed the work of both efforts as well as result in faster initiatives of higher quality.

CURRENT STATE OF BUSINESS

Business, Data and the Tower of Babel

"And they said, "Come, let us build ourselves a city, and a tower whose top is in the heavens; let us make a name for ourselves, lest we be scattered abroad over the face of the whole earth.

"But the Lord came down to see the city and the tower which the sons of men had built.

"And the Lord said, 'Indeed the people are one and they all have one language, and this is what they begin to do; now nothing that they propose to do will be withheld from them. Come, let Us go down and there confuse their language, that they may not understand one another's speech.'

"So the Lord scattered them abroad from there over the face of all the earth, and they ceased building the city.

"Therefore its name is called Babel, because there the Lord confused the language of all the earth; and from there the Lord scattered them abroad over the face of all the earth."[7]

Businesses often act like the people of the Tower of Babel, each party absorbed with their own projects, be it a business streamlining initiative, a data-centric initiative or another project with little concern, understanding of other efforts going on across the enterprise nor perspective as to their mutual or conflicting purposes. Programs and projects often lack a uniformity of purpose. This occurs often because the efforts are bottom-up, created to satisfy a particular problem or a singular opportunity within a particular function, process or business area.

This results in development of silos of business functionality and/or silos of information, which have little or no connection to other projects or programs in the enterprise. Efforts are often developed creating their own terminology or language which may serve the purpose of the individual project or program, but has little or no connection to the language or terminology used in other projects and programs. This *Tower of Babel* in the enterprise requires layers of translation among the projects and programs to resolve. Unanticipated overhead costs emerge each time there is a change which impacts multiple projects or programs. This increasing complexity causes a slowdown in the enterprise's ability to respond quickly to change.

Sisyphus and Bottom-up Architecture

As a punishment for his trickery, King Sisyphus was made to endlessly roll a huge boulder up a steep hill. The maddening nature of the punishment for King Sisyphus was due to his hubristic belief that his cleverness surpassed that of Zeus himself. Zeus accordingly displayed his own cleverness by enchanting the boulder into rolling away from King Sisyphus before he reached the top which ended up consigning Sisyphus to an eternity of useless efforts and unending frustration. Thus pointless or interminable activities are sometimes described as Sisyphean.[8]

Many development efforts within IT departments are built from the bottom up. Each project or programs begins individually without a clear understanding or holistic view of how the enterprise operates (an enterprise wide business architecture) nor a holistic view of what information is delivered or data required of the enterprise as a whole (an information and data architecture). In an attempt to unify or transform these individual efforts of the enterprise a call to standardize various components of the projects and programs occurs. This starts with a call to standardize the names and definitions of the entities (things) used within projects and programs. The standardization efforts begin at the bottom of the enterprise, and much like Sisyphus continually try to push their efforts further up the enterprise hill and like Sisyphus, their efforts often take two steps forward and fall one or more steps back.

Architecture and the Purpose of Architecture

Figure 1: Burj Kalifa, Dubai, UAE. Source: Author – Michael G. Miller

This is the Burj Kalifa, in Dubai, UAE, at present, the tallest building in the world with a height of 2,722 feet or 829.8m. This is often what people think about when they think of architecture; that architecture is all about the construction of tall buildings. But architecture began with the building of caves. The intent of architecture is and was to provide utility to people and parties with a collective understanding of the utility being provided to the customer for today and for the foreseeable future from each individual builder's perspective.

No one would consider building the Burj Kalifa or any large building without a series of models or blueprints of the various perspectives of the individual construction efforts combined together, such as the heating and ventilation blueprints, the electrical blueprints and the plumbing blueprints. Each blueprint needs to be combined and integrated in order to deliver the final design. Buildings require blueprints or architecture, airplanes require blueprints, and an automobile's construction requires blueprints. The construction of virtually every product requires blueprints or architectures. Why should an enterprise operate any differently?

NIST Enterprise Architecture Model

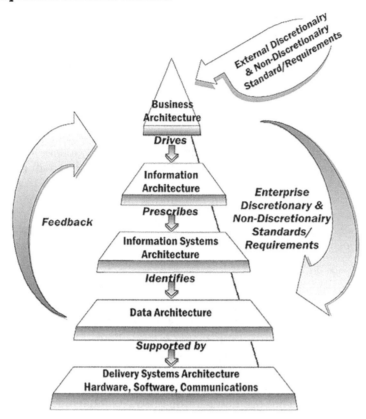

Figure 2: NIST (National Institute of Standards and Technology) Enterprise Architecture Model [9]

The NIST Enterprise Architecture Model (Figure 2) outlines the series of blueprints or architectures necessary to develop systems. Traditional IT system architecture often begins with the development of the hardware, software and communications architectures because when all you have is a hammer everything looks like a nail.

Technologists begin here because this is what they know. Like Sisyphus, they push the rock of development uphill, often again, taking two steps forward and falling one or more steps back. Without beginning with a business architecture, they lack the ability to view the end point of their efforts. Compromise occurs as they make assumptions of what business functionality they are really attempting to automate. In the meantime, while the information systems are being developed, the business requirement and thus the business architecture changes. When the information system is finally completed sometime later, the system fails to meet the present business requirements.

FUTURE STATE OF BUSINESS

Business Architecture and Information Architecture

"Always design a thing by considering it in its next larger context- a chair in a room, a room in a house, a house in an environment, an environment in a city plan." Eliel Saarinen [10]

Top-Down Business Architecture and Information Architecture

When all you have is a hammer, all the problems start to look like nails. When all you have are technologists, all the problems start to look like technology problems. What is happening is that we are, at last, realizing that while there are many nails (and many technologies), there are also many non-nails that cannot be solved with a hammer or technologists.

BUSINESS ARCHITECTURE

Business Architecture is where the architecture efforts of the enterprise should begin, top-down, rather than with the design of the hardware, software and communications architectures. Without a clearly-articulated holistic view of the business, as manifested by the business architecture, any development of architectures beneath the business architecture must make assumptions as to the business's current actual requirements. This results in architectures (delivery systems architecture, data architecture, information systems architecture, and information architecture), which fail to align to or meet the requirements of the business as manifested through the business architecture.

INFORMATION ARCHITECTURE

Information Architecture is the design of the information which is required by the business and is also the deliverable(s) (finished goods) of the Information Systems as manifested in the Information Systems Architecture.

The Information Architecture is the design of the specific information outputs to be delivered by the information systems to satisfy the information needs of the business. Lacking a clear holistic view of the business as defined by the business architecture, any attempt at an information architecture must make assumptions as to the true information requirements of the business. This results in the delivery of information systems which miss the mark in satisfying all the information requirements of the business.

Even if holistic (covering the breadth of the enterprise) business architecture and a holistic information architecture are developed in a sequential fashion as is traditionally done currently, the speed at which business is changes results in an architecture gap by the time the two efforts are completed. A better approach to architecture development is necessary in order to satisfy a rapidly changing business. Perhaps, examining how we manage other assets of the business, specifically money, can provide us with a better way to manage the information assets of the business.

Pacioli and Double Entry Accounting System

Figure 3: Portrait Luca Pacioli – Father of Accounting and Bookkeeping (1495) 11

Luca Pacioli, a Franciscan friar, is commonly known as the Father of Accounting. His book, 'Summa de arithmetica, geometria. Proportioni et proportionalita,' published in 1494, was a summary of all known mathematics, at this time and included a description of a bookkeeping method, known as the double-entry accounting system, which survives to this day.

Double-entry accounting can be applied to the development of enterprise architecture as well. If we undertake the development of both the business architecture and the information architecture simultaneously, we can apply the same technique by making sure that as we develop business architecture models such as a functional decomposition, in a verb-object format (for example, purchase raw materials, develop product, promote product, and receive product orders) and simultaneously develop the information architecture, that no object can be entered into one of the two architectures without also being entered into the other architecture.

By ensuring that the objects of interest to business show up in both the business architecture (which describes a business's *behavior*) and the information architecture (which describes a business's *structure*), we can better assure the completeness and accuracy of both models. In this way, we can operate the two models, in much the same way as Pacioli's double-entry accounting system operates to ensure the completeness of both of the architectures (business architecture and information architecture).

Conclusions

"Most transformation programs satisfy themselves with shifting the same old furniture about in the same old room. Some seek to throw some of the furniture away. But real transformation requires that we redesign the room itself. Perhaps even blow up the old room. It requires that we change the thinking behind our thinking — literally, that we learn to rewire our corporate brains." Danah Zohar (1997) [12]

Architecture in general is used to describe the utility of a structure collectively to all interested parties by showing the relationships among all its components.

Enterprise Architecture is used to describe the utility of an enterprise collectively to all interested parties, by showing the relationships among all its components (business architecture, information architecture, information systems architecture, data architecture, and the delivery systems architecture).

By starting at the top of the pyramid of enterprise architecture (i.e. the NIST Enterprise Architecture Model) with the business architecture and the information architecture simultaneously developed, we can better serve the needs of the business in a more timely fashion. By applying the simple double-entry bookkeeping method to the objects of the enterprise we can better ensure the completeness of both models and thus their quality and completeness to the enterprise.

Starting at the top of the enterprise, with the business architecture first, in explicably linked to the information architecture, we can better serve the enterprise in a timely manner against the data tsunami which is occurring as a result of all the new technologies (i.e. Big Data, Cloud, Mobile, etc.) coming into play. By turning upside down the way we normally develop enterprise architectures, by starting at the top, rather than the bottom, we can build a more complete holistic business view of the enterprise, as well as articulate the language of the enterprise through the information architecture, which will roll downhill from the top of the enterprise, rather than forced uphill from the bottom of the enterprise. In this way, we can build better businesses and build better business systems that meet the needs of the whole enterprise and all concerned parties.

"Make no little plans; they have no magic to stir men's blood and probably themselves will not be realized. Make big plans; aim high in hope and work, remembering that a noble, logical diagram once recorded will not die, but long after we are gone be a living thing, asserting itself with ever-growing insistence. Remember that our sons and our grandsons are going to do things that would stagger us. Let your watchword be order and your beacon beauty." Daniel Burnham – Chicago Architect 1907 [13]

References

1. The Perfect Storm Movie (2000) – Source: IMDb – Quotes - http://www.imdb.com/title/tt0177971/quotes)

2. The Digital Universe of Opportunities: Rich Data and the Increasing Value of the Internet of Things, April 2014, By EMC Digital Universe with Research and Analysis by IDC. - http://www.emc.com/leadership/digital-universe/2014iview/index.htm

3. The Business Imperatives - A Call to Action in "The Digital Universe of Opportunities: Rich Data and the In-creasing Value of the Internet of Things, April 2014, By EMC Digital Universe with Research and Analysis by IDC. - http://www.emc.com/leadership/digital-universe/2014iview/business-imperatives.htm)

4. High Value Data – in "The Digital Universe of Opportunities: Rich Data and the In-creasing Value of the Internet of Things, April 2014, By EMC Digital Universe with Re-search and Analysis by IDC. - http://www.emc.com/leadership/digital-universe/2014iview/high-value-data.htm)

5. Big Data: The Future of Information and Business. A Report by Harvard Business Review Analytic Services, 2013 Harvard Business School Publishing - https://hbr.org/resources/pdfs/comm/experian/hbr_serasa_experian_report.pdf)

6. Big Data: The Management Revolution by Andrew McAfee and Erik Brynjolfsson, Harvard Business Review October, 2012 - https://hbr.org/2012/10/big-data-the-management-revolution)

7. Genesis 11:4–9[1] King James Bible (http://en.wikipedia.org/wiki/Tower_of_Babel)

8. Sisyphus - From Wikipedia, the free encyclopedia, http://en.wikipedia.org/wiki/Sisyphus)

9. NIST Enterprise Architecture Model (Wikipedia - http://en.wikipedia.org/wiki/NIST_Enterprise_Architecture_Model)

10. Eliel Saarinen (Finnish Architect notable for his influence on modern architecture in the United States, particularly on skyscraper and church design. 1873-1950) (Quote from ThinkExist.com - http://thinkexist.com/quotation/always_design_a_thing_by_considering_it_in_its/204270.html)

11. Luca Pacioli - Wikipedia - http://en.wikipedia.org/wiki/Luca_Pacioli

12. Systems Thinking and Its Implications in Organizational Transformation by John Pourdehnad and Gnana K. Bharathy, Ackoff Collaboratory for Advancement of Systems Approaches (ACASA), University of Pennsylvania, [In the Proceedings for the 3rd International Conference on Systems Thinking in Management. May, 2004, Philadelphia, PA.] http://www.scholarism.net/FullText/2012101.pdf

13. Daniel Burnham - Wikiquote http://en.wikiquote.org/wiki/Daniel_Burnham

Business Architecture: Setting the Record Straight

William Ulrich, TSG, Inc., USA,
Whynde Kuehn, S2E Consulting Inc., USA

AN INTRODUCTION TO BUSINESS ARCHITECTURE

Business architecture is drawing significant interest from a wide variety of organizations worldwide. Yet, business architecture is often misperceived as to its uses, origins, and value proposition. These misperceptions are the biggest barrier to adoption, because it prevents businesses in many cases from getting a business architecture effort off the ground, and undercuts sponsorship and business engagement.

Business architecture is not a buzzword or a quick fix solution for a broken process, a computer system, or a single project or business unit. It is a holistic discipline that is most effective when applied across business units, practices, disciplines, and stakeholders.

The discussion that follows lays out a number of fundamental business architecture concepts. This includes an overview, beneficiaries, common myths, core and extended perspectives, interdisciplinary alignment, governance, getting started, and a vision for the future.

Business Architecture: What is it?

Formally defined, business architecture is a blueprint of the enterprise that provides a common understanding of the organization and is used to align strategic objectives and tactical demands.(1) It is an abstract set of standardized perspectives that represent a given business ecosystem. The foundational perspectives include the following core "domain" categories.

- What a business does (capability)
- The vocabulary it uses (information)
- How a business is organized (organization)
- How a business delivers value to key stakeholders (value stream)

Independently, each of these business perspectives has value, but when viewed in aggregate, they serve as an essential baseline that brings significant transparency from an internal and third party engagement perspective. Organizations that embrace business architecture shift more and more of their planning, impact analysis, operational delivery, and solution deployment towards relying on these standardized domain perspectives.

While the four core business architecture domains serve as the foundation for the business architecture, an extended set of perspectives offers even greater insights including:

- What a business should do to compete and thrive (strategy)
- What dictates strategy, investment, and actions (policy)
- Who are the internal and external players (stakeholders)
- How to achieve goals and objectives (initiatives)

- What to offer customers (products and services)
- What makes the business work (decisions and events)
- How well the business is performing (metrics and measures)

While each of these perspectives is built out with a specific focus, the overall eco-system allows for a wide variety of "cross-mapping" perspectives that provide a business with a rich set of business perspectives that inform planning through solution definition and deployment. When fully formed, an almost infinite variety of business blueprints and analysis viewpoints spring forth. Figure 1 depicts the core and extended business architecture perspectives.

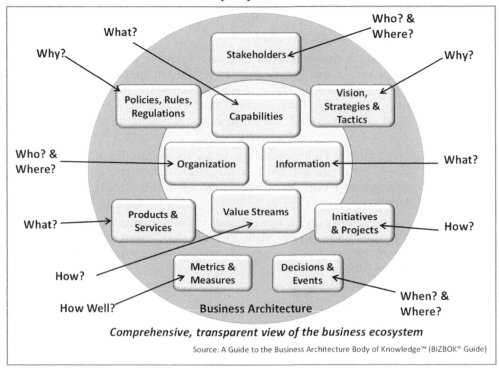

Figure 1: Comprehensive, transparent view of the business ecosystem.(2)

Business Architecture: What Is It Used For?

Business architecture is an all-purpose discipline that applies to many scenarios. Business architecture is not a goal in and of itself. Business architecture is, ra-ther, a means to an end for delivering any number of business scenarios. Con-sider the following sample uses for business architecture.

- Framing and communicating impacts of strategic business objectives
- Aligning strategies and plans across business units
- Realizing business model aspirations
- Determining cross-program, cross-project impacts and dependencies
- Assessing the impact of regulatory and policy changes
- Improving customer and third party engagement and experience
- Informing investment decisions within and across portfolios
- Framing, scoping, articulating, and reusing business requirements
- Scoping information technology investments
- Defining target state IT architectures
- Enabling strategic business transformation
- Integrating companies during a merger or acquisition

Business Architecture: Who is using it?

Business architecture is used by wide variety of business areas and minimally includes the following groups of people.

- **Business Strategists and Leaders:** Strategists and leaders leverage business architecture to influence and assess the impact on strategic planning, business modeling, and policy setting.
- **Planning Teams:** Planning teams use business architecture to interpret the impact of strategic plans and executive mandates on the business from a cross-portfolio perspective.
- **Portfolio Managers:** Portfolio planners must determine the programs or projects to fund, defer, or reject. Oftentimes, they end up funding multiple competing, conflicting, or misaligned projects due to lack of a formal business impact analysis. Business architecture offers horizontal transparency that identifies cross-program and cross-project impacts and dependencies.
- **Risk, Audit, and Oversight Teams:** Businesses need to manage risks more formally and business architecture provides a framework for assessing risk impacts across multiple business perspectives and additionally serves as a focal point for audit and oversight teams to proactively target risk prone areas.
- **IT Architects and Execution Teams:** Enterprise, data, application, and solution architects use business architecture as a basis for or input to IT asset management, data modeling, solution design, and transformation planning. Solution teams can track reusable software assets back to the business architecture, enabling services reuse on an enterprise scale.
- **Business Analysts:** Analysts use business architecture to scope, articulate, and track business requirements and ensure that analysis work is defined in a well-articulated business context and aligned across business units, programs, and projects.

Business Architecture: Where Does It Come From?

The business architecture comes from the business. The simplicity of this statement hides the power of a business-driven, business-owned business architecture. Experience has shown that business architectures created by third parties, IT organizations, or business surrogates with inadequate business knowledge or participation are limited in depth, content, accuracy, and usefulness. A poorly constructed business architecture that does not fully and accurately represent the business in its own language creates a framework that is of limited value.

Business Architecture: Why Now?

Business environments continue to become more volatile and more global. Competition is coming from innovation and unforeseeable directions. In addition, businesses are being called upon to engage more consistently and effectively with customers, move into new markets and regions, and streamline delivery of improved products and services.

A documented business architecture establishes a formal, consistent point of reference that is used to deliver value from planning through deployment, enabling innovative business designs and solutions. Without it, the ability to quickly and effectively introduce change into a business is dramatically diminished. When the competition leverages business architecture it makes it harder for those organizations ignoring this discipline to compete and thrive.

BUSINESS ARCHITECTURE: DISPELLING COMMON MYTHS

There are several misconceptions about business architecture that we want to dispel. Below are ten commonly held business architecture myths with appropriate counterpoints following each myth.

1. *A business architecture can be built with limited business engagement and commitment.*
   - Ineffective business architectures that do not reflect the business are the result of a lack of engagement with business subject matter experts, which in turn can be linked to a lack of business commitment and support.

2. *The business architecture capability map is **the** deliverable.*
   - The capability map is only one business architecture blueprint and of limited value when not incorporated with other aspects of business architecture. In addition, the real value is achieved when business architecture as a whole is integrated into broader business practices and management disciplines.

3. *Business architecture is complicated.*
   - Building the foundational business architecture is a straight forward discipline, requiring only a basic understanding of foundational principles. The real value and intellectually challenging aspects of business architecture occur once the foundational business architecture is established.

4. *There is no commonly defined approach to business architecture.*
   - There is a common approach, it is well-defined, and in use across numerous businesses and industries worldwide. This myth is propagated by those who benefit by keeping people confused, presenting business architecture more as art than science. As long as it is an art versus a science, self-interested parties will continue to prolong your journey towards deriving business architecture value.

5. *Business architecture is program, project, or business unit specific.*
   - Business architecture should not be restricted by project or business unit. The more narrowly defined, the less value business architecture delivers. Once the business architecture foundation is established, the results are leveraged over and over again, with sustainable value building as the discipline moves into more and more corners of the business.

6. *Business architecture can be licensed or acquired.*
   - A business architecture is unique to a given business. Prepackaged perspectives rarely, if ever, meet requisite levels of specificity and lack a useful vocabulary and structure. Customization is what makes business architecture valuable to organizations that want to differentiate themselves from the competition, improve customer value delivery, and standout as innovators.

7. *Business architecture is an IT discipline.*
   - Business architecture represents the business, not data, solution, application, or technical architectures. As a result, the business has to participate in, understand, and leverage business architecture in or-

der to capitalize on the discipline. Anyone confusing business architecture with IT architecture needs to understand its use in strategy
alignment, initiative management, and other business initiatives.

8. *Business architecture is expensive.*
   - Because it is managed in-house, business architecture costs "pennies
     on the dollar" compared with other major disciplines. This is why the
     concept of cost justifying or building a return-on-investment (ROI) on
     business architecture makes little sense. The value is significant and
     long-running, while the initial and ongoing investment is marginal.

9. *Businesses do not need business architecture because they already understand all they need to know about the business.*
   - Business architecture transparency delivers the most value when ap-
     plied on a cross-business unit, cross-program, and cross-project per-
     spective. Business vocabularies, mental models, and stakeholder en-
     gagement perspectives vary widely across business units and are of-
     ten fragmented. Business architecture surface issues that are often
     hidden from a given business unit's or executive's line of sight.

10. *Business architecture is fancy term for business analysis.*
    - Business analysis defines requirements and solutions for resolving
      specific business issues, often on a project-by-project basis. Business
      architecture provides the cross-portfolio transparency that enables
      business analysts to perform more effectively and deliver better solu-
      tions. The two disciplines are unique and distinct, but business ana-
      lysts should have access to and leverage business architecture.

BUSINESS ARCHITECTURE: KEY ASPECTS OF BUSINESS ARCHITECTURE

We address the core business architecture perspectives below and discuss the extended perspectives in the section titled "Business Architecture: Extended Business Architecture Domains."

Value Streams

Value streams represent end-to-end views on how value is achieved for a given
external or internal stakeholder. The two examples shown in Figure 2 depict a
stakeholder who wants to acquire a product, in this case a car, and a manager who
wants to hire an employee. The "value" in the value stream is in the eyes of the
triggering stakeholder. In the first example this is the car buyer and in the second
example it is the hiring manager.

Value stream is "an end-to-end view of how value is achieved
for a given stakeholder"

Acquire Product

Value streams may be externally triggered, such as a customer desiring a product

Onboard Human Resource

Value streams may be internally triggered, such as a manager desiring a new hire

Figure 2: Value streams and triggering stakeholders.

Value streams offer a rich and sophisticated way to prioritize and envision the impact of strategic plans, manage and streamline internal and external stakeholder
engagement, and visualize and deploy new business designs and related solutions.

They also provide a value context for other business architecture perspectives such as capabilities.

Value streams are not simply pretty pictures, but formal work transition frameworks, enabled by business capabilities at each stage of the transition. Figure 3 depicts a Process Claim Request value stream that highlights the stage-gate nature of how work transitions from the point where the value stream starts to where it ends, based on a series of state changes.

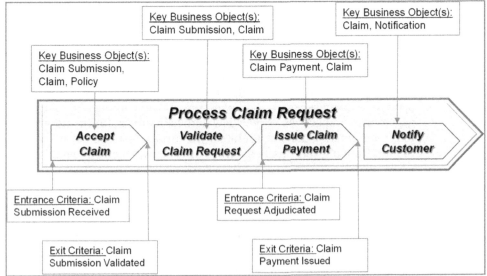

Figure 3: Transitioning of work through the Process Claim Request value stream.

Important value stream concepts may be summarized as follows.

1. Value streams represent every point of interaction with customers, third parties, and internal stakeholders, for every work transition within a business.
2. Value streams are the quickest way to get a snapshot of the business because they represent all work within a business in a value delivery context.
3. Value streams are a primary focus for strategic planning, investment analysis, portfolio planning and alignment, and project scoping.
4. Viewing capabilities through the lens of a value stream provides a very effective context for business analysis and planning.
5. Value streams provide a framework for business requirements analysis, case management, and solution design.
6. Value streams are NOT high level business processes or end-to-end life cycles as many processes typically map to multiple value stream stages.
7. Value streams are defined at an enterprise level for a given business, which means that an average business may only have 20-25 external and internal value streams.

Capabilities

Capabilities represent "what" a business does or has the capacity to do. A capability map in an ideal sense encompasses the totality of "what" a business does in a structured, non-redundant way. You may consider the capability map as the collective set of building blocks that define your business.

A good capability map provides the basis for assessing the impact and scope of strategic plans, defining the scope and impact of business initiatives and related investments, enabling stakeholder value delivery, insourcing and outsourcing, and defining automated solutions. Figure 4 represents a sample level 1 capability map for a business that is in the services industry. Note the three-tier structure that spreads the fourteen, level 1 capabilities across strategic, core or customer facing, and supporting tiers. These tiers are simply for reference purposes for planning teams.

Sample Level 1 Capability Map

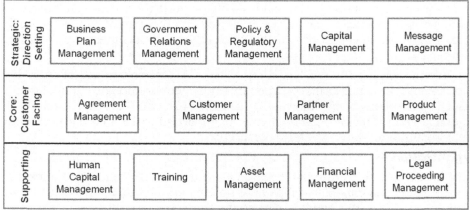

Figure 4: Sample level 1 capability map.

The following points address important capability concepts and challenge common misconceptions.

1. A capability map organizes level 1 business capabilities around specific business objects, otherwise it is likely to be fragmented and redundant.
2. A capability map is globally defined for an entire business and not specific to a given business unit or initiative.
3. A capability map may not appear "business friendly" to people with unique business dialects, but its business-wide nature allows it to serve as a Rosetta Stone for cross-business planning and deployment.
4. A capability map derived solely from an industry reference model rarely aligns to a given business or its vocabulary.
5. Capabilities decompose into more capabilities; relationships to other business domains are established in cross-mapping blueprints.
6. There are no technical capabilities, only business capabilities. Creating dual maps or competing maps results in redundancy and confusion.
7. A typical capability map will have hundreds of capabilities below the level 1 capabilities, but typically do not go below level 6.
8. The size and depth of the capability map increases with business model diversity, not necessarily with the size of the organization.
9. Capability maps take time to build, vet, refine, and socialize across a requisite cross-section of business professionals, but this is what establishes a robust map and business architecture centerpiece.

Information

Every business requires effective information management, and business architecture delivers a business vocabulary and related associations of this information. The information map is a separate business artifact in business architecture. It is initially derived from the capability map, assuming the capability map is based on well-defined business objects.

For example, the capability map in Figure 4 contains Agreement, Customer, Partner, Product, Asset, Human Capital, Financials, and other objects. These become the initial set of objects in the information map. These capabilities also have child capabilities that would include Submissions, Claims, Notifications, Payments, and other objects. The information map would also include these. Associations are then made across the "information concepts" based on child-parent capability relationships and capabilities that tie two objects together such as Agreement / Customer Matching.

The information map is not based on systems or technology and often includes information that is not formally stored in any system or database. In addition, the associations among these information concepts are often not expressed in information systems. The information map is an important tool in information planning and formalization from a strategic perspective.

Organization

Most business architecture perspectives are business unit agnostic. For example, value streams and capability maps have no inherent link to any particular organizational view. While this agnostic perspective is essential to holistic impact analysis, planning, and solution deployment, a business unit perspective is required for a number of reasons. This includes initiative funding, business engagement planning, organizational realignment, and asset ownership and tracking. Organization mapping brings the business unit perspective to business architecture.

Organization mapping goes beyond documenting the traditional organizational structure and provides views of the business unit decompositions and third party relationships. Organization maps are augmented with capabilities, which depict which business units or third parties have certain abilities. For example, an organization map would highlight which business units should be involved in a claims management improvement effort. Organization mapping also links stakeholder, location, and other perspectives to business units. Organization maps round out the core business architecture.

BUSINESS ARCHITECTURE: EXTENDED BUSINESS ARCHITECTURE DOMAINS

The extended business architecture domains shown in Figure 1 include stakeholder, strategy, initiative, policy, product, metrics and measures, and decisions and events. In this section we discuss the top three most critical domains; stakeholder, strategy, and initiative. These business perspectives are the most commonly used extended business perspectives, but exclusion of the other categories by no means diminishes their value.

The overall ecosystem integrates as shown in Figure 5, which shows how strategy is mapped to value stream and capability, which in turn are mapped to initiatives and business requirements. This is only one viewpoint and does not fully depict all cross-mappings, but provides a basic comprehensive perspective.

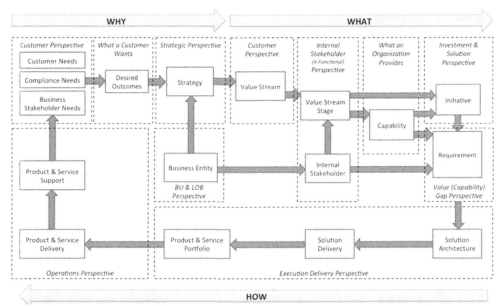

Figure 5: Traceability from strategy through solution deployment.(3)

Stakeholder Mapping

Stakeholder mapping begins with value mapping because each value stream stage must incorporate participating internal and external stakeholders. Stakeholder mapping extends this view and requires a rationalized set of internal and external stakeholders that is maintained as a key domain resource. For example, a stage within the Process Claim Request value stream shown in Figure 3 would include a claims agent, claims manager and attorney, along with external stakeholders such as the auto body manager, policyholder, and involved third parties. Stakeholders also can be used to extend the organization map and are essential in the related disciplines such as case management, business process management, and business requirements analysis.

Strategy Mapping

Strategy mapping articulates strategic goals, objectives, action items, outcomes, and other perspectives based on the mapping approach being used. There are several formal strategy mapping options available including Norton Kaplan's Strategy Map (4), Hoshin Kanri (5), Business Motivation Model (6), and a number of others.

Regardless of the strategy setting and mapping approach, business architecture must formally map the objectives and outcomes to value streams, capabilities, and business units to assess the scope and implications of deploying that strategy. Strategy traceability is shown in Figure 5.

Consider a situation where an insurance company wants to streamline and reduce the cost of claims processing. Minimal points of analysis include the Process Claim Request value stream, Claim Management capabilities, and all business units linked to the Claim Management capability. Impact analysis determines that this capability is linked to ten different business units and multiple software systems. The scope and impact of the strategic objective becomes much clearer based on this analysis. Follow-up traceability links the strategy to various initiatives and requirements, enabling formal tracking of implementation work.

Initiative Mapping

Initiative mapping provides a framework that benefits various practices within an organization such as strategic planning, portfolio management, and program and project management. It identifies and visualizes complex tradeoffs that would be otherwise difficult to achieve. Initiatives map to objectives, capabilities, value streams, processes, business units and assets.

Initiative mapping should explicitly link initiatives to the strategic objectives. This ensures that all planned and in-flight work aligns to business value and priorities, and is measurable. Figure 6 shows how capabilities and value streams can be used to define the scope of initiatives. They are also used to help articulate program roadmap sequences and identify dependencies across initiatives.

Figure 6: Using business architecture to scope initiatives.

Initiative mapping is also be used to show how well a portfolio aligns back to strategic objectives and may help refine prioritization of work on value streams and capabilities. Priorities are initially defined based on identification of value streams required to maintain competitive differentiation. When mapped to initiatives, however, prioritization may shift based on real-world resource constraints and dependencies across initiatives.

THE BUSINESS ARCHITECTURE FRAMEWORK

As business architecture matures, the usability is enabled by using the Business Architecture Framework, shown in Figure 7. The baseline created for each of the core and extended perspectives is maintained in the business architecture knowledgebase. Business blueprints can then be generated from the knowledgebase in support of various usage scenarios.

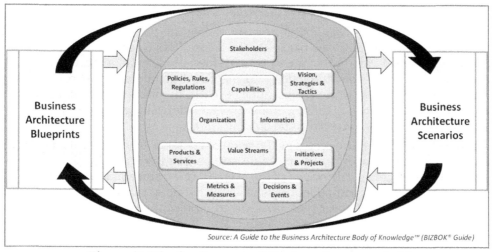

Source: A Guide to the Business Architecture Body of Knowledge™ (BIZBOK® Guide)

Figure 7: The business architecture framework.(7)

The Figure 7 framework represents a maturing business architecture practice, where a central knowledgebase is accessed by business leaders, planning teams, analysts, architects, portfolios managers, and solution teams to coordinate and deploy high priority business strategies.

BUSINESS ARCHITECTURE: ALIGNING BUSINESS ARCHITECTURE WITH COMMON BUSINESS PRACTICES AND DISCIPLINES?

Business architecture is occasionally perceived as a competing discipline, which is a false notion. Business architecture enables other disciplines to be more effective. Business architecture receives input from or provides output to other disciplines, or is purely complementary. For example, business architecture receives input from strategy development, provides output to requirements management and is complementary to change management. In this section, we selected three high visibility disciplines commonly aligned with business architecture.

Business Process Management Alignment

Business Process Management (BPM) is a "discipline involving any combination of modeling, automation, execution, control, measurement and optimization of business activity flows, in support of enterprise goals, spanning systems, employees, customers and partners within and beyond the enterprise boundaries,"(8) When integrated, BPM and business architecture can be of mutual benefit to each other. For example, business architecture provides a framework to streamline processes, prioritize process improvements and establish process governance at an enterprise level. On the other hand, business architecture is often implemented through business process definition, consolidation, deployment, and automation.

To enable these benefits, business processes can be mapped to business architecture value streams and capabilities. Value streams map well to processes because they both move from left to right and have the end goal of accomplishing something for the business. Process / value stream mapping provides context for where certain capabilities should be considered within the context of a given value stream stage.(9) Business processes also map to capabilities, which in turn highlights where certain processes can be improved or consolidated.

Business Architecture and Case Management

Case management is a "method or practice of coordinating work by organizing all of the relevant pieces into one place – called a case."(10) Business architecture establishes the ideal framework for case management. Value streams are a business-wide perspective on work transition and may be decomposed to represent state-based, case transition at a very granular level. In addition, capability and information definitions provide the underpinnings for establishing the business objects that will move through a given value stream.

The business architecture serves as the point of reference for defining the next level of detail related to case transition. Value stream stages are not black boxes, but can be exploded into a microcosm of the overall work transition that occurs across the value stream spectrum. Figure 8 shows the dynamic rules-based routing map and routing map worksheet typically used to represent case transition in a case management business design.(11)

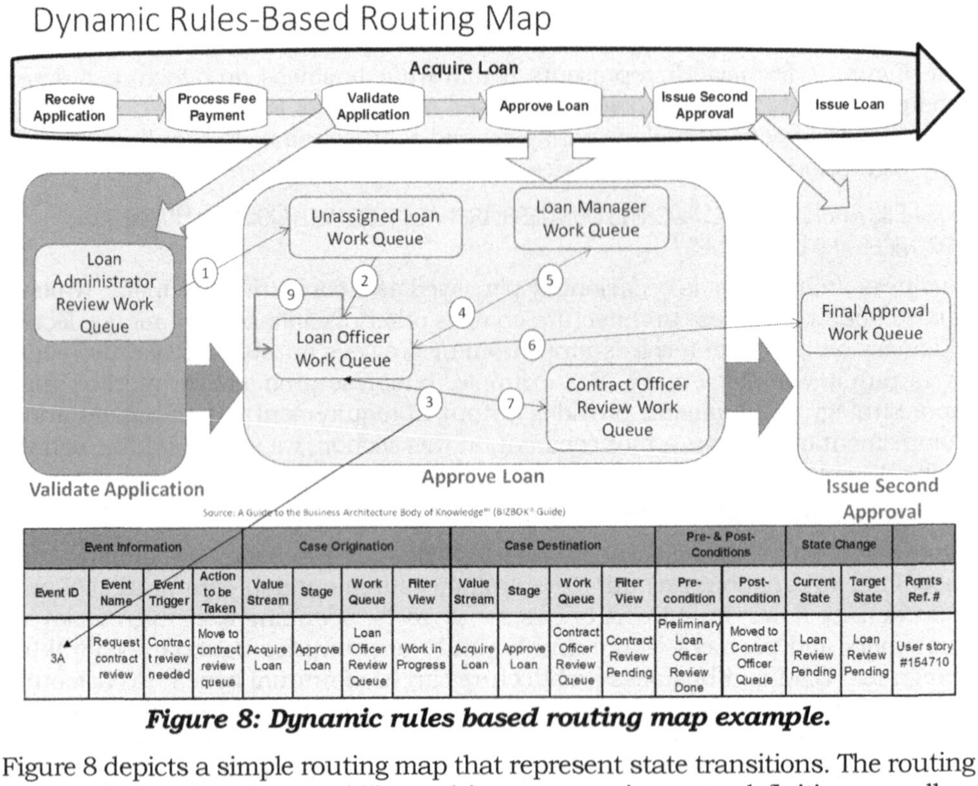

Dynamic Rules-Based Routing Map

Event Information				Case Origination				Case Destination				Pre- & Post- Conditions		State Change		
Event ID	Event Name	Event Trigger	Action to be Taken	Value Stream	Stage	Work Queue	Filter View	Value Stream	Stage	Work Queue	Filter View	Pre-condition	Post-condition	Current State	Target State	Rqmts Ref. #
3A	Request contract review	Contract review needed	Move to contract review queue	Acquire Loan	Approve Loan	Loan Officer Review Queue	Work in Progress	Acquire Loan	Approve Loan	Contract Officer Review Queue	Contract Review Pending	Preliminary Loan Officer Review Done	Moved to Contract Officer Queue	Loan Review Pending	Loan Review Pending	User story #154710

Figure 8: Dynamic rules based routing map example.

Figure 8 depicts a simple routing map that represent state transitions. The routing map worksheet has the capability to drive user requirements definition as well as case management automation solutions.

Use in Business Requirements Analysis

Business architecture assists with framing, scoping, articulating, and reusing business requirements. Figure 5 depicts the link between a requirement and the impacted value stream stage, capability, stakeholder, and initiative. Because a business requirement would be tied to something the business does or wishes to do, by definition every requirement addresses an implementation of a capability. In addition, since requirements are very specific, the capability would be framed in the context of the value stream stage it enables and the stakeholder working within that stage. The business analyst, therefore, leverages the dynamic rules-based routing map shown in Figure 8 to inform analysis efforts.

Business architecture also assists with tracking requirements and identifying where they may be reused. Requirements are mapped to capabilities so that any analyst seeking to implement a capability on any project, within any business unit, can quickly see if a set of requirements have been crafted for that capability elsewhere. Solutions may also be tied directly to the capability so developers can reuse deployed services where applicable.

The requirements approach, whether agile, waterfall, or hybrid, is not relevant, but business architecture works very effectively with an agile requirements approach. The important point is that business architecture provides a formal framing that delivers significant value to the practice of business requirements analysis.

ALIGNMENT WITH IT ARCHITECTURE AND SOLUTIONS

Business architecture delivers significant value to IT because it delivers a formal business perspective for all aspects of IT architecture conceptualization, design, and deployment. Business architecture ensures that planned changes to the business are readily interpreted and translated into IT architecture impacts. This includes small scale changes as well as major transformation work.

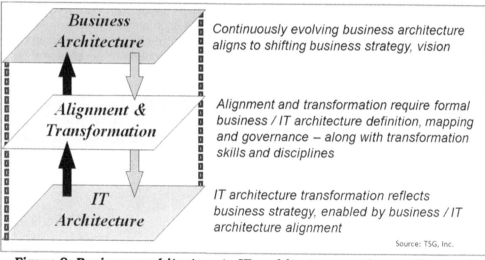

Figure 9: Business architecture to IT architecture continous alignment.

Figure 9 represents a bidirectional impact analysis, change management environment. When value streams, capabilities, and information are targeted by a strategy for small scale changes or major transformation, a business / IT cross-mapping provides rapid input to the impacted IT artifacts. These artifacts span business units, systems, databases, and user perspectives. Conversely, when IT systems change, because one business unit requires value stream, capability, or information related improvements, business architecture identifies the other potential impacted areas across business units.

The business / IT cross-mapping that enables the alignment and transformation change impact perspective is very specific. Capabilities have a direct relationship to application systems and IT services, as framed in a services oriented architecture (SOA). Information maps directly to data architecture. Value streams have a relationship to service and application orchestration, user interfaces, and case management automation. The enabling cross-mappings between business and IT architecture streamline IT architecture planning, design, and solution definition, and solution deployment. An organization builds out these cross-mappings incrementally on an as needed basis.

BUSINESS ARCHITECTURE: GOVERNANCE AND BUSINESS ENGAGEMENT

Establishing the business architecture discipline within an organization requires governance, tight integration and championship. Maturing a business architecture practice takes time, but as business architecture maturity increases, so does its value to the organization.

Business Architecture Governance

When establishing business architecture within an organization, there are multiple aspects to balance and mature over time. This includes not just developing and using the business architecture maps, but also defining business architecture governance, defining the processes and methods necessary to ensure consistent execution of the discipline, developing competent business architecture practitioners, implementing tools, and integrating with related practices and disciplines. Another critical aspect is sponsorship, change management and communication to ensure that business architecture is embraced across the organization.

A standard industry Business Architecture Maturity Model can be used to assess the current maturity of an organization's business architecture practice across all of these aspects.(12) The maturity model is also used to chart a course for improving practice maturity over time, and informs on the methods, processes and practices needed to get there.

Business architecture team structures vary across organizations and can evolve over time. While the best structure for an organization is the one that aligns with its goals and culture, a common structure is shown in Figure 10. This Center of Excellence (COE) structure has been successful because the business architecture team reports to a business executive, but incorporates key participants such as business subject matter experts and IT architects as virtual team members.

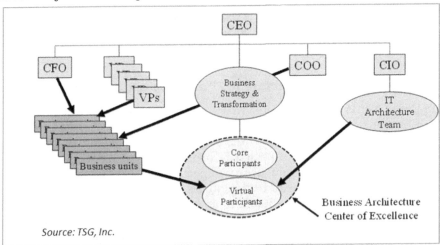

Source: TSG, Inc.

Figure 10: Sample business architecture governance structure.(13)

To fully leverage business architecture, business architecture practitioners require strong mapping skills and much more. They need to have a solid understanding of the business and the environment it operates in, as well as emotional intelligence and other soft skills such as influencing and story-telling. They also require cognitive abilities such as strategic thinking, design thinking, and problem solving. The discipline of business architecture is best learned through apprenticeship over time with experienced practitioners.

Getting Started

To establish business architecture within an organization, the first step is to define clear objectives for the business architecture discipline that tie back to strategic priorities and other key business needs within the organization. Since the business is the ultimate owner and consumer of the business architecture this will help to ensure engagement and priority.

Opportunities to leverage business architecture in support of the objectives should then be identified and a governance structure should be created. Once the initial structure is in place, the initial business architecture baseline can be developed and leveraged to deliver business value. The business architecture knowledgebase can be expanded over time to capture more information and support more usage scenarios. The process of institutionalizing business architecture within an organization takes time, but once the business recognizes its value, they will proactively request business architecture and seek out business architecture practitioners as trusted advisors.

BUSINESS ARCHITECTURE: VISION FOR THE FUTURE

What does the future of business architecture look like? We have to consider the evolution of the discipline to visualize the future. The industry is still in the early stages of capitalizing on business architecture, but maturing at unusually rapid pace. Business architecture has evolved much more quickly than other business disciplines that are decades old in many cases. Five years ago there was little adoption of a formal framework for business architecture and today a generally accepted framework is in place, a widely leveraged body of knowledge is in widespread and growing use, and a formal, business architecture certification program was rolled out in 2015.(14)

Tools are evolving to support the formalization of the business architecture practice. Those tools will continue to evolve to provide a sophisticated impact analysis framework that will enable a wide variety of assessment and impact analysis scenarios. These tools will eventually link to requirements analysis, program management, and solution design and delivery solutions.

Long-term, business architecture will be woven into the fabric of numerous business practices and disciplines. As foundational business architectures are established, strategic planning, portfolio management, change and risk management, business analysis, IT architecture definition, and solution design, and deployment will incorporate business architecture. Business architecture will become a critical, indispensable discipline in the business community.

Business can begin to capitalize on this rapid evolution by formalizing their business architecture now. As the industry matures, these organizations will be well out in front of their competition, while providing new, innovative solutions to their customers.

REFERENCES

(1) Business Architecture Guild, "A Guide to the Business Architecture Body of Knowledge™" (BIZBOK® Guide), Version 4.1. Part 1. 2014.

(2) ibid.

(3) Randell, Alex, Spellman, Eric, Ulrich, William and Wallk, Jeff. "Leveraging Business Architecture to Improve Business Requirements Analysis". March, 2014.

(4) R. S. Kaplan and D. P. Norton. "Strategy Maps: Converting Intangible Assets into Tangible Outcomes" (Boston: Harvard Business School Press, 2004).

(5) Hoshin Kanri. "Visual Strategic Mapping". 1997-2013, http://www.hoshinkanripro.com.

(6) Business Motivation Model. Version 1.1. Object Management Group. May 2010. http://www.omg.org/spec/BMM/1.1/PDF/

(7) Business Architecture Guild, "A Guide to the Business Architecture Body of Knowledge™" (BIZBOK® Guide). Version 4.1. Part 1. 2014.

(8) "One Common Definition for BPM". Collaborative Planning and Social Business. January 27, 2014. http://socialbiz.org/2014/01/27/one-common-definition-for-bpm/

(9) Dugan, Lloyd and McWhorter, Neal. "Business Architecture and BPM - Differentiation and Reconciliation." 2015.

(10) Swenson, Keith D. and Palmer, Nathaniel. "Taming the Unpredictable: Real World Adaptive Case Management: Case Studies and Practical Guidance". (Lighthouse Point, FL: Future Strategies, 2011), 2014. http://futstrat.com/books/eip11.php

(11) Business Architecture Guild, "A Guide to the Business Architecture Body of Knowledge™" (BIZBOK® Guide). Version 4.1. Section 3.5. 2014.

(12) Business Architecture Guild, "A Guide to the Business Architecture Body of Knowledge™" (BIZBOK® Guide). Version 4.1. Appendix B.3. 2014.

(13) Business Architecture Guild, "A Guide to the Business Architecture Body of Knowledge™" (BIZBOK® Guide). Version 4.1. Section 3.2. 2014.

(14) Business Architecture Guild. www.businessarchitectureguild.org

Making Sense of the Architecture Jungle

Frank F. Kowalkowski,
Knowledge Consultants, Inc., USA

Summary: Managing to work your way through all the different perspectives on business, enterprise and other architectures is a daunting task. It would be useful to organize some of the current viewpoints into a few simple categories that are applied in sequence and indicate what the outcomes are from each to the next. These are the issues addressed in this chapter.

The terms 'business architecture' and 'enterprise architecture' are rapidly emerging as phrases that are meant to depict the structure of an enterprise. There are numerous definitions of business architecture and as many architecture methodologies as there are consulting firms and consultants. However, architectures can be grouped into 3 basic categories; 1) that which deal with the 'business strategic architecture' of the enterprise, 2) the 'business architecture' that deals with transforming the operation of the business, and interpreting the direction that is identified by the business strategic architecture and finally 3) the 'enterprise architecture' which encompasses the execution of the business, especially the process flow and the enablement by information technology. This paper sorts out some of the differences, similarities and connections between these architectures and proposes what types of things belong to each type of architecture.

The emphasis in this writing is on the business strategic architecture which may be the least known of the three types. Business strategic architecture spans three basic views of an organization; 1) the external perspective of what influences the organization, 2) the response that management proposes, often embodied in the strategic plan and 3) the direction with change initiatives that management gives to the operation of the organization.

A key linkage to the business architecture is the connection between the strategic business architecture and the process architecture that is part of the business architecture. Along with the process architecture are the enablers that support the process architecture such as the policies, procedures, skills, systems and digitization aspects of the enterprise.

The linkages between these views are not always clear especially when looking at the process architecture. Further, architectures are related and require quantitative and qualitative analytics to assess responses to the influences that cascade across the architectures and impact realization. Finally there are analytics for additional assessment such as comparative analytics and rankings of options that are used to identify impacts and alternatives relating to the operation of the enterprise.

1. PRELUDE

Over the last 5 decades there have been several attempts to describe analyzing an enterprise by separating the effort into various categories, layers, levels and focus. One of the most popular has been the Strategic, Tactical and Operational view (the STO view) as a means of layering the analysis by scope and time. The external view of the landscape around the enterprise was left to the competitive analysis part of marketing and strategic planning.

The organization of these the views provides a focal point for analytical techniques that provide management with options arrived at in a systematic manner. Along with the STO approach are the many management models or disciplines that have emerged to assist managers through decision making on alternatives. This also keeps the analysis from becoming overwhelming to an analyst, limits the skills needed and the time frame to get an analysis completed.

The layers also have a focus such as balanced scorecard for performance, value chain and value streams for process analysis that improves efficiency and effectiveness, five forces for strategic competitive analysis, environmental scanning for strategic analysis, process mapping and modeling for operations and enterprise architecture for IT planning and execution, the digital part of the enterprise. In all cases there is some connection between layers. For example, balanced scorecard while tactical and operational, links back to strategies through objectives.

More recently the approaches to understanding the enterprise have taken on the term 'architecture' as a means of articulating the structure of the enterprise. Much of how we view this today originated in the IT need to link to the business in an orderly manner, hence the development of enterprise architecture as an IT focused perspective, intended to deliver good, reliable applications for the enterprise. By and large, this effort has become successful, with still some distance to go before it is accepted completely.

'Business Architecture' has emerged as a means to encapsulate the business linkage to the digital enterprise perspective. All this evolution of architecture prompts a cleaner view of architecture as applied to an enterprise. There have evolved a number of differences on what constitutes a business architecture, how it links with enterprise architecture and what is the scope of such an architecture.

These differences also prompt some thinking about how to define architecture for an enterprise. The point of this article is to provide a suggested approach to architecture and to identify what is in the architectures and what analytics may be applied to help management through complex decisions in today's world.

There are many perspectives of what is called architecture. Architecture is applied to organizations, enterprises, businesses (profit or non-profit, private or public) or whatever term is used to define a structure that delivers goods and/or services to a constituency. This constituency consists of citizenry or customers, products or services, governments, educational institutions and so on. In any event, what we are talking about is some structure that consists of component parts and relationships that are used to deliver the goods and services. Many of the ideas, concepts and techniques for architecture of an organization are taken from historical uses of architecture in construction of building, cities and neighborhoods.

2. A SUGGESTED ARCHITECTURE PERSPECTIVE:

The post-World War II era has seen the advent of many types of business models and methods of quantitative analysis. It has also seen the growth of organizations both organically and via merger or acquisition. In addition, recent economic conditions have pressured consolidations, divestitures, disposals and spinoffs. On top of all that, the past 50 years have seen a number of opportunities and issues evolve that confront organizations today, such as:

1. Transitioning from local to global markets and delivery points
2. Increasing competitive pressure to streamline processes
3. Drowning in huge amounts of disparate data with many different formats and media
4. Exponential growth and proliferation of the data
5. Integrating the merged and acquired organizations
6. Assessing risk in a more complex environment
7. Governance of the organization, processes and data
8. Integrating agencies and ministries of governments
9. Dealing with regulation and compliance
10. New types of analytics
11. Consolidating operations, *and the list goes on...*

Techniques are emerging to deal with many of these issues under a common umbrella. One of the key techniques is to view the structures of organization in terms of their components, models and relationships. This is what is meant by the structure of the organization, its *architecture*. Management uses multiple descriptive structures to show context aspects of the components and relationships. This is how the delivery of goods and services happens. These descriptive structures have been called Architectures. For products, we call it a "Bill of Materials. For an organizational structure, we've got an organization chart. For a process, it's a value chain, value stream, workflow, or process flowchart. Each is a form of architectural representation consisting of phrases and their relationships. This diagram provides a picture of some of the components and structure of interest in understanding an organization. This diagram is focused on business and enterprise architecture. However, phrase-based models also make up the external and strategic architectures of an organization. The models are more general, and often not operationally oriented, but direction, decision or situation oriented.

Phrase-based models represent the structure of the enterprise... the business and enterprise architecture

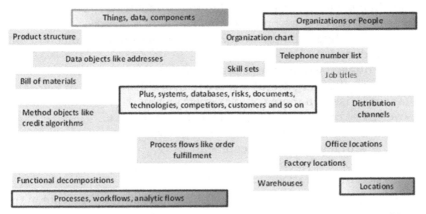

Some are tree structures like bill of materials, some are flows, some are matrices, some are big networks and some are simple lists but all have phrases.

3. THE GOAL OF ARCHITECTURE TODAY

The goal is to pull together various perspectives of architecture to get a type of 'Unified Approach to Architecture' that ties the various perspectives of the enterprise together. This unified approach provides for an architecture view of enterprises, including orchestrating 4 architectural perspectives and 3 linkages between the perspectives. The four perspectives are defined by:

1. External architecture and the linkage to Strategic Architecture
2. Strategic Architecture and the linkage to business architecture
3. Business Architecture and the linkage to enterprise architecture
4. Enterprise architecture to formalize the operational execution of the business
5. Linkages are required for semantic consistency across architectures

The least understood right now is articulating and using architecture that is a view of the external and strategic perspectives of an organization. This is separate from the idea of strategic planning, although an overlap exists. This is the area along with the external view that is receiving a lot of attention today.

In order to define the strategic business architecture the following is needed:

- Showing what a core external architecture might look like
- Showing the linkage to the strategic business architecture
- Defining generic actions, object, decisions and other components in the Strategic Architecture
- Addressing the linkage needed to connect with the business architecture
- Identifying what types of transitional architectures might be needed.
- Providing a set of standard and common analytics to assess impact, comparative analysis, clustering for predictive/hidden relationships and ranking of options and business structural action as the architectures and analytics for transition are orchestrated.

The 4 views of architecture are described in the next several sections.

The 4 types of architecture we have today and the 3 types of linkage

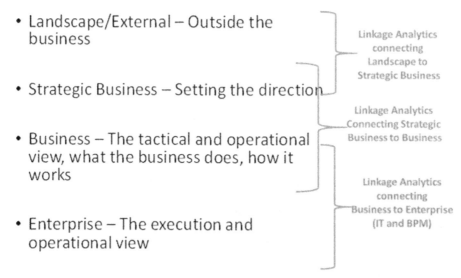

- Landscape/External – Outside the business

  Linkage Analytics connecting Landscape to Strategic Business

- Strategic Business – Setting the direction

  Linkage Analytics Connecting Strategic Business to Business

- Business – The tactical and operational view, what the business does, how it works

  Linkage Analytics connecting Business to Enterprise (IT and BPM)

- Enterprise – The execution and operational view

There are a number of different ways architectures can be organized. Organizing architecture for the business is much like architecture for a building, neighborhood, city or region. For organizing architecture we are using the classic STO approach plus the external or landscape perspective. The diagram below shows the basic idea for identifying the architectures that describe an enterprise.

Viewing Architecture Context...

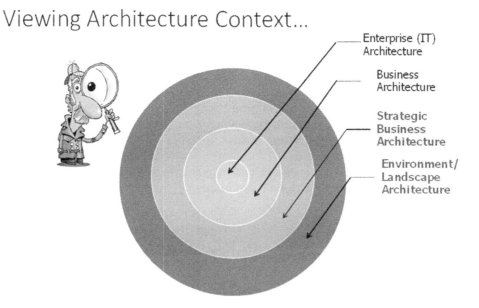

Enterprise (IT) Architecture

Business Architecture

Strategic Business Architecture

Environment/ Landscape Architecture

The bold architectures are the focus of this chapter.

4. ANALYTICS FOR ARCHITECTURE INSIGHT

There are three ways analytics can be used with architecture:

1. *Between models inside an architecture* – Used as a form of assessing degree of impact between components, ferreting out hidden relationships, simplifying models and inferring impacts across multiple component types. Classical ranking and 4-box (9, 16 and 25 box graphics also) types of analytics along with heat maps are also used to arrive at conclusions involving looking at multiple components at one time. This has value in confirming the consistent use of common terms, looking for hidden relationships, ranking of opportunities, risk analysis and a number of other outcomes.

2. *Between architectures in the same perspective especially versions of models and architectures* – This is a means of assessing the gap between architecture states especially 'As-Is' with the 'To-Be' types of assessment. Also used when the change is incremental, involving all or just part of an architecture. This has value in contrasting or comparing the structures of two operating units or a merger acquisition pair, inferring impact across categories of analysis. An architecture may not represent clear states in some industries and may resemble fluid change as some parts change faster than others.

3. *Between architecture perspectives* – As a means of cascading linkage where one architecture drives another as in external architecture providing the driving force for the strategic business architecture. This is a key use of analytics to link the architecture perspectives together for impact assessment, consistent use of terms, model and architecture simplification to focus on where to take the 'deep dive' and bind the analysis and other efforts, a means of reducing analysis costs. The use of Inferencing techniques to assess impact is also key here such as in linking Strategic to Initiatives to Value Streams or Capabilities and eventually to Processes and Systems. A change in strategy can be assessed for impact on any other category in any other architecture.

Space limitations in this chapter restrict the number of examples that can be shown. At least one analytic example is shown for External to Strategic Business Architecture Linkage and for Strategic Business to Business Architecture. Also, at least one analytic is shown that compares architectural components to assess the best fit of an acquisition – merger situation.

The typical analytics used but not limited to, are:

- Rankings of various types
- Calculated values and trend projections
- Impact analysis using Inference across component sets
- Comparative analysis using phrase analytics
- 4-Box types of analysis
- Basic statistical analysis such as regression and correlation
- Cluster analysis for hidden relationships
- Best fit analysis
- Affinity analysis
- Simulation
- Decision analysis including influence calculations
- Tornado diagrams

5. WHAT ARE THESE ARCHITECTURE TYPES ABOUT?

Describing an architecture requires the definition of the things that make up the architecture and describe it in a manner that management and others can understand. The components of the architecture must have some basic way that analytics are applied. In this case we are looking at the quantitative and qualitative analytics. Quantitative analytics are well known, although it can be argued that it is questionable if they are well used and properly used. For qualitative analytics we use the semantic approach with phrases as described earlier.

Describing an architecture

The following are needed to describe an architecture:

1. *Components,* for want of a better word, that make up the architecture, the things of the business or that the business is interested in, such as products, services, markets etc. These vary according to the type of architecture but they can be related to each other for analysis.
2. *Models* that describe the relationships of the components. The types of models also vary based on the type of architecture. There are some model types that naturally evolve into other, and some that have use only in the architecture type you are focused on.
3. *Methodology* that describes how results are achieved through constructing models from the components, applying analytics and reaching a conclusion.
4. *Analytics* that work on the components and the models both quantitative and phrase analytic semantic types of analytics.
5. *Desired end results or outcomes*, the motive for doing architecture and applying analytics. This can be to solve a problem, take advantage of an opportunity, and reconfigure the structure of the organization to accomplish a new goal.

The motives may change as an architecture is developed and the types of architecture are navigated. While you may start with solving a problem at the strategic business architecture level, you may end up assessing the impact of change to the Enterprise architecture.

Linking architectures

The 4 architecture types have components in common such that the architectures can be linked together. This creates an overlap of component types in the architectures. For example, the strategic business architecture has customers in common with all 4 architectures. This is how connection is maintained. So components are of 2 types:

1. Those components or parts that are unique to an architecture and do not appear in another architecture
2. Those components that span two or more architectures and provide for the linkage between the architectures.

The use of the components in each architecture may be at different levels of detail but the linkage will be at the same level in the two connecting architectures.

There are also linkages that are made between architectures that use unlike components. For example, it is common to link certain external components like government regulations directly to value chains or objectives. How the components are used depends on the interest of management and the style of management. The linkages can be shown as in the diagram below.

While this diagram looks neat and clean in terms of how the architectures are connected in reality it is usually a mix with organizations using parts or all of 1, 2 3 or all 4 architectures. So, the diagram represents a target or an ideal in articulating and managing architectures. Also, the arrows are not meant to convey a 'waterfall' type of approach but only that the architecture must be linked for impact assessment.

Architecture today

Architectures often are developed without concern for any type of sequence except what serves planning purposes. Parts, or all, of an architecture may be developed in parallel or in some sequence that suits the need of the organization. They are linked with whatever method the organization or a consulting firm can identify. This is what prompts the description of architecture as a **'Jungle.'**

Many organizations are currently focused on enterprise architecture. At the same time they do parts of the other architectures and use various components and connect them together using various model types. For an organization to *survive* it must do parts of all these architectures, whether or not they are formally structured and analyzed.

Formally organizing the material provides the organization with an advantage in terms of analyzing options and making changes rapidly to respond to external pressures. This diagram provides a template for the formal organization.

The Relationship of Architectures

Architecture of organizations is an emerging formal discipline and will undergo many changes in the future.

The External Architecture

The external architecture describes what happens outside the organization. The external architecture has many more names such as the landscape architecture, the business ecosystem, the business environment and others. It describes the external influences on the organization that impact the direction the organization will take going forward. Sometimes the view is many years long and sometimes it can be days depending on the type of business. Utilities, for example, have a long term view and are often impacted by long term changes in their environment such as legislation, deep social trends, major technology shifts and other market forces. On line businesses such as music downloads, video, digital media and financial institutions may be impacted by short term social trends and need a much more rapid reaction time to the environment.

External architecture is critical to articulating what the external world looks like. Focusing on items of interest gives the organization an advantage over others who are not focusing or have a limited view of the external environment. The reason is simple; if you can anticipate the influences you can determine a strategy to take advantage of, or neutralize, the influence. This gives the organization more and better information than the competition has. This is called asymmetric information, which means you know more than your competitors and hence can make better decisions. Big words that mean 'I know more about significant influences about a topic than you' and hence have an *advantage*. The opposite view when everyone has equal information is similar to what is often called a 'level playing field' which may not exist in reality.

External influences also interact with each other. In many organizations, analysis and understanding of what goes on outside the organization is the responsibility of the senior (including C-Level) management together with the competitive analysis effort, strategic planning and marketing organizations. Creating an external architecture view means coordinating the different perspectives and models and defining how they interact. When this is done it is necessary to define the specific outputs that will influence the organization in short, medium and long term timeframes as the type of business requires.

The external architecture produces some key outputs that drive the Strategic Business Architecture (SBA).

Components of the External Architecture

The external environment consists of many components such as:

Components of the External Environment	Typical Model Types Used with the Components
<ul><li>Customers/Buyers</li><li>Potential Customers</li><li>Markets</li><li>Competitors direct, new entrants, suppliers, customers, substitutes</li><li>Suppliers</li><li>Potential suppliers</li><li>Governments/Politics</li><li>Geographies</li><li>Economics</li><li>Markets</li><li>Industries</li><li>Commodities</li><li>Social Groupings<ul><li>Demographic</li><li>Ethnic</li><li>Religious</li></ul></li></ul>	<ul><li>Lists</li><li>Matrices:<ul><li>Input/output (usually by industry or by commodity)</li><li>Association and Adjacency used to show relationships</li><li>Impact with attributes that characterize the impacts</li></ul></li><li>Influence Diagrams</li><li>Feedback models</li><li>Econometric equations</li><li>Key Influence Indicators (KII)</li><li>Documents (data structure)<ul><li>Annual reports</li><li>Technology Forecasts</li><li>Economic Forecasts</li></ul></li><li>External Data Base Sources (data structures)</li></ul>

o Criminal o Militia • Technologies • Laws/Legislation • Risks, etc.	o The Economist o World Health Organization o United Nations o Dunn and Bradstreet o Government Studies, etc.

Analytics to work on the components and the models were initially quantitative and mostly consisted of forecast trends, based on country's economic data gathered by governments. The data is not consistent across the world and even today the data from many countries is unreliable. Newer analytic techniques such as dynamic modeling, simulation and phrase analytics have added considerably to the analysis insight that can be extracted from the models.

While this list is not complete it represents the major items of interest to mist organizations that do strategic planning, competitive intelligence and market research.

A methodology for linking components, models and analytics to get an External Architecture

Connecting the components, models and analytics into a simple methodology provides some guidance to an analyst regarding how to go about doing this type of work. The diagram below shows a typical methodology that links the components and models together.

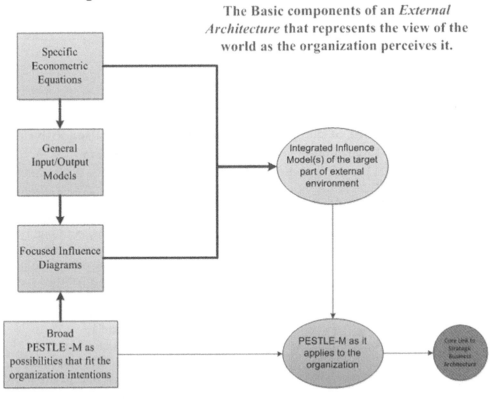

The Basic components of an *External Architecture* that represents the view of the world as the organization perceives it.

The outcome of the architecture; an organization has a limited view of the world with respect to what it can identify that is significant to the organization. Skill in external architecture is focusing on those external components of significance to the enterprise and anticipating as best as possible those things that may be overlooked thereby reducing the uncertainty of the information used.

This external architecture view represents the most common components used in an external view. In some cases other techniques may be applied such as feedback models that may be used in place of or with influence models

- *Specific Econometric Equations* - History and Prediction on those factors that are significant to the organization, e.g. heating degree days for power estimation, disposable income for consumer buying power, etc.
- *General Input/output Models:* Relationships of those factors of interest to the organization modified by econometrics, consists of current as well as future possibilities
- *Focused Influence Diagrams:* Local models that reflect proprietary views such as regional, country, market, product, service, technology etc.
- *Broad PESTLE –M:* PESTLE-M as it applies to the broader environment, used to identify all potential relationships and impacts
- *Integrated Influence Models:* An influence model that represents the context of the enterprise that filters the broad PESTLE-M to a specific PESTLE - M. The influence diagram is converted to a PESTLE-M set of lists and matrices that link to SBA
- *PESTLE –M for the organization:* PESTLE-M as it applies to the specific focus of the enterprise that would support strategic direction

This type of modeling and representation of the external environment has been available since the early 1970s. The US State Department used such an approach called the 'Status of the World' in support of the Secretary of State during overseas missions. In the early 1980s the concept of environmental scanning was developed as a means of assessing the competitive environment as part of competitive intelligence. These concepts are based on intelligence gathering. Of course, the strategic planning groups in many companies picked up these ideas and used them as part of strategic planning.

An analytic example applied to the external architecture itself

One of the key pieces of insight in working with external architectures is understanding the impact of changes from one component to another. For example, the external environment contains information about the commodities that belong to an economy in a country, region or world. The scope depends on the size and breadth of the organization doing the architecture.

We thus consider the following:

- *Legal actions* in a country, region or the world such as banking regulations, pollution rules on commodities or even embargos on countries that impact the availability of a commodity or strategic resource.
- *Commodities* that are available from various parts of the country, region or world and that are used by industries. Commodities are in agriculture, energy, metals and others. Commodities are impacted by changes in laws and regulatory action by governments. These can be within a country or region or applied to commodities entering the country by using such mechanisms as tariffs.
- *Industries* that commodities serve and changes in commodities impact the industries.

If we focus on one country such as the US, we see that there are 12 major agencies that impact various commodities and industries. This is not a complete list and is not intended to be one, it is only to illustrate what analytic can be used and how the analytic is applied. The industries are industry groups. There may be 10 to 20 subdivisions in an industry. In reality you would pick the more detailed industry classifications that relate to your organization.

Legal Agency	Commodity	Industry
CPSC	Grains - Corn	Investing
EPA	Grains - Oats	Personal Finance
EEOC	Grains – Soybeans	News and Opinion
FAA	Grains – Wheat	Basic Materials
FCC	Meat – Hogs	Services
FDIC	Meat – Cattle	Consumer Goods
FED	Energy – Oil	Financial
FTC	Energy – Natural Gas	Technology
FDA	Energy – Ethanol	Healthcare
ICC	Energy – Propane	Utilities
NLRB	Metals – Copper	Industrial goods
NRC	Metals – Lead	
OSHA	Metals – Zinc	
SEC	Metals – Steel	
	Metals – Gold	
	Metals – Platinum	
	Rubber	
	Wool	
	Palm Oil	

The list of agencies is provided at the end of the chapter.

The technique used to analyze impact of change is an inference-based technique that uses matrix models that contain relationships. These matrices are used to inference potential impacts across architecture components. A simple example is shown below. In practice the first matrix would be 14 rows (14 Agencies) by 19 columns (19 Commodities) and the second matrix would be 19 by 11 (11 industry groups) with a result that would be 14 by 11 and this is a pretty simple example.

At the end of the day you have some idea of what happens when a regulatory agency changes its position. What you see in the sample is that Federal Regulation number 4 is the most frequently impacted and Federal Regulation 4 does the most impacting. Of course, there is more to do such as including the degree of impact on industries using attributes in the intersections such as Impact, Importance, Risk, etc.

Several of these types of inferences are done when analyzing the external architecture. The matrices are filled out in management workshops so some of the relationship data is subjective but still useful.

In linking this to the strategic business architecture you then ask 'what is the impact on a product or products that we sell into the consumer goods industry, say automobiles'? This way you can trace impacts from government action to the products you market. Many companies don't go through such efforts as they take time. While there are limited tools for this type of analysis the ones that are available make the analysis easier.

The Matrix Inference Technique

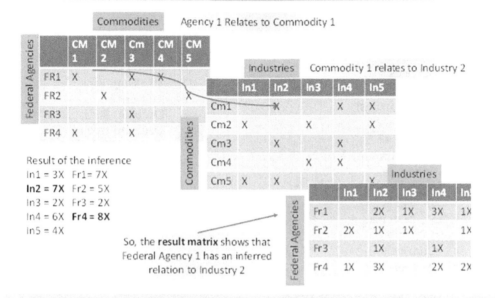

The external view has the Key Influence Indicators (KII) often econometric, Influence diagrams, Input-Output or association matrices plus PESTLE, Political, Economic, Social, Technological, Environment and Legislative influences on the enterprise.

The Strategic Business Architecture

Strategic Business Architecture is the starting point for the business response to the external environment. The work starts with simple models that are lists of the things that are of interest to the organization. When analyzing the organization relationships between the lists, they are defined through matrix models relating the members of one list to another. The scope of the lists and matrices is defined by the boundaries of the analysis such as an operating unit, a geographic area, a product, a market and so on.

A typical business or strategic plan is best represented and typically contains the lists and models that are the result of this architecture. So, this is where you see structures like process hierarchies, business oriented flow models like value chains, distribution networks, policies and decision structures that eventually become rules.

Components of the Strategic Business Architecture

Components of the Strategic Business Architecture	Typical Model Types Used with the Components

• Strategies
• Goals (KRI)
• Objectives
• Initiatives
• Key Performance Indicators (KPI)
• Key Influence Indicators (KII)
• Customers
• Suppliers
• Products
• Services
• Knowledge
• Polices (rules)
• Risks
• Facilities
• Locations
• Resources
  o Revenue/Costs
  o Skills
  o Material
  o Data
• Channels
• Partners
• Capabilities
• Etc.
	• Lists
	• Decompositions (hierarchies/ trees)
	  o Products
	  o Locations
	  o Services, etc.
	• Matrices:
	  o Association
	  o Adjacency
	  o Impact
	  o Inference
	• Decision Diagrams
	  o Influence
	  o Decision structures
	  o Decision trees
	  o Decision tables
	• Performance Indicators and trends (KRI)
	  o Profit/Loss
	  o Revenue
	  o Market growth and penetration trends, etc.
	• Documents (structured data)
	  o Annual reports
	  o Strategic Plan
	  o Focused Technology Forecasts (including IT)
	• Value Chains (Flows)
	• Value Streams
	• Strategy Maps
	• Supply Chains (network models)
	• Capabilities
	• Scorecards (balanced and otherwise)

There are a large range of business models, or as some call them business disciplines, that are used in constructing the strategic business architecture. Fortunately, most organizations used a subset of 4 to 8 disciplines to assist their planning. These disciplines are also used at different points in the methodology

A methodology for linking components, models and analytics to get a Strategic Business Architecture

While the diagram below looks simple, the actual execution can be quite complicated depending on the size of company, number of products and services, what their transformation issues are, the structure of the business such as conglomerate or single industry or product family and so on. A few words about the parts of the methodology are needed.

Competitive intelligence: Provides the basic 5 -Forces assessment of the business landscape but focused specifically on the needs of the organization.

External Architecture: Contains all the focused results of the external architecture effort usually focused on PESTLE types of analysis narrowed to fit the business.

Management interests: This represents the direction in which the management would like to take the organization. This group consists of the C-Level managers and their direct reports. They are typically the group that is putting together the Strategic plan and the related strategic business architecture.

Other Stakeholder Interests: The management of the organization must take into account certain groups of interested parties such as the Board of Directors, Major stakeholders, financial analysts that issue commentaries on the business and special interest groups.

Management Disciplines: Often the management is using several management disciplines such as value chains, balanced scorecards, blue ocean strategy or one of the other 65+ disciplines that have emerged over the last 50 years or so. These must be integrated into the strategic business architecture by extracting their meta-models and content making them part of the architecture.

Reference Models: Finally there are often industry, association or vendor reference models that are part of a transformation effort or a startup part of the business. Consideration must be given to these as they may form a key part of the business architecture defining the operational and tactical views of the organization.

The basic method of putting together a Strategic Business Architecture

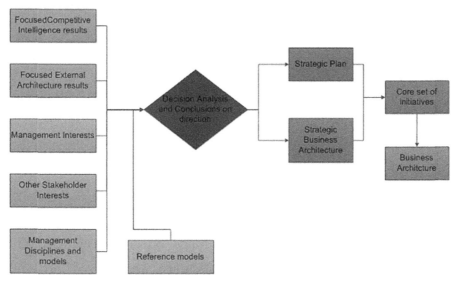

Input from the results of external architecture development enters an iterative decision making effort using a number of different tools and methods to arrive at the strategic plan and strategic business architecture. This material makes up a focused view from the more general view that is developed in the external architecture effort. It is filtered for the organization such that it can be used for a strategic plan

From the strategic plan and strategic business architecture we get a set of strategies and initiatives that drive the business architecture. The concept of business architecture developed by the Business Architecture Guild describes the components and their relationships quite well.

Analytics help map the strategic business architecture to key parts of the business architecture such as value streams, capabilities, policies (governance and rules), information (data sets), measures, organizations units, locations and other pieces necessary to complete a business structure.

An analytic example applied to the Strategic Business Architecture itself

Below we see a setup of an assessment involving the acquisition and merger of another operating unit for a company. The key question to ask is whether the target is a good match. Usually all the due diligence involving financial, legal and assets have been done. Often markets and customers are included in the assessment. But as studies show the biggest problem is in the operations and culture. Currently this is assessed by interviewing the management of the target.

So an assessment that takes into account some of the components may provide clues as to the likelihood of success of the merger or acquisition.

Category of Information	Abbr.	Companies	...	
Comparison # 1 - 100 %		**Alpha**	**Beta**	...	Choice
Processes	PRC				
Documents	DOC				
Applications	APP				
Locations	LOC				
...					
Comparison # 2 - 65 %		**Alpha**	**Beta**	...	Choice
Processes	PRC				
Documents	DOC				
Applications	APP				
Locations	LOC				
...					

Legend: ... means other categories and companies

Here we see 4 types of components that typically cause the most problems in combining business structures. There are semantic phrase analytics that can help determine if the two organizations at least use similar language. This would help identify how close a match they are. Not a perfect technique but better than none, which is what most businesses do right now.

Phrase analytics need some control over the degree of match to be really useful. Sometimes, looking for perfect semantic matches can be misleading and loosening up the matching criteria can provide better insight. Some skill and experience in determining this is needed by the analyst.

Comparative Analysis – An Example

4 Key categories were used for the comparison

Alpha – Merger candidate A
Beta – Merger candidate B

Comparison is done against
same categories from acquiring
company

PRC – Processes
LOCS – Locations
DOCS – Documents
APPS – Applications

Comparison was done on
a **100** % match basis and
again on a **65** % match
basis

Comparative Analysis of 2 Acquisition Candidates Using Architecture Components				
100% Match		Alpha	Beta	Choice
	PRC	63%	60%	A
	LOCS	95%	68%	A
	DOCS	57%	68%	B
	APPS	75%	66%	A
65% Match				
	PRC	68.50%	60%	A
	LOCS	100%	100%	Both	Tie?
	DOCS	71.50%	84%	B
	APPS	82%	83%	B	Tie?

Which candidate would you choose ?

Initially it looks like there is a large mismatch in the locations, mainly using the names of cities and countries. Since the names can be presented in several ways such as with an extra word appended to the name, it is useful to look for partial matches. In this case, matching will result in improved suggestions to the analyst to look at the data and make sure this is not a false positive. Looking at the sets of results, the question to be answered is which is the better match Candidate: A or B?

A is the better match if you are concerned with the processes, B might be a better match if it is the data side. Some might reject both and look for a third candidate. Clearly someone sets up the criteria for this and provides a rank for which is the most important. If the applications are the main concern or locations, then it looks like a tie. Again this depends on the criteria set by the management.

This type of analysis is done on a high level such as using 20 to 25 major applications, 40 to 50 processes deemed important, key locations and 30 to 40 documents. Similar types of comparisons can be done in more detail to resolve the choice issues. Of course you need to have this material from both targets but it is easy to get in interviews with their managers as well as the other typical material that comes out of the interviews.

Business Architecture

Business architecture may sometimes be called transformation architecture as it relates to redesign of the business based on directional changes. Transformation architecture encompasses the stages of transforming the direction and overall structure of the enterprise into design components. Input to this stage is the result of applying the management disciplines and formatting them in a manner useful to the transformation architect. This is the 'design' part of bringing an enterprise structure into existence. Management disciplines often make this linkage. Many companies do not use the transformation architecture idea yet and just go from business needs to executable and back.

The transformation architecture may contain several versions or variations of the enterprise structure as it goes from the current to future state. A **transformation**

or business architect works in this space and is responsible for maintaining the evolving intermediate architecture. There are several approaches to accomplishing this task including the one that fragments the structure. Fragments are transformed individually. This approach is used often in IT transformation, HR transformation and so on.

An analytic example applied to linking Strategic Business Architecture to the Business Architecture

One linkage that can be used is to connect between architectures using the products or services of an organization. Here we are connecting the strategies to the products and then product to knowledge. Knowledge is considered a critical component of many products especially products based on proprietary intellectual property. What you want to know is which strategies impact which products. We could also use initiatives instead of strategies which would be more explicit, especially if they come from a discipline like balanced scorecard. Once we have the strategy to product relationships we can identify the product to knowledge relationships.

Impact Analysis – An Example Linking Strategy to Business Architecture

Relating the Business Strategy-to-Products

Tying Strategy to knowledge to see impact

Then, relating Products-to-Knowledge

Impact Analysis – An Example of the Inferred Result

The Strategies doing the most impacting are:
Create Value Added, Improve Return and Increase Market Presence

A simple inferred impact analysis that allows you to see the impact of strategy changes on knowledge

| 5 | 2 | 2 | 6 | 5 | 2 | 6 | 3 | 4 | 4 |

The most impacted KM nuggets are: Pictures & Product Data Sheets

What does this mean? Like an alert...
If you change the "Create Value Added" strategy you may impact many knowledge nuggets

Now we have two matrices that can be analyzed for impact such as in previous examples. In this case we are linking across architecture types from strategic business architecture to business architecture.

This is the result of the starting inference, which is a simple one to first identify where the impact lies.

Enterprise Architecture

The Enterprise Architecture encompasses the stages of transforming the design structure of the enterprise into detailed executable components. Input to this architecture is the result of applying the management disciplines and formatting them in a manner useful to the enterprise architect. This is the 'construction' part of bringing an enterprise structure into existence. If there is a specific solution that is to be used, then the solution architecture idea is used. This approach is typically used when the solution is an IT solution.

The enterprise architecture is driven by the use of development, engineering, project management, other disciplines, and tools. Enterprise architecture is used for converting the artifacts of the transformation architecture into executable and measurable components. The Enterprise Architect works in this space and is responsible for maintaining the executable architecture.

There are several approaches for achieving an executable and operational structure. In fact, it may include choosing a part of the structure (a fragment) and transforming that fragment as is done often in agile approaches to implementation. The fragment may follow enterprise functional boundaries, such as: IT transformation, HR transformation etc. About 80% of the effort of the Enterprise Architect is spent on the execution architecture and 20% linking to the transformation or business architecture.

The enterprise architecture also includes the operational aspects of the organization, like the need to make sure the constructed result works. This might include follow up measurements and analysis to make sure operational targets are reached, quality levels are acceptable and resources are properly used.

6. WHO DOES THE WORK?

Of course, when there are so many models and structures, someone is needed that understands how to put them together and analyze them. In the past, this has fallen to the management of the organization. Today, the issues and analytical methods are sufficiently complex that specialists are needed to support management. This has caused the emergence of the business architect as well as other architects for data, systems, process, products, IT (the enterprise architect) and so on.

External Architecture

The work of defining and analyzing the external architecture falls to and depends on the *senior management and planning specialists* today. They do the competitive analysis, PESTLE types of assessments and assess any econometric descriptions that are relevant.

Strategic Business Architecture

The *strategic business architect* works in this space and has the responsibility of working with senior and upper middle management to articulate a description of the organization that has all the components and their relationships on a high-level. Often this effort includes consultants with specific capabilities that augment the senior management input.

Business Architecture

The *business architect* identifies the components of the business and their relationships, creates the lists and models and the relationships between the models. Often the business architecture is actually done by the senior management with help from consultants. About 80% of the architecture effort is spent on the business perspective and about 20% on the transformation (design) perspective.

The *Business Analysts* at this point is often a domain analyst, that is, skilled in an analysis specialty that can be function oriented such as distribution, inventory, loan and policy types of analysts. They can also be in an analytical discipline such as financial, process, quantitative, qualitative and operational analysts. Sometimes an analyst team is put together of internal analysts and external consultants.

The Subject Area Expert analysts work with the Transformation or Business Architecture artifacts produced by the Transformation or Business Architect. The architect documents requirements defined by architecture components and relationships needed for business execution implementation. The architect and engineer perspectives provide for the translation of the direction of the enterprise to requirements considering the interrogatives that are typically required for executing business initiatives.

Enterprise Architecture

Enterprise Architect and Implementer roles: The Implementer works with the Enterprise Architecture produced by the Enterprise Architect. The Enterprise Architect develops and implements the requirements defined by the Enterprise Architecture ensuring that the architecture components and relationships meet the needs for business operations. The technician and enterprise perspectives provide for the construction and operation of the enterprise requirements.

Architects produce architecture artifacts, descriptions of the structure of the organization. Analysts apply analytical techniques to the artifacts to evaluate alternatives and draw conclusions resulting in recommendations for actions available to management. Hence, there is a relationship between architects and analysts.

Business Architect and Business Analyst role

As a business architect/consultant supporting the organization the architect performs the following types of analytical tasks. It deals with the subject area and the business analyst's deliverable that can result from the analysis.

As a business architect supporting the organization in this role, the architect performs the following types of tasks:

- Supports the management in the assessment of major business functions, goals, objectives and initiatives through the use of management disciplines
- Constructs all the artifacts such as value streams, value chains, list of categories and matrices needed to describe the organization
- Collaborates with business analysts (subject matter experts) to understand and document quantitative and qualitative decisions to make
- Identifies and documents specific instances where existing business capability such as process performance or asset turnover may be streamlined or improved;
- Develops, maintains, and distributes business architecture such as matrices and flows to stakeholders and involved parties

- Serves as team representative at designated meetings and responds to questions/tasks related to business analysis, modeling and business level decision rationale.

Enterprise Architect and Analyst roles

A Transformation Architect may be responsible for the following types of tasks:

- Leading the assessment of business
- Integrated Business Architecture with the Enterprise IT architecture transformation
- Building the business case for technology variants to process baseline
- Cross-value-stream integration; establishing performance metrics and monitoring
- Solution/technology requirements definition; process/data mapping; project management
- Use of other standard methods and techniques to facilitate the chosen transformation.
- Also, an implementer works with the Enterprise Architecture produced by the Enterprise Architect. The Enterprise Architect develops and implements the requirements defined by the Enterprise Architecture ensuring that the architecture components and relationships meet the needs for business operations. The technician and enterprise perspectives provide for the construction and operation of the enterprise requirements.

Roles of those working on these architectures often overlap. In workshops, over 35 different types of 'analysts' were identified that have some input to the architectures with the business analyst the most general.

WHAT DO YOU GET FROM THESE ARCHITECTURE EFFORTS?

The 4 perspective architecture approaches decide business direction and move it through a series of transformations, that produce usable and executable business system implementations. This includes the digital part of the business as well as the manual parts of business systems.

Management, business analysts and architects work together on the artifacts of the architecture, the relationship of the artifacts to each other, the context of the artifacts and the architecture linkages. They also apply the analytics needed in making key decisions for implementation. Therefore the explicit architecture components, relationships and artifacts support informed decision-making and analysis. This provides the following key benefits:

1. A focus on what is important to the organization in terms of responding to changing environments outside the organization.
2. An orderly and cost effective approach to define transformation of an organization.
3. Analytic based inputs to decision making that reduce uncertainty through better information.
4. A reduction in the complexity of documenting an architecture by separating it into different areas of interest, namely external, strategic, business and enterprise execution

7. LIST OF GOVERNMENT AGENCIES:
    1. CPSC- Consumer Product Safety
    2. EPA - Environmental Protection Agency
    3. EEOC - Equal Employment Opportunity Commission

4. FAA - Federal Aviation Administration
5. FCC – Federal Communication Commission
6. FDIC – Federal Deposit Insurance Corporation
7. FED - Federal Reserve System
8. FTC – Federal Trade Commission
9. FDA – Food and Drug Administration
10. ICC – Interstate Commerce Commission
11. NLRB – National Labor Relations Board
12. NRC – Nuclear Regulatory Commission
13. OSHA – Occupational Safety and Health ministration
14. SEC – Securities and Exchange Commission

Converting Decision to Action

Gil Laware, Information By Design, USA

Summary: Transitioning from a current environment to a future environment requires the examination of four architecture-based areas. Each are seemingly independent but are mapped to each other to enable the transformational change. These mappings help to dynamically assess and evaluate the solution alternatives available. These managed architectures become a new management tool as they influence the decisions about the desired future organizational/enterprise environment. This chapter addresses specific challenges in this environment.

INTRODUCTION

Management is faced with various challenges such as making effective and efficient decisions, facilitating change and managing the changes throughout the organization, and transitioning from its current position into the future. These decisions dramatically affect the reaction and the organization's ability to respond to external changes. Making effective and efficient decisions is most difficult because there are no right decisions, only satisfactory decisions! Most decisions are uncertain, incomplete, and must constantly evolve due to the acquisition of new information that relates to the decision choices, daily. Impact assessments address the change across the whole organization. Simply put, decision-making is choosing the best solution based on the acceptable level of risk, uncertainty, and satisfaction given the current resources. Once a decision is made, project and change management approaches are used to ensure changes are thoroughly and smoothly implemented to achieve the desired long-term benefit.

Most organizations today are faced with significant change that are driven by external architectural forces, such as worldwide market influences, increased competition, legislative and environmental regulations, and technological changes that affect both products and services. Management usually adopts various disciplines and techniques to mitigate the effects of these changes. Management can assess organizational risks by using different architectures, gathering appropriate content; perform analytics on the architectural content to assess the long-term impact of a decision on the organization.

Making the transition from the current business model to a future business model affects many sets of architectures within the organization. These architectures show how different components and relationships may be impacted because of the change. Examples of architectures include a strategic and business architecture, product architecture, manufacturing and process architecture, information/data architecture, enterprise architecture, partner/supplier architectures to name a few. Every current operational implementation has an architecture which is either implicitly or explicitly documented. To reach a desired future or targeted architectural environment, a transformation is required. It is achieved by a transitive architecture that maps the necessary details to move from current state to the future architecture. Transitive architecture enables change that affect the whole organization/enterprise not just some of the pieces!

This chapter highlights four architectural perspectives. Each are seemingly independent but are mapped to each other enabling transformational change. These mappings help to dynamically assess and evaluate the solution alternatives available. As managed architectures, they become a new management tool as they influence the decisions about the desired future organizational/enterprise environment.

EXECUTIVE ENVIRONMENT

Focused on making Decisions, Decisions, Decisions

Executives and management engage in a process that commits resources to seek some competitive advantage or to resolve a business issue. But all decisions are based on uncertain, incomplete, inconsistent, and ever changing information. The implications of every decision-making situation is what do we do next.

The value of making a decision is predicated on the relationships of information and data (numbers, text, graphics, audio, or videos) that are structured and formulated into some model. The model allows the decision-maker(s) to frame knowledge and make judgments that are involved in the decision process. Figure 1 shows the hierarchy of information and data supporting the development of the decision.

The decision-making process is one of understanding what is required to clarify the opportunity or issue that will yield a satisfactory solution, exploring alternatives that are potential solutions, developing criteria to measure each alternative, and evaluating or comparing the alternatives based on the criteria chosen. Once an alternative is chosen, the decision has been made. Documenting the decision can come in many forms, i.e., the annual report, a strategic plan, or a list of initiatives with supporting project plans, etc. The decision-making process can be implemented in a number of ways: top-down, bottom-up, middle-out or a combination of these using decision-making techniques.

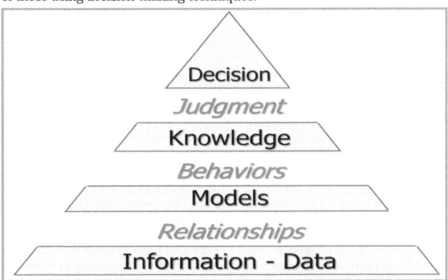

Figure 1: Hierarchy of Information/Data for Decisions

The next step in decision-making is determining what to do next in order to make the decision most effective by incorporating it into standard work processes, using the business architecture, communicating its purpose, and implementing a BPM approach throughout the organizations affected. Even though the decision made is timely, the management task involves making trade-offs of resources.

Management of Resources

Executives and management's responsibilities include successfully obtaining, directing, and allocating resources to meet certain organization goals and objectives. These impose certain constraints on the decision-making process. Each constraint needs to be examined with data and analytics need to be considered in the decision-making process. For example, the following areas and questions are considered.

People

Does the staff have the training, skills, abilities and capabilities to achieve the desired goals and objectives? Would a merger, divestiture, or consolidation facilitate the change faster? Do we have partners who can help us? Are our people willing to accept the desired change? Can external resources be used to educate, train, and mentor new skills? What is an acceptable timeframe for such a transition?

Places

Can the desired plan or change be accomplished with our existing locations? Can we utilize external suppliers or partners and transition to a new business structure? Do we have to upgrade or purchase new locations to support desired goals? From a marketing perspective, do we change our sales locations? Do we need sales locations? Can we market and sell directly to our prospects/customer? Where are the best markets globally?

Products or Services

Will we have to change our product mix or services rendered? Will we have to upgrade existing products and services? Do we have to invest in new products and/or services to remain competitive? Can the desired plan or change be accomplished with our existing locations? Can we utilize partners or suppliers to expand our products and services?

Technology

How can technology be incorporated into our products and services to improve our image, brand, capabilities, service, and market growth? What technology is the best fit for the market we serve? When will that technology be available at what cost? What technologies will enable our organization to become more customer centric, process effectively and efficiently, and be responsive to the market trends?

So the analysis that one does in decision-making process can significantly impact the outcome because of the contextual situation being examined.

Using the Analysis Triangle in Decision-making

In producing an analysis, the person who is assigned responsibilities to examine multiple alternatives or solutions usually creates, develops, produces, documents and recommends a solution. Each analysis encompasses a minimum of three factors that include a:

Narrative: a qualitative description of the contextual understanding of the opportunity or issue.

Quantitative: a collection of data that summarizes numerical aspects of the situation.

Financial: a financial analysis that summarizes criteria used by the organization to evaluate the worth of the opportunity or solution to an issue.

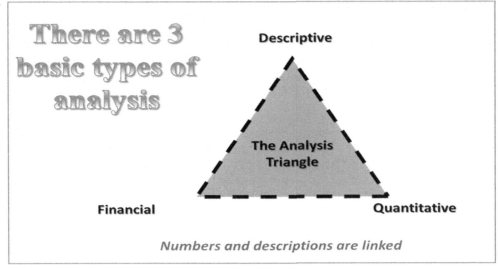

Figure 2: Analysis Triangle

The person works with the management team and staff to recognize there is a decision to be made stating what it is in a single clear statement. Once this is framed, they do a number of tasks: seek multiple alternatives for resolving the opportunity/issue, list all stakeholders, generate a set of discriminating criteria and their targets, evaluate or rank criteria in terms of importance, evaluate alternatives against chosen criteria, assess risk scenarios to ensure selected recommendation minimizes risk and maximizes satisfaction, list what needs to done next. Finally, document the reason and assumptions made for the decision made.[1]

Even though these aspects are considered in the decision-making process and are timely, something changes. That is, the information about the external environment dynamically changes affecting some of the assumptions made in the decision-making process.

ORGANIZATIONAL ENVIRONMENT

Today's environment has changed dramatically with the beginning of the 21st century. Several technological factors have altered the world. They include: miniaturization of electronic components while increasing their speed and capacities resulting in increased computer and mobile device adoptions, world-wide communication networks bring about almost instantaneous communications and commerce, faster and easier adoption of software changes impacting Internet of Things (IoT) and computing devices, all affecting the way markets are defined, product capabilities and features delivered, and services are rendered.

Survival of the Fittest

Executives and management teams are in a race for survival. They have to have the capabilities to not only survive but win. Most recently, in McKinsey's recent report: *"Digital is in: Disrupt or Be Disrupted,"*[2] management will be constantly changed by digital competition. Coupled with this competition is the challenge of

---

[1] Making Robust Decisions, Ullman, David G., Trafford Publishing, Victoria, CA, 2006.

[2] Competition at the digital edge: 'Hyperscale' businesses. Michael Chui and James Manyika. McKinsey Quarterly, March 2015, http://www.mckinsey.com/insights/high_tech_telecoms_internet/competition_at_the_digital_edge_hyperscale_businesses

assessing the quality of the information and data used from external sources for decision-making like:

Variety

The information and data can be either structured, unstructured, or both; providing the content as desired. For example: Twitter/Facebook communications.

Velocity

The speed at which the information and data is updated (from hours to seconds). Ex: Stock market transactions per second.

Volume

The size of the information and data is massive compared to traditional sources. Ex: scanned Walmart's data.

Veracity

The accuracy, timeliness, correctness, and meaning affect the degree of certainty one has about the data's quality.

Together, these affect the quality of the decision and assessment of what's next. How can technology be incorporated into our products and services to improve our image?

These changes increase the complexity of decision-making. Why? Because of the interdependencies that exist across these products or services, executive management's confidence in decision-making is mitigated by the degree of uncertainty about the reliability, risk, and adaptability of all of these elements. One reason how executives are seeking a way to minimize risk is to use architecture and architecture analytics. What is architecture?

The term architecture has many meanings. One definition is the: *"formation or construction resulting from or as if from a conscious act or a unifying or coherent form or structure."*[3] It is in this context that the categorization and organization of various organizational items and their relationships is used implicitly or explicitly by executive management. For example, common things like an organization chart, a chart of accounts, a project plan or a bill of material are forms of architecture. Let's examine other architecture forms.

THE STRUCTURE OF BUSINESS –SUITES OF ARCHITECTURE

Every organization operates in an environment in which they have to understand their external market, customers, citizens, partners, suppliers, and report to owners, Boards of Directors, legal (Governmental, Regional, and Local) entities and stockholders. These interested parties have various relationships that affect the operations and performance of the organization.

---

[3] http://www.merriam-webster.com/dictionary/architecture, 2015-03-15.

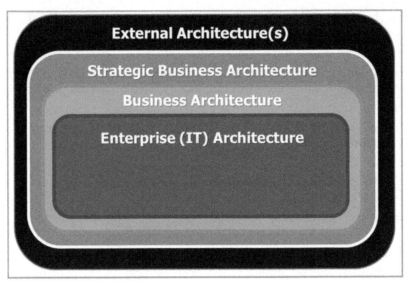

Figure 3: Architecture Suite

From these influences and factors, the executives and management formulate their business model. The business model drives the strategic vision, mission, goals, strategies, and initiatives that set the operational direction of the organization. The formulation of the strategic direction establishes a more refined view of the business process (actions) that are executed at an operational level. Business Architecture captures and executes these actions in the most efficient and effective manner.

Lastly, Enterprise Architecture (instituted by Information Technology organization) is a business practice whose role is to maintain various data about the different business processes, resources (people, costs, etc.), systems, data, and technology being used throughout the organization. The role is to facilitate better analysis and understanding of the "digital" environment supporting the organization by clearly showing various economic, technological interdependencies across the organization in decision-making scenarios.

External Suite of Architecture(s):

The external business environment contains a number of different types of architectural structures that may influence your particular organization. A management technique often used to examine different factors affecting the organization is called **PESTLE- M** analysis. Factors included in the analysis cover: political; economic; social factors in a country; technological factors in the market; legal and regulatory items; and environmental influences upon the organization. In this example, **M** is the market's influence.

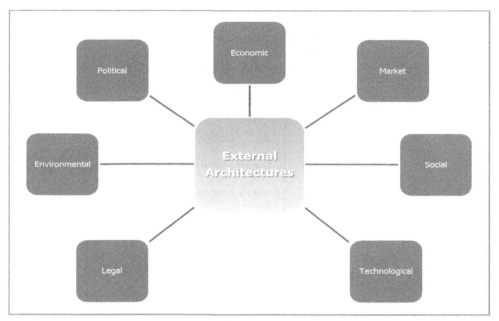

Figure 4: PESTLE- M Framework

As an example, the Digital Appliance Company (DAC) might use these descriptive factors structured into representative models to provide an analytical context for your organization.

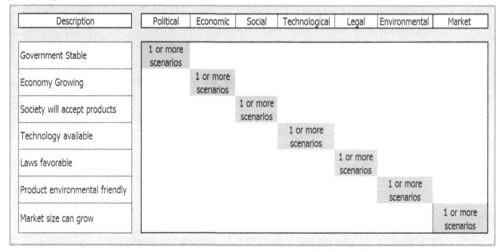

Description	Political	Economic	Social	Technological	Legal	Environmental	Market
Government Stable	1 or more scenarios						
Economy Growing		1 or more scenarios					
Society will accept products			1 or more scenarios				
Technology available				1 or more scenarios			
Laws favorable					1 or more scenarios		
Product environmental friendly						1 or more scenarios	
Market size can grow							1 or more scenarios

Figure 4: PESTLE- M Scenario Matrix

Results from this analysis affect the assumptions and the risk profile management uses in the development of the Strategic Business Architecture. The border surrounding the Strategic Business Architecture (in Figure 1 - 3?) is the capturing of the structured scenarios with models that position the executive team in the development of the Strategic Business Architecture. The intent is for these models to continually assess the dynamics of the external environment that may influence the resulting Strategic Business Architecture.

Strategic Business Architecture

The Strategic Business Architecture connects and resolves the relationship of the enterprise to its external environment. This work is often done by the senior management as part of strategic planning and competitive intelligence. The outline below shows typical content of the strategic plan.

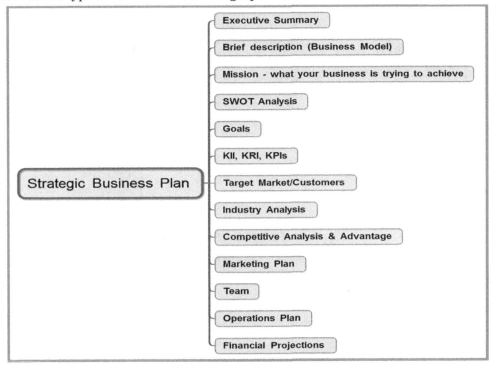

Figure 5: Example of Strategic Business Plan Outline

There are the following parts to this linkage:
1. Developing the relationship of the enterprise to the external environment including markets, products, services etc.
2. Analyzing the options to respond to the external environment. This may require the mapping of certain management disciplines currently in vogue such as Five Forces, SWOT analysis, Blue Ocean Strategy, BCG analysis and other of the 18 strategic disciplines.
3. Generating the strategic structure that drives the business. This often uses some management discipline to develop the options and determine the strategic imperatives. Value chain, Balanced Scorecard, Rummler-Brache[4] and other techniques provide such structuring mechanisms.
4. Establishing the linkages to the business architecture. This might include relationships of Strategies, Products or Major Functions to capabilities, value streams, policies (governance) and other essential business components. There are multiple views of how this can be done today.

The border surrounding the Strategic Business Architecture (in Figure 3) is the capturing of the structured scenarios with descriptive and analytical models that define one or more decision trade-offs, which are made to assess the satisfaction about the chosen course of strategic actions. Basically, they provide a measure of

---

[4] Retrieved on 4/13/2015 from http://www.rummler-brache.com/the-nine-boxes-model

the degree of certainty and risk that satisfy the executives in executing the strategic plan and the supporting Strategic Business Architecture.

In this process, criteria are evaluated for importance and certainty against the alternatives by the team. Trade-offs evaluated by the team. The alternatives examined by DAC'S management team are shown in Figure 6[5] below: "Locally Build-Sell, Regionally Manufacture-Ship, or Build here, Ship There." In this example, the management team selected "Build here, Ship there" since it satisfied most of the criteria examined, although there were differences of opinion.

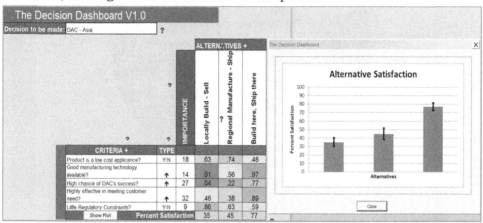

Figure 6: Satisfaction associated with Decision Alternatives

When a decision is made, one management team member takes on the responsibility to deliver this initiative with a supporting high-level business process architecture project.

Business Architecture Definition:

Business architecture is the set of representations showing the structuring of organizational parts that are put in place to deliver valued products, services or both. These representations describe "Why" the parts exit and "What" it wants to achieve; "What" the business does (its operations), "How" it interacts with its environment (relationships with other things), and "How" it expects to make the transition over time.

The Business Architecture Guild[6] has portrayed the following "gray-color" components of business architecture shown in the Figure 7 below. In the Guide to Business Architecture Book of Knowledge (Bizbok), the guild focuses on the capabilities, value streams, organization, and information that an organization uses to address the Strategic Business Architecture.

---

[5] Image from Decision Architecture, www.davidullman.com/DecisionDashboard

[6] Business Architecture Guild, http://www.businessarchitectureguild.org/

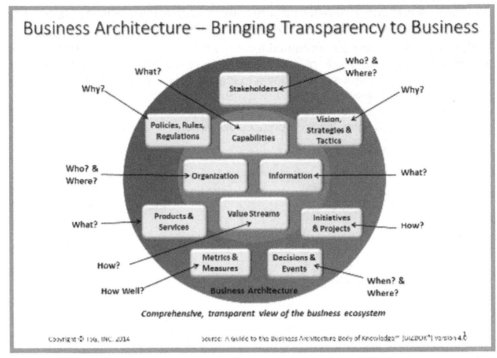

Figure 7: A view of Business Architecture Elements

Figure 7 shows various elements or components with the interrogative reasoning for each element being shown. What is not shown? The interconnection (relationship) or linkages of each component to another component are not shown. Not knowing the purpose behind interconnection with the degree of importance, risk, resources, and costs makes it difficult to develop the transition or transformation required for the Enterprise (IT) Architecture.

Architectures within the suite have components with their relationships that:

1. Can be defined by lists, matrices, and maybe a few other model types (UML, BPMN, etc.)
2. Can be graphically illustrated by using some architecture framework or form to represent the elements and relationships.
3. Can be analyzed in anyway: ranked, compared, inferred, and easily reported.
4. Can be dynamically changed to assess impact across the whole organization.

In either case, the architecture development process also includes a set of methods, analytics, and deliverables (etc. a suite of things or artifacts).

The border (in Figure 3) that surrounds the Enterprise (IT) Architecture captures the descriptive and analytical models of the chosen alternative which defines one or more Business Architecture solutions. It must be much more inclusive of the supporting details to transition to the Enterprise Architecture.

Enterprise (IT) Architecture

Enterprise Architecture (instituted to support the Information Technology (IT) organization) is a business practice whose role is to maintain information about the different processes, resources (people, costs, etc.), systems, data, and technology that is being used throughout the organization.

Here is where Enterprise (IT) Architecture comes into play. As the organization becomes more digitized with information systems implementations, various architectural elements have been built into IT's tooling to deliver automated software components supporting the organization's capabilities. IT's tooling captures information about the organization's operations (organization, functions, processes, decisions, information, roles of people, systems, applications, and services, etc.). This practice with its various methodologies and tools is to be used to show various technological interdependencies across the organization in decision-making scenarios. Having this type of information, IT is better able to analyze and understand the "digital" environment supporting the organization (see Wikipedia[7] for a list of some tools). Figure 9 shows an approach to show relationships mapped from the business to IT goals and objectives by Avolution[8].

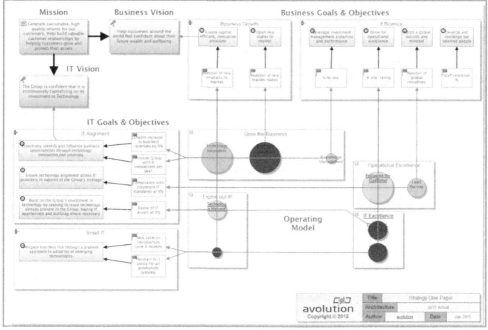

Figure 9: Mapping of Business Goals – Objectives to Information Technologies'

Other relationships are typically mapped using IT tooling that requires models that describe the following:

- Parts of the strategic business architecture – value chain, business canvas, or other management discipline used
- Information/data architecture
- System/application architecture
- Infrastructure/digital Technology
- Communications architecture
- Process architecture
- Business Rules architecture

A number of EA tools referenced in the appendix provide templates and reporting features that cover information technology views of enterprise architecture: Federal

---

[7] https://en.wikipedia.org/wiki/Enterprise_architecture

[8] Avolution (2015). ABACUS [Computer Software]. Retrieved from http://www.avolutionsoftware.com

Enterprise Architecture Framework ITIL, CoBIT, Open Group Architectural Framework (TOGAF), MoDAF, DoDAF, Zachman Framework for Enterprise Architectures, etc.

DECISION-TO-ACTION SCENARIO

Formulating the Architectural Content

There are various ways to acquire the content to support architectural/business analysis. They include management interviews, extracting content from strategic plans or corporate reporting requirements from quarterly or annual reports, deconstructing management disciplines like balanced scorecard, value based management, value chain and even inferring the list from operation models, such as process flows. The gathered material is sorted into each category of interest. Content can be imported from various tools (Access, Excel, Visio, databases, or other tools) that may contain desired information. Models of components (subjects) and relationships are created for analysis.

Difference between Structure and Architectural Content

There are two assertions that can be made about architecture and business analysis:

1. You can perform analytics on the architecture itself. This uses techniques that analyze the structure represented by the architecture using discovery, diagnostics, prescriptive and predictive analytics. After that you can look at content of what is actually in the architecture. This is useful for analysis of the impact of change on the content. For example, we see what the impact of strategic change is, find the organizations (who), stakeholders (who), information/data (what), processes (how) and applications (how) that are related to the change, then assess impact on the structure of the supporting models, not on the content of the database itself. That comes later.

2. Most analyses are focused on using the architecture to analyze content. Like looking at the furniture in a house and ignoring the structure of the house itself, using the structure to locate types of furniture like the sofas, chairs, and tables in the living room, beds, nightstands, TV in the bedroom etc. The equivalent is asking the question 'how do you find things in a database by using the structure (architecture) of the data?' The content is analyzed through the architecture and then some impact on the structure is identified backwards. Most navigation occurs through the architecture relationships to find some grouping of content often based on a keyword or phrase or data point as the focus of grouping. To find some grouping of text or quantitative content, an individual uses the relationships as defined by the enterprise architectural representation.

The Structure (the Architecture) versus the Content of the Architecture

Architecture provides the fundamental structure of the enterprise, whereas, the content of the architecture represents the specific items or instances related to the operational aspects of the enterprise.

Architecture is the Structure of the Enterprise

The architecture of the enterprise is defined and described by the relationships that exist in the enterprise. Most of this information is contained in the metadata (information about the data) of the enterprise. A pictorial characterization of the architecture might look like a high-level model. Other representations may contain more levels of detail.

Architecture is shown from different perspectives or levels of abstraction of the Enterprise with Content

When content is added to the structure of the architecture and related to other structures, the architecture becomes meaningful. For example, if one looks at a chair's bill of materials, one high-level view or perspective looks reasonably simple, but breaking it down into its individual pieces and connections is quite different. That is because of the unique combination of parts and pieces that make up the chair. We also need to describe the sequence, location of parts and pieces in order to make the chair.

In comparing two chair's bill of materials semantically, a similar view must be chosen to determine the similarity or differences that exist between them. It is only with content that a comparison becomes meaningful! That is also true when comparing organizations as well.

Architecture Content is the Execution of the Architecture

The content of the architecture is the items (instances) that occur when you collect and store the architecture itself. This is most obvious when looking at the data of the enterprise (i.e., data model). It is less obvious when looking at things like the process architecture. The process information about flow includes the name of the flow and the supporting details about the process flow (start time, connection from/to, participants who use content, frequency, participants, etc.) for each step in a flow.

Collecting Architectural Content

Using the concept of the business model, the contemporary definition varies greatly. Making explicit your business model can take on many forms. For example, the Business Model Canvas[9] focuses on four (4) major areas for consideration: infrastructure, offering, customers, and finances with nine (9) sub-areas being used in its template. For each sub-area of the template, one describes the specific activities. For infrastructure, key activities (i.e., value chain), key resources and the partner network is described. Likewise, the offering describes the value proposition as proposed by the organization. For the customers, a description of the segments, channels, and type of customer relationship being used. Finally, finances describe the cost structure and revenue stream. All of these elements are part of a business model definition. This ontological framework is quite inclusive of the elements of a business model.

Others have defined business model as simply: Customer Value Proposition, Profit Formula, Key Processes and Resources as four interlocking elements that, taken together, create and deliver value.[10] Joan Magretta describes the model as a story that explains how organizations work[11]. Of course, most business models have to answer the questions that Peter Drucker cited: "Who is the customer? What does the customer value? How do we make money? How do we deliver value to the customer at an appropriate cost?" Given these various definitions, no wonder architects find it difficult to position and align their architecture (s) with their business model. Note that all these approaches explain the business model from the point of execution. The architecture approach described here uses phrases (qualitative)

---

[9] Alexander Osterwalder (2004). *The Business Model Ontology - A Proposition In A Design Science Approach.* PhD thesis University of Lausanne, http://en.wikipedia.org/wiki/Business_Model_Canvas.

[10] Johnson, Mark W., Christensen, Clayton M. and Kagermann, Henning. *Reinventing Your Business Model,* Harvard Business Review, Dec., 2008.

[11] Magretta, Joan. *Why Business Models Matter.* Harvard Business Review, May, 2002.

with quantitative models to do more than the execution of the enterprise. This approach also helps to align the performance and knowledge perspectives of the organization as you cascade through the various architectures. By asking some very fundamental questions about the organization and its goals, one can separate and categorize the various components of the business and the environment it operates. This is portrayed in the following diagram.

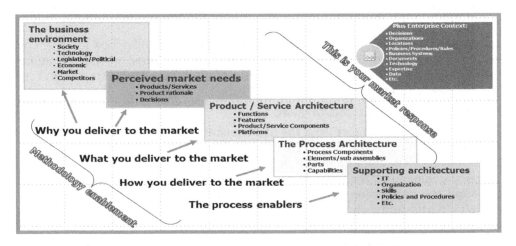

Figure 9: Business Methodology – Architecture References

In discussing architectural analysis, it is focuses on the subject areas with supporting detail content that need to be assessed effectively and efficiently. For example, a wide range of subjects or components (shown below) may be involved in doing the analysis:

Components used in Architecture(s)	Business Model Subject	External Architecture(s)	Strategic Business Architecture (Linkage)	Business Architecture (Linkage)	Enterprise IT Architecture (Digital)
Applications	Maybe	Maybe	Maybe	Maybe	Yes
Capabilities	Maybe		Yes	Yes	Yes
Communications				Yes	Yes
Content	Yes	Yes	Yes	Yes	Yes
Data	Yes	Yes	Maybe	Yes	Yes
Databases				Maybe	Yes
Decisions (Alternatives)	Yes	Yes	Yes	Yes	Yes
Documents				Maybe	Yes
Economics	Yes	Yes	Yes	Yes	Maybe
Entities	Yes	Yes	Yes	Yes	Yes
Functions		Maybe	Maybe	Yes	Yes
Goals	Yes		Yes	Yes	Yes
Information	Yes	Yes	Yes	Yes	Yes
Initiatives			Yes		Yes
Knowledge	Maybe	Maybe	Maybe	Maybe	Yes
Legislation	Yes	Yes	Maybe	Yes	
Locations	Yes	Yes	Maybe	Yes	Yes
Markets	Yes	Yes	Yes	Yes	Maybe
Money	Maybe	Maybe	Yes	Maybe	Yes
Organizations	Maybe	Maybe	Maybe	Maybe	Yes
Policies	Yes	Yes	Yes	Yes	
Procedures				Yes	Yes
Processes	Yes	Yes	Yes	Yes	Yes
Projects	Maybe	Maybe	Maybe	Maybe	Yes
Products / Services	Yes	Yes	Yes	Yes	Maybe
Rules (Governance)	Yes	Yes	Yes	Yes	Yes
Social Trends	Yes	Yes	Yes	Yes	Maybe
Strategies	Yes	Yes	Maybe	Maybe	Maybe
Systems			Maybe	Maybe	Yes
Taxonomies		Maybe	Maybe	Maybe	Yes
Time	Maybe	Yes	Yes	Yes	Yes
Technologies	Yes	Yes	Yes	Yes	
Technologies - Information	Maybe	Maybe	Maybe	Yes	Yes

Figure 10: Subject-Components used in Architecture(s)

Note: A "Yes" indicates that there should be some representation for that category. Not all architectures with the supporting methodologies include all the components shown here. Over time, the organization chooses from the various methodologies and converges on a representative set of architectural components. Because there are number of different descriptions of business model content, no two approaches are the same. Unfortunately, some of the business model references are implicit and not made explicit. A "*Maybe*" designation is indicated and may be applicable based upon the type of industry, management disciplines used and size of the organization.

At the end of the day the business model for execution is critical for strategic direction success. The executive team has the responsibility to clearly communicate the intent and the transitions (the linkages) between these architectures. They can use simple business analysis methods/techniques to address the required transformations. These methods and techniques help to describe artifacts needed to draw conclusions, selecting categories of analysis to use and providing traceable linkages between these architectures. By identifying, ranking, assessing impact and providing solution options for execution, management and staff can assess applicable knowledge to make the decision appropriate for the opportunity or performance problem that management wants solved. Given that these are available, phrase analytics coupled with quantitative methods will provide the insight needed for effective restructuring of execution along with the knowledge and performance whether major or minor.

Actually, doing it

Using a Step-by-Step Approach

To complete a supporting analysis, the management team has to address: (1) What subject areas (components) need to be analyzed, (2) capture relevant information/data about those subject areas, (3) identify key relationships between the subject areas, (4) produce relevant analysis and analytics (comparisons, contrasts, ranking, etc.), (5) understand the similarities and differences from analytics (6) develop solutions alternatives and recommendations, (7) make decision choice, (8) document rationale, and (9) transfer into a project.

There are various ways to acquire the content to support architectural/business analysis: including: management interviews, extracting content from strategic plans or corporate reporting requirements from quarterly or annual reports, deconstructing management disciplines like balanced scorecard, value based management, value chain and even inferring the list from operation models, such as process flows. Importing content from other electronic sources can be used to gather material for each category of interest.

A focal point for the analysis of an opportunity or issue requires choosing the components of interest. For example, using a process (the How) as a focal point it needs to be related to the other interrogatives:

- How and What (information/data: documents, databases, sensor data etc.)
- How and Who (who does the work)
- How and Why (why are you doing it)
- How and Where (where is it done)
- How and When (when do you do it, what triggers it, and any metrics about that process)

Relationships are mapped. Data is collected and verified. Models are built to examine the various semantics, rankings, and impacts because of the sundry relationships.

Selecting the Analytic Option(s) to Use

Based upon the business perspective (Strategic, Tactical, or Operational) various analytics can be applied to the architectural content. Each of these techniques uses subjective (qualitative) or factual (quantitative) data to produce the analytic assessments. These items can be organized in subjects and categories so typical evaluations (in matrices) can be used for organization ranking in terms of importance, certainty, risk, likelihood (probability), resources required/used, time (duration), costs, and the degree of satisfaction in the decision-making process.

Business Perspective	Quantitative	Money (A special form of Quantity)	Text (Model Phrase Analytics, a special form of text analytics)	Big Data Video, Audio, Pictures, large data sets, sensor data etc.
Strategic (Value Chain, Business Models)	Cluster analysis Data Mining Influence diagrams	Risk analysis Component analysis Comparative analysis	Model comparative analysis Inference analysis	Pattern matching Clustering
Tactical (Functional models, reference models, large models like Supply Chain, Order Fulfillment)	Comparative Analysis Cause and effect Control Limits	Cause and effect Influence diagrams	Affinity analysis Adjacency Matrices Clustering Impact analysis Ranking Process Mining	What If Analysis Scenarios
Operational (Specific group and individual processes)	Optimization Sensitivity analysis	Decision Trees Simulation	Impact degree ranking Affinity	Simulation

Figure 11: Architecture Analytics used for Operational Perspectives

Different approaches to problem-solving can be used. A combination of divergent and convergence thinking is used to explore all the alternatives and then select only those alternatives that are most promising for solution implementation.

In a typical merger and acquisition scenario, components and relationships for the models would be chosen. Let's assume two banking organizations are merging and the management team wants to consolidate their demand deposit operation. They must look at both operations and collect information about: locations, people, roles, regulations, processes, procedures, rules, information, data, applications, systems, costs, and metrics that relate to performance. Obviously, a comparison of financials is important to such a merged operation. They are usually examined first. Certainly capabilities are evaluated to seek improvement in the market, customer satisfaction, and the possibility of new opportunities.

One important factor is the regulations potentially affecting the operational locations of the "to-be" bank. If the operation spans countries or states, not only are the systems more complex but the business process with operational support of those systems become more complex. The regulations impact the staff, business processes, systems, applications, rules, data, and decisions that require change. By performing the comparisons of the processes across locations, the bank was able to identify 35 very complex operations due to the regulations that needed to be streamlined and agreed upon prior to the merger. Since the cultures of both of the organizations were quite different, this analysis highlighted the difficulty it was going to be to make the merger work in the long term.

In the manufacturing industry, Computer Integrated Manufacturing (CIM) was a concept in the 80's, the 90's brought the efforts to model various elements of the architecture, and in the 2000's various manufacturers have implemented highly sophisticated CIM manufacturing systems. The models created focused on the data interchanges that are required to enable intercommunication between people and machines. Descriptive and quantitative models with supporting analytics have become a critical part of making CIM successful today. The mastery of CIM has occurred over 40 years. Now we are starting to do design via different modeling techniques and delivering results via linked technology. The current application of the 3D printer on the engineering design process and the executional process is dramatically more effective and efficient.

On a side note, for example, going to your dentist for a crown may only take an hour using some of the same manufacturing technologies (machine with software, take pictures for dimensions, a numerical control milling machine to shape crown, and only a few minutes for dentist to complete final fitting).

Executive management is going through a similar transformation. The use of various models and analytics is just starting to impact the decision-making process. The science behind management is the search for new knowledge; technology is that application of that new knowledge in practical ways. The use of descriptive modeling and supporting analytics is at the forefront of a new management paradigm driven by big data, predictive analytics, and the necessity to make faster, opportunistic, but less risk-adverse decisions for the organization.

Analytic Results

Figure 12 shows a number of architectural touch points across the organization. It provides us with some understanding of the scope and complexity of "whole" architectural representation. The number of touch points has significantly increased in recent years due to computer and mobile communication that is readily available. It shows a typical organizational environment where management is challenged to organize decision-based information for analytical purposes. But, architecture components can be gathered in small chunks by the use of lists and matrices to identify key relationships. Using inference across matrices technique, an impact analysis can readily identify those areas of key management concern.

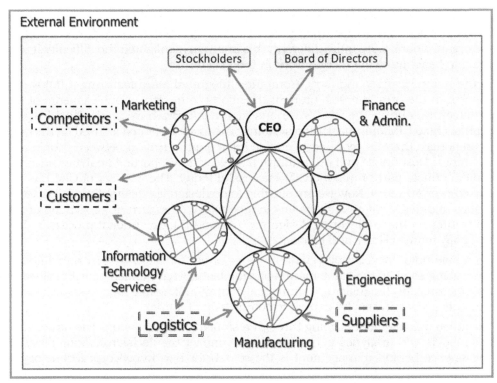

Figure 12: Architecture based Communications

The impact of building small architectural components and mapping them provides Business Architects and C-level management a way to change the current models to a new targeted model and explore alternatives. This capability provides the management team to greater insight to assess the risks associated with the scenario being examined.

As each scenario unfolds, finding the best possible choice by eliminating uncertainty given available resources, and choosing with a known and acceptable level of satisfaction and risk is the key point of architectural decision-making. Generically, most commercial organization scenarios include a progression of architectural components as shown in Figure 13. For governmental and non-profit organizations, a number of the same components are used but are mitigated by the culture and industry factors that need to be considered in formulating the underlying models.

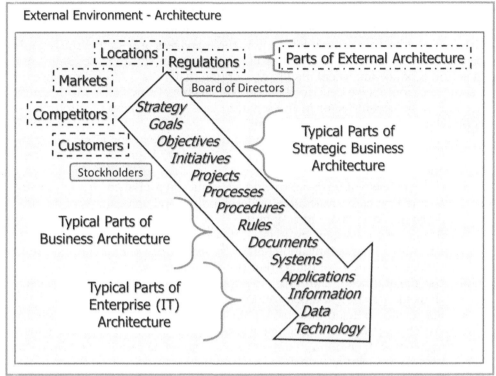

Figure 13: Architecture Suites for Transformational Change

These architectures and models certainly have a "current" representation with their implementations. To achieve a desired future or targeted environment, a transformation is required. Such a transformation has a transitive state prior to reaching the future/targeted architecture. Management should understand the degree of uncertainty about the reliability, risk, and adaptability of the architecture elements. Key intermediate or long-term architecture, with associated analytics highlights the breadth of the organization's resource challenges in a way that executives can minimize the overall risk.

WHAT DOES ALL THIS MEAN?

The value of one approach (structural) versus the other (content) depends on the problem.

When considering a merger, acquisition, consolidation or any other structural change, the value is in looking at the structure independent of the content. Whereas, if you are looking for specific things like correlating consumer buying habits then using the architecture to search content is more important.

Sometimes companies start with structure and sometimes with content. Whichever one an enterprise starts with, eventually both are impacted and both need articulation. The good news is these can be done incrementally and updated incrementally. So a 'big bang' project is not needed! So, you need to understand both ways of doing the analysis.

Most of the interest today is in short-term analysis that uses *content* to find things out. Long-term impact deals with the *structure* of the enterprise which translates into the architecture components themselves.

CONCLUSIONS

One of the issues with architecture today is its relevance to management. Whatever is done in architecture must relate to how the managers and staff of the organization identify with the architectural results that they can see and use. Suites of architecture produce analytical results as working materials that lead management to some decision. As we described earlier, the degree of satisfaction with solution chosen is a significant factor in the organizational commitment of resources and action taken. Some key observations are:

- Always store and maintain architecture materials in one integrated convenient place for ease of analytics for discovery, diagnostic, prescriptive and predictive analysis.
- Using consistent terminology and semantics in architecture analyses to ensure that communication, understanding, and agreements of the underlying concepts are meaningful.
- Structuring the architecture (s) so they are representative of the existing structure of the organization/enterprise and including content that represents the operational things that run the enterprise.
- Use the architecture analyses to support executive and managerial decisions in improving the performance of the enterprise.
- For no other reason than having the architecture (s) stored in a repository and the capabilities to produce the associated analytics, it provides management with creditable content to understand, assess impacts, and evaluate scenarios that help manage the business.

In demonstrating how a set of descriptive and quantitative architectural analytic results related various architectural components, the assertion being made is that providing the relationships and components through suites of architecture is the new management direction. It provides a transformational technique addressing the long-term interests, more than just operational problem solving. As such, architecture results become a significant instrument for management decision-to-actions while presenting any opportunity for long-term organizational performance and improvement.

Design and Reengineering of Business: An Engineering Approach

Brian K Seitz, Intellectual Arbitrage Group, USA

Abstract: Other engineering disciplines have long matured to a basic set of practices to design a product and validate its fitness for use. This has not been the case within the Business Process Reengineering (BPR) community. Business reengineering, when practiced well, has been more about optimization than innovation. Management Consulting's Strategic Planning has been unable to keep up with the rapid market changes, so what is left? The author has developed an approach that enables business leaders and IT professional to work on common group to "design" the business with common and popular methods such as Business Model Canvas, BPMN and others to yield models which visualize the needed attributes of a business that affect its capabilities and performance. Currently the author is using this approach to reengineer his employer's internal value stream.

WHY BUSINESS DESIGN AND REENGINEERING IS IMPORTANT

The objective behind business design is to provide the planning necessary to build and evolve an enterprise in the most efficient and effective way possible to be successful in the marketplace. This demands business architects that should be intentional with regard to the resources as much as practical, given the constraints of the business environment. Similar to product design, resources (people, technology, funding, time) are rapidly becoming constrained and the efficient use of such has become a mandate.

While *technology* and *funding* have always been managed resources, *people* and *time* have also increased in importance. The realities of the marketplace have positioned knowledge and learning as scarce resources. The domain of human knowledge now is so large it is impossible for a single person or team have the complete expertise needed to function in today's ecosystem.

Similarly time usage was at a slower rate of consumption; time-to-market has now become crucial, making time a critical resource to manage. An enterprise can no longer afford the luxury of careful methodological process as in the 1950s.

> *"Today, only 15 percent of product developers know the cost of delay associated with their products"* [1]

Business now must deal with uncertainty like merchants during the renaissance and take calculated risks if they are to meet time-to-market needs. Dotting all the "I's" and crossing all the "T's" has given way to the agile mantra "fail fast and learn." However, if the broader enterprise infrastructure cannot support the rapid change of components, Agile without a business-based architecture is a recipe for disaster. A business will likely implode from all the inert materials (i.e., Technical Debt) that builds up over time.

---

[1] (Reinertsen, 2009)

This has become the innovators' theme song; what organization does not want to be seen as innovative? Not every business venture is an innovation effort however, and using the wrong business model can spell disaster for an enterprise. Knowing which type of model to develop has become as important as which offering to provide to the market. This is the rational for Business Design and Reengineering.

Business Design Dilemmas

One of the classic dilemmas often cited in design books is the potential conflict between form and function. This conflict is often discussed in many human endeavors: Art vs. Science, etc. These boil down to aesthetics vs. functionality. The discipline of designing and reengineering business is no exception to such debates.

There are often many ways to accomplish the same functional task; it can become a trade-off between the aesthetic vs. efficiency and effectiveness. However, effectiveness starts one on that slippery slope to the aesthetic. Effectiveness means that the results desired are achieved. Those results are not necessarily functional and often are conditional to the observer's value system. As such for the Architect, Engineer or other Design Professional the trade-off between aesthetics and functionality is a constantly-evolving dialog as values are clarified and/or change over time.

In the Design Engineering Disciplines it is not uncommon for these practitioners to use trade-off matrices to establish the optimum balance between functional attributes of a product, leaving aesthetic decisions to stylist and other types of design professionals. In the case of business design, aesthetic concerns are only now starting to be address through sub-disciplines UX/UI.

Business Design and Reengineering a Maturing Discipline

Business Design and Reengineering, like other design disciplines, is on a path to higher levels of maturity. What that end of that maturity lifecycle will be is too early to tell. Like science's examination of physics, the forces there were originally theorized have been merged into one. So, too, the design praxis of all disciplines may have a single root from which others have emerged.

Proposed Discipline Lifcycle

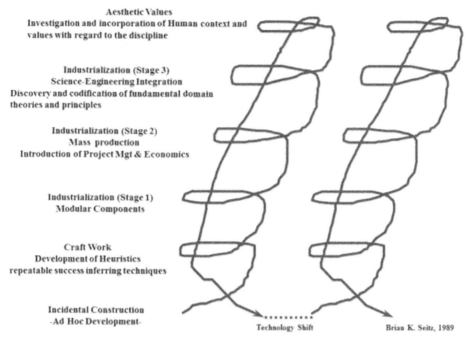

Aesthetic Values
Investigation and incorporation of Human context and values with regard to the discipline

Industrialization (Stage 3)
Science-Engineering Integration
Discovery and codification of fundamental domain theories and principles

Industrialization (Stage 2)
Mass production
Introduction of Project Mgt & Economics

Industrialization (Stage 1)
Modular Components

Craft Work
Development of Heuristics
repeatable success inferring techniques

Incidental Construction
-Ad Hoc Development-

Technology Shift   Brian K. Seitz, 1989

Figure 1. Discipline Maturity Lifecycle

The author has observed that all the design disciplines' praxis over the decades of evolution follow a similar lifecycle. This is where an individual discipline is in its lifecycle and maturity level.

Business Environment and market are changing

The environment in which businesses compete today has significantly changed. A once slowly-evolving market and ecosystem have moved to a dynamic, rapid-pace world where change is the new normal. Delays to entry or delivery are now costly as competitors can rapidly replicate offerings with added features. Thus a first-mover advantage can be quickly eroded if they lack rapid and continual market refresh of both product and business model.

Business needs to be more efficient, effective, and adaptable

The scarcity of resources, all types of resources, dictates that businesses need to be more efficient and effective with the resources they control. Waste is punished severely in the market as is an inability to quickly adapt.

Where scaling-up based upon mass production concepts such as economic order quantity (EOQ) was the order of the day, now time-to-market and agility is the corporate watchword. Corporate powerhouses that took time to optimize production are now being overtaken by smaller, faster, and lighter competitors that can move with changes in the ecosystem and customer preferences.

Businesses needs to be more intentional

This infers that businesses must be more intentional with how resources are used. Which in turn infers that having an efficient process is not enough. Today it's a matter of *Doing the Right Things* as well as *Doing Things Right*. However, to achieve this goal, businesses need to design not only what they deliver to the market but how they do so. As predicted several decades ago, businesses will need to compete not only on the offering, but on the business model that produces it.

WHAT IS BUSINESS DESIGN AND REENGINEERING

Business Design and Reengineering is the practice behind business architecture. The strategic core of Business Design and Reengineering is Business Model Innovation and Optimization

Approach to designing a business like any other product

The problem with Business Architecture and Designing Enterprises is that the products are typically not visible. Only the design artifacts that represent the abstract constructs of business organization. Thus, unlike design in other disciplines, the results of implementation are indirectly visible through operations only.

Metrics and Measurement

A CAUTIONARY TALE

Less than a decade ago I was witness to an organization that had over two hundred metrics that were being measured. When asked: What was done with all of these measures? I heard crickets around the table. The awful truth was these measurements were collected because the COO asked to have metrics. However, nothing was done with these. No reviews, no analysis, no decisions, and no actions other than collecting and charting these at significant cost to the organization.

Years later the metric list had been trimmed and measurements were reviewed for conformance. However, a risk-adverse culture created a system that always reported "Green" even when projects were obviously failing. This disabled their ability for learning and adapting to change.

There are a lot of measurements available to an enterprise today. A dialect has been developed around enterprise metrics and measures. One must have been buried not to have heard of Key Performance Indicators (KPIs) or Six Sigma. While measurement is important, measurement without a purpose is a waste of resources. Too often measures are taken to justify activity, not to provide management control information.

If one takes a cue from the manufacturing industry which is highly focused on production then core metrics an enterprise should use are those that directly enable understanding time, cost, and quality. These metrics are interrelated; that is, changes to one metric impacts the others and thus improving or maintaining these becomes a balancing act in the context of an ever-changing ecosystem in which the enterprise operates in.

Indirect measurement

Measurement at times seems more like a puzzle in physics. If you can't see it how do you know it's there or can measure it. Astronomers have long since discovered you can measure something indirectly by measuring the effects it has on other objects. So too can Entrepreneurs and Business Executives. An effective business design is measured by how well it operates and obtains its objectives.

However, measurement of *how well* is a subjective evaluation that should be determined ahead of actual measurement. The reason for such can be illustrated by the results of a study decades ago. In this study the act of measuring affected the outcome. This coined the term the "Hawthorne Effect.[2]"

Value Measurement

While an enterprise is typically measured by investors by ROI, an enterprise's rational to exist is more than simply capturing revenue. For an enterprise to be successful long term it must provide utility and value to others in the ecosystem; customers, suppliers, and other stakeholders. While a noted economist suggested the only obligation a corporation has is to increase shareholder value, one has to question such a single metric. If corporations are as established by court interpretation as class of person and profess to be citizens then shouldn't they too should be measuring themselves by additional standards other that net worth? A single-minded philosophy negates its effects on the ecosystem and environment and often employs strategies that will eventually poison the well, so to speak. Thus strategies to maximize externalities is a curved blade that points back to the business.

Value to these others in the ecosystem may not be a financial measure (e.g., a car can provide multiple benefits to a purchaser other than basic transportation utility as illustrated in Customer$APPEALS). If measured solely on transportation efficiency a car would likely lose out to mass transportation. Thus there are other values which are under consideration by car purchasers.

> Business Performance is based on values, ROI is not the only value of concern.

Business Modeling and Simulation – Business Design Artifacts

Modeling and Simulation are activities that assist the business designer in creating a new or reengineering an old enterprise. Through these activities design artifacts are created and hopefully used for analysis to determine fitness and appropriateness for use. As with design artifacts in other disciplines a questions of qualities these artifacts must have is a matter of opinion.

Business Value

Business Value can be measured in other than financial gains. However, the majority of enterprises translate business value into economic terms using such as the "lingua franca" of business. However, this measurement may becoming a lagging indicator a scorecard of a more significant driving force.

Cost of Time

The financial success both internally and externally for enterprises now has two masters: Money and Time. The later appears to be the more dominate master at this moment. What this suggests is that optimization around time

---

2 https://en.wikipedia.org/wiki/Hawthorne_effect. The Hawthorne effect (also referred to as the observer effect) is a type of reactivity in which individuals modify or improve an aspect of their behavior in response to their awareness of being observed

both internally and externally has become the driving force. Development concepts such as LEAN and AGILE are becoming the dominate philosophy around offering realization.

The current economics model underpinning these concepts are that LEAN and AGILE propionates advocate are applied to only the production portion of offering realization. Much time and effort is focused around queue sizing and scheduling of the software development (DEVOPS) portion of offering realization. This is based upon the concept of Lifecycle Value. The assumption is an asset (offering) will depreciate in value over time and that the later its induction to use the less total value can be captured (See Figure 2. Lifecycle Value).

Lifecycle Value $LCP = I\phi \sum_{t=1}^{n} \frac{S\tau}{(1+\kappa)\tau} + \frac{R\eta}{(1+\kappa)\eta}$

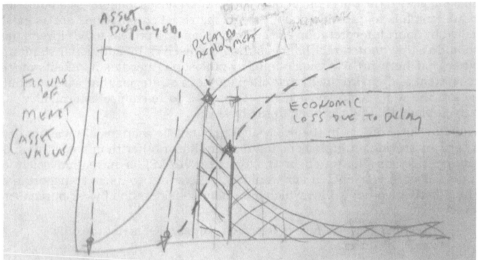

Figure 2. Lifecycle Value

It is my belief that what is missing from such a model is the ability to account for ideas and conceptualization. Offering Realization actually starts further upstream and while accounting systems still have problems addressing the value of intellectual property. These none-the-less have value or patents or would not be of any value. This issue and how to determine value-add as ideas move through the development process from problem identification through design is an area rich in future research potential that I only scratched the surface on years ago (Seitz B. K., CIM Architect Notebook, 1986). In terms of perceived worth people know that solving a problem or a design to address a problem is worth more than identifying the problem. However, accounting systems today do not effectively value or manage such intellectual inventories within a firm.

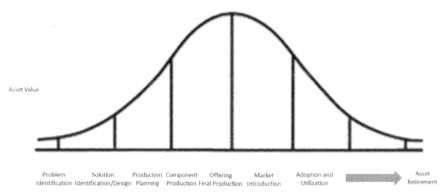

Figure 3. Product Lifecycle

As Enterprises continue to move toward more information content and services as part of their offerings the Work-in-Process (WIP) becomes harder to measure as do other factors. Economist and Accountants all discuss the time value of money as a basis for investment measurement. "A dollar now is worth more than a dollar a year from now". However, there is the corollary to such a theory, the *money value of time*. Time is the one resource in business that is completely perishable. Once it passes it cannot recovered or salvaged. Once it is gone it is gone.

In the mid-1900s, during the heyday of mass production, economists developed the concept of economic order quantity (EOQ). This simple construct was used to justify and drive creation of large production facilities. People often talk about "scaling up." This is the derivative of that concept. If a corporation invests in large production product runs, product costs can be lowered, thus increasing profits. This concept was based upon costly equipment and materials and low-cost labor. At that time optimizing around these two resources equipment and materials made sense.

However, as the market has changed so has the economic system that operates it. Today *time-to-market* is the driving force. Exclusivity of markets and offerings is vanishing. An unknown competitor half the globe away could replicate an offering at a potentially lower price and ship it to your domestic markets within months. GM is still reeling from Toyota's and other's focus on reducing time-to-market. This issue becomes more pronounced in areas of "intellectual offerings" such as software and information. The advent of the internet as made these markets hyper-competitive. An offering introduced Monday could very well have several competitors within days or weeks.

BUSINESS MODELING AND SIMULATION – BUSINESS DESIGN ARTIFACTS

Modeling and Simulation are activities that assist the business designer in creating a new or reengineering an old enterprise. Through these activities design artifacts are created and hopefully used for analysis to determine fitness and appropriateness for use. As with design artifacts in other disciplines a questions of qualities these artifacts must have is a matter of opinion.

Artifact Qualities

Much can be discusses around qualities of a design. Most often is engineering design quality and checks are often limited to presentation standards rather than the qualities of the intellectual construct these represent. The one factor key to success of business design models is *fidelity*; how closely does the model represent the behavior of the actual real world article?

Fidelity

A key quality of any artifact is that of fidelity. Fidelity has been defined as "accuracy, or exact correspondence to some given quality or fact." Fidelity can be decomposed into two subordinate and related qualities; accuracy and precision.

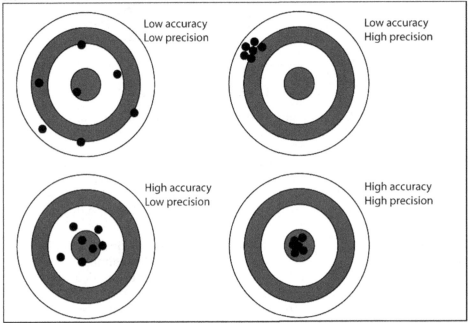

Figure 4. Accuracy and Precision

Accuracy: The degree of conformity and correctness of something when compared to a true or absolute value.

Precision: A state of strict exactness—how often something is strictly exact.

Together these define how well a model or simulation resembles or predicts the behavior or outcome of the real object under examination. The degree of fidelity required, like beauty. is subjective and often is a tradeoff between cost and benefit. **A model with more fidelity may not be worth the added cost to produce for the additional information.** *The bottom line to this concept is to select the minimum level of detail necessary to make an effective decision and no more. This enables an enterprise to be more agile and adaptive.*

An example: Definition of business requirements often is expressed in product feature terms rather than what the business is trying to achieve. While using a common construct between the "customer" and "builder,, this limits those that build and manifest solutions needed. Using such a construct often limits the thinking of those developing the solution to *optimizing* rather than *innovating*. Changing the construct using business models changes the discussion from "how" to achieve to a "what" needs to be achieve. Such a change limits the level of detail product design communicated between "customer" and "builder" but establishes the success context that the business will ultimately use to assess the products and service purchase criteria[3].

Business Models

Business design has not evolved much past Sloan's organizational model until the recent past when Michael Porter introduced his Value Stream model. The Sloan model was concerned with formal organizational structure based upon business functions. These functions were primarily internally based.

More recently Slywotzky, Osterwalder and Ries have introduced models that expanded the perspective of how to describe a business's operation in context to the markets in it participates.

Holistic and Multi-dimensional

As these models have evolved, so has the thinking around the various attributes of a business structure. Those concerned with business strategy and operations advocate looking at the business from multiple perspectives.

Advancing from this concept of perspectives, we propose creating a framework similar to architecture and mechanical engineering. While the *Zachman Framework for Information Systems* provides a generic set of dimensions it leaves short of the integration of these dimensions into a holistic system like descriptive geometry. In geometric systems dimensions are combined to create perspectives (views). Thus a change of a dimension in one perspective will affect the object under examination in other perspectives. This suggests that design space is prescriptive and calculable.

Systematic

Advancing from a framework to organize the design space, one is left with the requirement to develop a repeatable approach to address working in this space intentionally altering the objects attributes. In other design disciplines this systematic approach has been called a *praxis*, practice or methodology. In usage this approach is simply a sequence of activities that yields a repeatable result.

Simulations

Simulations provide something that Frameworks and static models cannot. These types of tools and methods enable visualization of the interactions of components. It is one thing to know there is a relationship among various components; it is another to see the dynamics of that interaction.

During the 70s and early 80s simulation tools suffered from two flaws:

- First, the level of effort to create a simulation was almost as much as the effort to build the real thing.
- Second, the data necessary to drive simulations required significant effort to find or generate or was not well understood.

Thus simulation—even in mechanical product design—was not used as an everyday tool. Only products or issues of high value or risk were subject to such analysis. Given the value and risks inferred by business models it surprising that more simulation tools and simulations are not used.

---

[3] Refer to Customer$APPEALS

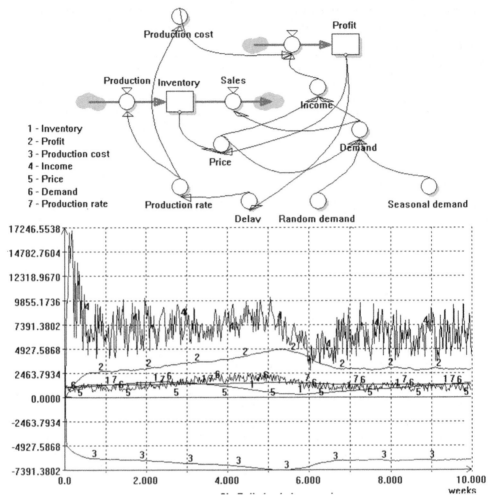

Figure 5. Systems Dynamics Model and Simulation

BUSINESS DESIGN AND REENGINEERING PRAXIS

Designing and Reengineering are about determining how to improve business performance. This can be accomplished through innovation, optimization or both. These improvement strategies can be applied to the offering the enterprise delivers or the means by which the enterprise delivers value to the customer (business model). This section of the paper primary addresses the later.

The author uses a question first approach towards methodology creation rather than a tools first approach. This enables a practitioner to select and/or modify the methods and tools that work best for him or her.

The visual methodology (refer to Figure 6. Visual Methodology) is one possible set of methods/tools to populate the methodology.

HOW TO DESIGN AND REENGINEER A BUSINESS (PROCESS/METHODOLOGY)

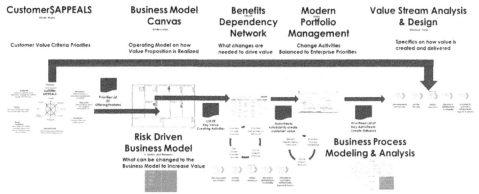

Figure 6. Visual Methodology

Business Model Innovation and Optimization

Innovation and Optimization are two sides of the same coin. Innovation is concerned with creating something unique and different from before, while optimization is concern with removing unneeded activities from an existing endeavor.

Prioritization

Prioritization Problem

Prioritization happens at many stages and levels within an enterprise. The concerns around how to prioritize are typically not addressed by the same methods or people. Thus selecting a prioritization approach becomes a task of identifying the prioritization problem, the decision makers and stakeholders involved.

Stakeholder

Executive levels are typically looking to balance gains vs. investments thus a method to show tradeoffs that provide the optimum tradeoff are best. However, presenting such multifactor tradeoffs is problematic. The time needed to understand such optimization weighs heavy on executives thus they typically ask for simple binary decisions. The hoped-for assumption is that enough due diligence has been done prior to being presented with these options.

Supporting staff typically provide the due diligence needed to provide executives with a recommended prioritization. Multiple spreadsheets of analysis summary data are often used. A master spreadsheet enabling weighting of factors gathered from these analysis is the typical best practice.

Execution staff manage capacity and throughput. As such simpler methods that balance corporate priority, schedule and capacity are the order of the day.

Methods

Methods such as Balanced Scorecard and BEAM are multifactor prioritizations methods that are typically used by supporting staff. Real Options and Options Theory are usually reserved for financial analysis however, more applications of these within other parts of the enterprise are gaining favor.

Weighted Shortest Job First (WSJF)[4] is one of the preferred methods of those practicing Agile as it enables working on activities that are easiest to deliver with the greatest benefit.

Tradeoffs

Enterprises like others do not have unlimited resources as such they must make tradeoff between Opportunities, Benefits, Liabilities and Risks. Often these tradeoff are made without realizing same. Risks, such as interdependencies, need to be explicitly addressed lest these create a risk to the business's continuity.

In the design of an Enterprise there are many tradeoffs that need to be made. These are around the values, priorities of business management, customers within the ecosystem and the resources available to each. Several methods are needed to address the various tradeoffs as no enterprise has unlimited resources.

What methods/tools to use and what each does

Customer$APPEALS

Customer$APPEALS examines the priority of product/service attributes that influences a customer-purchase decision.[5]

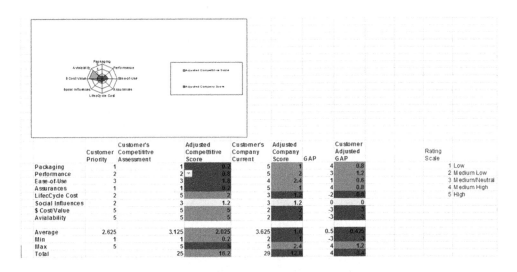

Figure 7. Customer$APPEALS

Business Model / Lean Canvases

Both Canvases provide a visualization of the operating model of the enterprise. The Business Model Canvas is more suited toward understanding an existing business design and focuses on optimizing the design. While the Lean Canvas is focused upon leaning and discovery of a business design. Lean Canvas is also effective in *innovation* (reimaging) of an existing business.

---

[4] WSJF = [User Value + Time Value + Risk Reducation | Opportunity Enablement Value] / Job Size – Principles of Product Development Flow, Donald G. Reinertsen, Celeritas Publishing, 2009

[5] Customer$APPEALS developed by Peter Marks of Design Insight

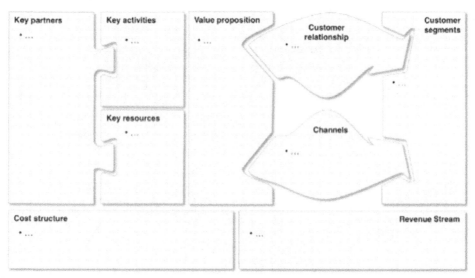

Figure 8. Business Model Canvas

Problem	Solution	Unique Value Proposition	Unfair Advantage	Customer Segments
Top 3 problems	Top 3 features	Single, clear, compelling message that states why you are different and worth paying attention	Can't be easily copied or bought	Target customers
	Key Metrics		Channels	
	Key activities you measure		Path to customers	

Cost Structure	Revenue Streams
Customer Acquisition costs	Revenue Model
Distribution costs	Life Time Value
Hosting	Revenue
People, etc.	Gross Margin

PRODUCT · MARKET

Lean Canvas is adapted from The Business Model Canvas (http://www.businessmodelgeneration.com) and is licensed under the Creative Commons Attribution-Share Alike 3.0 Un-ported License.

Figure 9. Lean Canvas

Cause-Effect Diagrams

Cause-Effect Diagrams provide a visualization of events, actions or decisions and consequences. There are many types that provide the business design insights to the various aspects of a design. Chief among these are Strategic Capabilities Network, Results Chain, and Benefits Dependency Networks. Usage of these diagrams provides insight to how elements are linked within an enterprise's course of action.

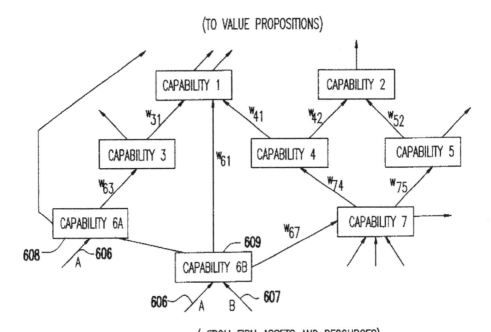

Figure 10. Strategic Capabilities Network (IBM)

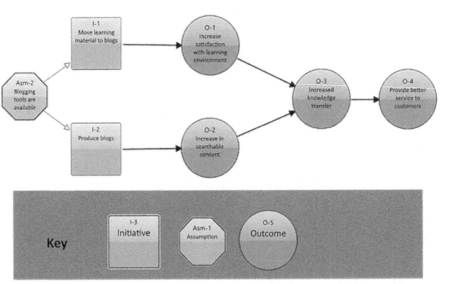

Figure 11. Results Chain (DMR Consulting)

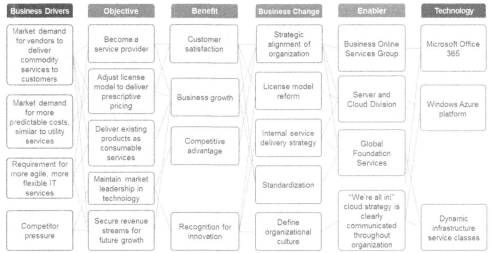

Figure 12. Benefits Dependency Network (Canfield University)

Matrix Analysis Methods

Matrix Analysis methods, similar to cause-effect diagrams, provide visualization of interactions among elements. Unlike cause-effect diagrams, matrices are limited to pairwise comparisons. However, matrix analysis allows for mathematical values to be displayed indicating magnitudes of interactions.

Strategic Position Analysis / Financial Analysis (SPAN/FAN)

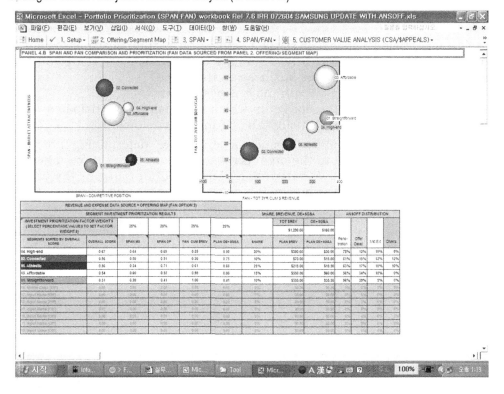

SPAN/FAN is an evalution to the Boston Consulting Matrix. These two matrices provide an indication as to the relative financial desirablity as well as strategic positioning of a strategy.

Business Model Analysis

While many may *dispute* that internal markets of Information Technology organizations behave the same as external; it is the author's contention that they do indeed behave the same. However, the dynamics of behaviors manifest themselves differently. Example, the "Shadow IT" problem that most CIO have to deal with is an example of the internal market finding solutions and resources the IT organization failed to deliver per customer priorities.

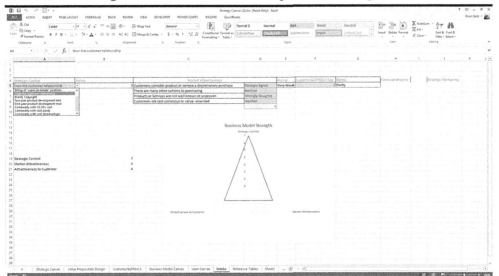

Analyzing a business model gives the business owner and designer insight as to the current and possibly future viability of the business. The evaluation model suggested examines the business on three axis:

- Strategic Control Strength the business exerts
- Attractiveness of the market in which the business participates
- Attractiveness of the business's offerings to customers

The first two axes are from the business's perspective, determining if the area to be served is beneficial to the organization. The last of the three takes the customer/client perspective, determining how important/urgent the area of concern is and how well the business meets those needs and wants.

Design Structure Matrix

Design Structure Matrix Analysis provides a stronger visualization of interactions between elements. It can be used effectively to visualize interaction depth and/or risks between those elements.

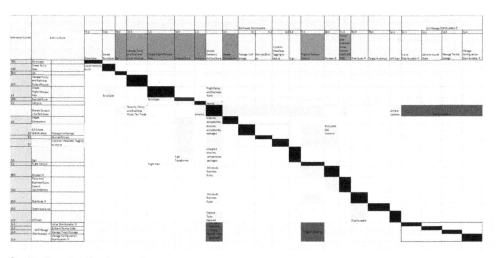

Quality Function Deployment

[Functional Allocation and Tradeoffs] QFD or its popular incarnation *House of Quality* provides an effective means by which to allocate requirements and strategy across the development cycle. Its visualization also enables the designer to gain insights on how best to allocate requirements thus making it an effective design tradeoff tool.

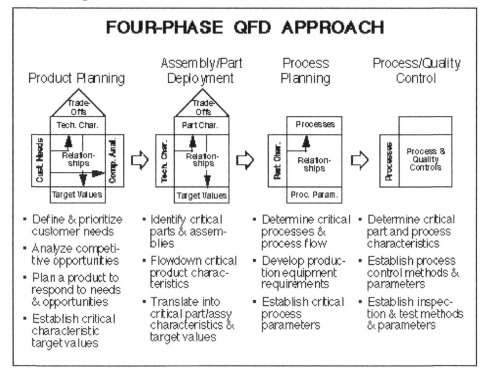

BIBLIOGRAPHY

Akao , Y. (n.d.). QFD: Quality Function Deployment - Integrating Customer Requirements into Product Design . 2004: Productivity Press.

Baghai, M., Coley, S., & White, D. (1999). The Alchemy of Growth --kickstarting and sustaining growth in your company. London, England: Orion Business.

Blank, S. (2013). The Four Steps to the Epiphany --Successful Strategies for Products that Win. K&S Ranch, Inc

Blank, S. (2014). Holding a Cat by the Tail --Lessons from an Entrepreneurial Life. K&S Ranch Publishing LLC

Blank, S., & Dorf, B. (2012). The Startup Owner's Manual—The step by step guide to building a great company. K&S Ranch, Inc

Bovet , D., & Martha, J. (2000). Value Nets: Breaking the Supply Chain to Unlock Hidden. Wiley

Burton, R. M., Obel, B., & DeSanctis, G. (2011). Organizational Design -a step by step approach (2nd Ed. ed.). Cambridge, UK: Cambridge University Press

Cohen , L. (1995). Quality Function Deployment: How to Make QFD Work for You. Prentice Hall

Guinta, L. R., & Praizler, N. C. (n.d.). The QFD Book: The Team Approach to Solving Problems and Satisfying Customers Through Quality Function Deployment. 1993: AMACOM

Hedley, G. (2009). Get your business to work. Benbella

Humble, J., Molesky, J., & O'Reilly, B. (2015). Lean Enterprise --How High Performance Organizations Innovate at Scale. O'Reilly

Kesler, G., & Kates, A. (2011). Leading Organization Design. San Francisco, CA: Jossey-Bass

Markowitz, H. M. (1968). Portfolio Selection: Efficient Diversification of Investments. New York, New York: Yale University Press

Marks, P. (n.d.). Winning Products (understanding the psychology of customer buying decisions)

Maurya , A. (2012). Running Lean: Iterate from Plan A to a Plan That Works. O'Reilly Media

Netessine, S., & Girotra, K. (2014). The Risk-Driven Business Model: Four Questions That Will Define Your Company. Harvard Business Review Press

Osterwalder, A., & Pigneur, Y. (2010). Business Model Generation: A Handbook for Visionaries, Game Changers, and Challengers. Wiley

Palfrey, J., & Gasser, U. (2012). Interop -the promise and perils of highly interconnected systems. New York, New York: Basic Books

Reinertsen, D. G. (2009). The Principle of Product Development Flow –Second Generation Lean Product Development. Celeritas Publishing

Ries, E. (2011). The Lean Startup: How Today's Entrepreneurs Use Continuous Innovation to Create Radically Successful Businesses. Crown Business

Seitz, B. (2015). Metrics Version1 --Value Management Metrics in Practice. Microsoft

Seitz, B. K. (1985). Investment Strategies for Information Systems (Areospace Edition). IBM

Seitz, B. K., & Mascarella, G. (1998). Rapid Economic Justification. Microsof.

Slywotzky , A., & Morrison, D. (1997). The Profit Zone: How Strategic Business Design Will Lead You to Tomorrow's Profits. Crown Business

Slywotzky, A. (1995). Value Migration: How to Think Several Moves Ahead of the Competition (Management of Innovation and Change). Harvard Business Review Press

Ward, J., & Daniel , E. (n.d.). Benefits Management: Delivering Value from IS and IT Investments (John Wiley Series in Information Systems). 2006: Wiley

Building a Foundation for Business Architecture

Martin Klubeck, Michael Langthorne, Donald Padgett

THE FULL PICTURE

To begin a conversation on Business Architecture, it's necessary to first recognize its role and relationship as a part of the whole. A business consists of three interrelated systems that define an organization: Business Architecture, Business Model, and Key Influencers.

Understanding how these three systems interrelate is critical to successfully growing your organization. We'll be focusing on Business Architecture here, providing a foundation for future growth. But before we dive into the architecture, we will provide a brief description of the three systems. Later we'll discuss why focusing on architecture alone will not necessarily enhance an organization's chances of long term success.

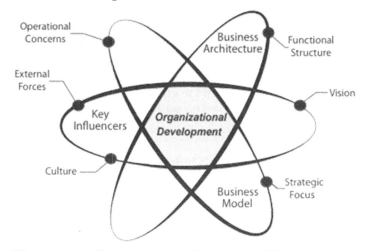

The Atomic Structure of a Business: Three Systems

SOME BASIC DEFINITIONS

Business Architecture: A good Business Architecture emphasizes the "what" by purposefully defining the functional structure of an organization, including the clear identification of its core components.

Business Model: The Business Model focuses on the "how". The how of designing and fulfilling the architectural components is also the area which leads to the greatest opportunities for innovation and creativity. This how is captured in the Business Model – the purposeful application of the Business Architecture in order to meet the organization's mission. In a mature organization the business model also makes it possible to achieve the organization's vision.

Key Influencers: The Key Influencers are where a business learns "why" it's doing what it does. The Key Influencers include the organization's culture, environmental (external) forces, and leadership's vision for the future.

To be a healthy and mature business, an organization has to do more than focus on the three systems. To truly grow, the organization has to also understand and nurture the relationships between them.

BREAKING DOWN THE DEFINITION

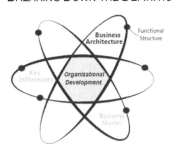

Let's spend some more time with the definition of Business Architecture. When we work with clients on developing a vision, defining goals, or identifying a root question, we follow a common time-tested (and simple) process. To fully understand what we're working with, we do a breakdown of the definition.

A good Business Architecture is the purposefully defined functional structure of an organization, including the clear identification of its core components.

Purposefully Defined

By "purposefully defined," we want to emphasize the importance of having a reason for creating and defining the functional structure. This is what makes the architecture a "good" one. Because the structure is consciously created, it drives the organization to align the architecture with the business model and its key influencers. If you don't purposefully define the structure, there's a good chance it will lack alignment with the other two systems. The lack of a plan or design greatly increases the risk the structure will evolve "by accident," with no purpose. Lacking both purpose and alignment with the other systems, the architecture will usually follow the path of least resistance which is rarely the right path to take.

Functional Structure

The next part of the definition is the "functional structure" of an organization. The use of the word "functional" is critical to a good architecture. We're not overly concerned with the physical structure — like who fills what position. We are much more focused on how the functions interrelate and create a synergy that supports and drives the organization. While professional development, personnel selection, facilities, and physical location of resources are valid considerations, they aren't part of the architecture. Of course when we look at lean-six-sigma, these factors do come into play, but again they're not part of this story. The physical structure on its own is not what we're examining.

Clear Identification

The "clear identification of its core components" means more than listing what the core components are. We will do that momentarily. A Business Architecture's definition spells out how each of the core components in your organization is implemented. It is important to not only identify them, but to do so thoroughly and clearly, for each component will have an assessable level of maturity.

As a recap, there are two ways to look at a business's architecture. There is the identification of what comprises an architecture - this is the encyclopedic definition. What exactly are the components, the pieces of the puzzle that go into defining it. This level is easy to capture - it's easy to write an article, chapter, or book on what these are.

The second way to look at a business's architecture is to look at how each of the components is implemented - this is the functionally-centered view. An organization is a living organism. To improve a business, you have to first understand the systems which make up the organism. An example of a living organism we should all be familiar with — the human body — makes a good analogy for this discussion. Before a doctor can advise us on how to improve our health, she has to understand that the body is made up of multiple systems; circulatory, nervous, pulmonary, etc. It's ok for your doctor to specialize in one of these systems, but to be effective she has to know what the systems are and how they interact (even if only at a high level). For our analogy, let's say the system you decide to focus on is Business Architecture. Like the doctor who specializes, you still have to understand all of the components of that system to effectively diagnose a problem or determine its overall health.

Being a doctor in this sense is easier than being a business improvement consultant. There are fewer variations to how each of the components work. In business the core components can be wildly different in their implementation, but still effective. This is why we focus on the functional structure vs. the physical. We care less about the bricks and mortar and more about how they function. One of your authors has personal experience with form vs. function. While in the military, he found out that he has an abnormal heart. One of the parts is larger than "normal." When he found out about this during his induction physical, he was distraught because all he heard was "abnormal." Later the doctor explained that it was actually a positive condition. So while we don't redesign the human body, we frequently reconstruct what makes up the best implementation of the business' architecture.

Even so, the key to determining the health of the organism isn't to identify the existence of the components - but instead understand how the existing components function. This is the same for any living organism. So, while we have to first define the components, when we discuss an organization's architecture, it's important for us to also look into how those components are implemented and how they interact. And, as with a larger organism (like the human body), we have to also look at how the different systems interact.

Let's start with identifying the individual parts of the Business Architecture.

WHAT ARE THE CORE COMPONENTS?

In our book, "Why Organizations Struggle So Hard To Improve So Little: Overcoming Organizational Immaturity" (ABC-Clio 2009) we wrote about the way the core components were implemented. We didn't even call them components since we were focused on the how, not the what. We knew there were many different ways to implement a component, and we didn't recommend one over another — after all, it's situational. What we did suggest was a way of measuring the maturity of how each was implemented.

Simply put, if your organization didn't consciously address a component (you may or may not even realize it exists), the implementation would have to be rated as immature. The more you know about the component and purposefully implement it, the more mature the organization. The maturity of your implementation of the components of the Business Architecture is a universal way to assess an organization's potential for success. In "Why Organizations Struggle" we focused on the overall maturity which directly affects the ability to implement organization-wide improvements. This treatise is focused on the definition of what actually comprises an architecture and the maturity of each individual component. Which components you have implemented and how you implemented them defines the basic health of your architecture. Poor definition or weak implementation spells an unhealthy Business Architecture.

The core components of Business Architecture are:

1. Organizational structure (the physical structure)
2. The organization's mission (why it exists)
3. Strategic thinking and planning (ability to look ahead)
4. Project Management (how well you deal with large scale efforts)
5. Process Management (how well the organization does its work)
6. Analytics (how well the organization uses measures for improvement)
7. Professional Development (learning players make the team better)
8. Reward and Recognition (showing you value the workforce)
9. Organizational Development (focus on maturing the organization)
10. Process Asset Library (how well you store and use your assets)
11. Service Catalog (with Service Level Agreements)
12. Collaboration and Communication (how well you work together)

ANALYZING YOUR CURRENT ARCHITECTURE

There are two foundational ways we assess a Business Architecture.

FORM VS. FUNCTION

Each component within a Business Architecture can be assessed as somewhere between totally immature to fully mature. As an immature organization, with immature components, the weakest levels are when the components are not recognized as part of the architecture. Within Form and Function, we will measure maturity of each. But first let's clarify the difference between Form and Function.

Form

If the component is documented, it has form. How well it's documented speaks of the level of maturity of the form. Well documented components not only explicitly describe the item, but also document how it relates to other components. Who is responsible for carrying out the component? Who "owns" it and who are the stakeholders? It may seem needless to say, but experience tells us it actually is necessary; to be mature, the documentation in question has to actually match reality. Form addresses the what, a clear definition of the component. And here is where it can become confusing. The Form also includes documented processes — how the component is supposed to be executed.

By documenting the process, the implementation, you can obtain repeatability. This allows for standardization and purposeful improvements. It also enables more innovation and creativity in the implementation. By having a well-defined form, you can change the way it's done — from small tweaks to total reengineering — and you can learn from the change. You can share that change across the organization because it's well documented.

Function

Function is a lot like well-documented form, it addresses the how. Function is different, in that it is how things are actually done. So, if you perform the same way the documentation says you do, you have the mature state of Form equaling Function. But that's rarer than you'd think (and less common than we desire). Rather than evaluate Function in terms of maturity, we look at it primarily based on its levels of effectiveness.

Function is all about the process, not just the documentation of the process but the reality of how it is actually done. Process improvement is founded on having repeatable processes, but they actually have to be repeated to reap the benefits. The function is about how it is actually conducted, not how it should or could be. When you look at improving an organization by addressing the Business' Architecture, you ensure that you are dealing with the function, not only the form. The form is a step, but it's not where you get the return for your investment. The return comes from the function.

When you analyze a component, it's very easy to review the existing documentation. But to say that an organization is mature as a result of a document audit is ludicrous. Putting documentation in place is only a step in the right direction. You have to ensure that documentation actually reflects reality. The purpose of documentation is to help make the processes and implementation of the components more effective. The documentation is not the goal. The goal is to improve the reality, and the reality is represented by the function.

MEASURING MATURITY

In varying degrees every business and organization has an architecture. In most cases the components are minimally documented (if at all) and often not really given purposeful consideration.

Think of the core components as boxes or containers; they might be empty, partially full, stuffed with old junk, or filled perfectly with no wasted space. An empty container or box with little-to-no definition would reflect a high level of immaturity. You may be able to fill some boxes by simply focusing on the size of the box, the structure, and what goes into it. Partially full-to-overflowing boxes can also represent immaturity if they haven't been filled purposefully. To add value, the containers have to be periodically examined, evaluated, and cleaned out when necessary.

But how can you measure the maturity of the architectural components? Leadership could take a quiz — describe what is currently in each box, each core component. You could measure what percentage of staff knows about each component within your business and how it functions.

Another measure is how frequently staff make use of policies or procedures contained in those containers. Not knowing about the documented processes is an indicator of immaturity, but worse would be if the staff know about them, but purposely avoid following them.

What's the quality of information in each component, in terms of general best practices, or in terms of customization to your specific organization? There are lots of ways you can measure maturity; here are some basics:

1. Determine if the architectural component is defined
2. Is that definition documented?
3. Is the document readily accessible to all who touch the component (owners, stakeholders, end users)?
4. Does the documentation reflect reality (or is it out-of-date)?
5. Is the documentation updated? Is it a living thing or is it shelfware?

6. Is the implementation of the component repeatable?
7. Is the implementation actually repeated (or adversely, are there any indications of staff avoidance)?
8. Are improvements to the implementation captured, added to the documentation, shared, and leveraged?

ORGANIZATIONAL STRUCTURE – AN EXAMPLE CORE COMPONENT

Rather than go through all twelve Business Architecture components in detail, we'll use Organizational structure as an example. You can apply the concepts we present to each of the components. If you want to fully assess the health (maturity) of your business architecture, you can use this as a template for the other components.

Let's apply the eight steps for measuring maturity to the organizational structure.

The first task is to "determine if the architectural component is defined." In its simplest form, Organizational Structure is just the "org chart." What the departments are, how they align across the organization, and who reports to whom comprises the physical structure. We find that the organizational structure (along with a select few other components) usually exists and is known. There's always at least a semblance of an org chart.

But knowing that the component (org chart) exists doesn't raise the organization out of immaturity. It's only one step above not being aware of the component at all.

Our second question is, "Is that definition documented?" This one is easier for organizational structure than for some of the other components. Chances are, if you have a defined structure, it's captured somewhere. But you can see that having an org chart doesn't mean much by itself. Not only does it have to exist, but it also has to be readily accessible to all who touch the component (owners, stakeholders, end users).

If you have a documented organizational structure, you have to check to ensure it's accurate. Is it out of date? You might be surprised how often the Org Chart changes and how few people in the organization could describe the latest version. Do the members of the organization actually know what's on the current Org Chart? Or do they have to refer to a copy they've printed out? If they have a hard copy, is there a version posted electronically? Do they still match? One sign of low maturity is that changes to the component are not communicated in a timely manner.

So far we've measured maturity (actually everything so far points to immaturity) by determining if the component is defined, documented, shared, and accurate. If you are a maturing organization, not only will these four factors be covered, but the document will be updated frequently. Perhaps it's communicated through the company website and updates to it generate an automated message to everyone that it has been changed. A maturing organization's processes, and documentation of those processes, are living things. They are tweaked, improved, and updated regularly.

Our next issue is around repeatability. But, an Org Chart itself isn't actually a process-centric component. There's usually little implementation around an Org Chart. But the currency and accuracy is a tell-tale sign. Is the chain of command reflected in the Org Chart actually used? Are changes made in a repeatable, logical manner? Are those changes communicated in a repeatable manner? And while it may be repeatable, is it actually repeated? Are these practices carried out?

And if it is repeatable, and repeated, finally we have to determine if changes are being made. Is it a truly living component? Are those improvements shared and leveraged across the organization. Again, the Org Chart is a very simple example, but it still works. Are changes in structure reflected? Are improvements in reporting chains and interrelations reflected so others can benefit from them?

The eight factors can help you determine the maturity of the Business Architecture component and that's primarily focused on the Form. You will also want to determine the functional effectiveness. While we had eight specific steps to measuring Form, Function is more difficult. It's all about how well things work.

Using the organizational structure as our continuing example, you will need to analyze the effectiveness of that structure. It's interesting that most organizations, when looking to improve, start (and many end) with changing only this aspect of the architecture. This may be the best example of why focusing only on business architecture, when trying to improve a whole organization, fails to produce the desired outcome or systemic change.

When reorganization (changing the organizational structure) is the improvement focus, the workforce normally likens the effort to "rearranging deck chairs on the Titanic." It may improve the "look" of the organization (on paper), but it doesn't really change anything. It doesn't change or improve how things work, especially if the changes to the structure are only cosmetic.

So, why doesn't it change how things work? Because one of the key influencers, the culture of the organization, didn't change. Over time people's behaviors toward work and toward co-workers becomes streamlined and then jelled. People figure out where and how to take short-cuts with procedures based both on positive and negative rewards from supervisors, and simply by observing whether or not their supervisors (and others in the organization) follow procedures. The Key Influencers are an entire system, which is also true of the Business Model. The question is, was the new org chart meant to represent an improved way to apply the previously-known business model, or has the business model changed to accommodate new customers or new products?

History suggests that, even if you drastically change the org chart, chances are the work will still get done the same way. The workers will circumvent your attempts at forcing new relationships and chains-of-command because the focus and motivation is on getting the job done — and they know who will get it done for them. You seldom change relationships by moving boxes or lines on a chart. Unless the root of your problem was the organizational structure, changing that structure won't solve your problems. In spite of this, management continues to use this method as its most common improvement effort.

Treating the organizational structure in a mature way takes a lot of insight and effort. To actually understand how each of the elements in the organization works together isn't easy. To correctly analyze how changes to the structure can result in positive results takes even more effort and a keen insight. To fully understand the underlying way the organization gets things done — regardless of the physical structure — takes a level of engagement most leaders can't claim to have achieved.

The hardest part of using the organizational structure as a means for improvement may be the difficulty in seeing past the org chart and seeing how inter-relationships between the three systems function in your environment.

MYTHS AND MISNOMERS

We've attempted to describe what Business Architecture is and how it can be documented, understood, analyzed, and assessed. It is worth it (and fun) to dispel a few of the myths and misnomers which have surrounded the concept of BA throughout the concept's young existence.

BUSINESS ARCHITECTURE APPROACH IS A NEW CONCEPT

Business Architecture is new, right? We just called it a young concept. It's so new that it requires this book of definitions compiled to help clarify its meaning, right? What if we told you that BA isn't that new?

Here's a brief history lesson. In 1982 John Zachman, while working for IBM, put forward the phrase Enterprise Architecture, referring to IT systems, and in 1987 published a paper entitled "A Framework for Information Systems Architecture." He considered "enterprise" to be synonymous with "business," but did not actually examine businesses as organizations — only IT architectures within a business environment. While that might be the genesis of the term "business architecture," this book is not in any way limited to Information Technology.

BUSINESS ARCHITECTURE APPROACH IS A MEANS OF IMPROVING THE ORGANIZATION

Business Architecture is actually a means of understanding the organization. Specifically, understanding the critical components, and in a well-defined architecture, how those components interact, depend on, and work with each other. However, most existing theories on how to improve organizations have taken extremely narrow focuses. Consultants have told businesses for many years that they can solve their problems by re-defining units within a business and reorganizing how those units supposedly interact based on a paper diagram of functional unit names. The first flaw is attempting to "drive" change all at once across an entire enterprise that is too immature to cope. Quite literally, the culture will kill 75% of such attempts. The second flaw is believing that Business Architecture Approach (BAA) is all that needs to be considered in order to drive organizational improvement.

IT ALLOWS YOU TO OVERCOME ORGANIZATIONAL IMMATURITY

No, it won't. Like any of the three systems, focusing on any one of them (or components therein) will not in itself overcome Organizational Immaturity. You have to take into consideration your organization's level of maturity as a factor in determining how best to implement any improvement effort.

The effective use and adoption of a Business Architecture Approach for improvement is dependent upon an organization's maturity, not the other way around.

FOCUSING ON JUST ONE OF THE THREE SYSTEMS TO IMPROVE

A very common myth is that you have to pick one improvement solution. You'll have advisors tell you to pick a single approach (Business Architecture or Business Model or Voice-of-the-Customer, or Vision Setting) for your improvement solution. They may encourage you to adopt a capability maturity model, Six Sigma, Lean, or a combination. The problem is that we are looking at the organization as a simple one-cell organism when in reality it is an extremely complex multi-dimensional living thing.

You wouldn't try to become healthier by only focusing on one of the systems that make up the human body. You have to develop indicators across the spectrum, pay attention to warning signs, establish an overall baseline and then work to improve the entire body. Actually, you shouldn't even focus only on the body as your mind, body, and soul all work together to define who you are and how healthy you are. Organizations are the same.

Should your organization adopt a Business Architecture Approach? The simple answer is "no." The organization should use Business Architecture to help focus on the components, and more importantly focus on the mature behaviors which define how well you implement each component. It's not an either/or discussion. Business Architecture was (and is) an important aspect that up until now has been under-valued and ignored, but it is not a stand-alone view. So feel free to focus on it, but remember, if you want to improve on a grand scale, you'll have to think a lot bigger than just one of the systems that comprise an organization.

WHY NOT FOCUS ON ONE SYSTEM?

We went into detail already why you should not focus solely on a Business Architecture Approach. But what about focusing on just one (or both) of the other two systems?

Business Model

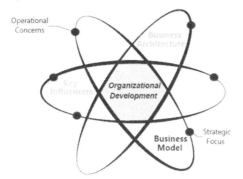

The business model has been the flagship approach to organizational improvement for decades. You had to define your business model, sell it to investors, and religiously defend it whenever a change in the environment pushed you toward a new horizon. The Business Model is the purposeful application of the Business Architecture in order to meet the organization's mission, and in a mature organization, to achieve the organization's vision. How you build the org-chart is a tiny fraction of Business Architecture. But the critical aspect is how. In an immature organization, one (or a select few) leaders close the doors and re-draw the boxes, then inform the employees with the date the new structure takes effect. In a highly mature organization, all areas of the existing organization are represented in designing the improvement, with an understanding of why the change is necessary, how customers will benefit, how the employees will benefit, and ultimately how the business will benefit.

Key Influencers

If you only focus on one of the three Key Influencers such as external forces which affect the organization, you will fall far short of fully understanding, analyzing, and affecting the future of the whole organization. Here are a couple of examples.

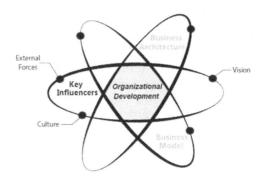

Voice of the customer (All Stakeholders)

The first mention of "Voice of the Customer" we've found is the 1997 book "Voices Into Choices: Acting on the Voice of the Customer" (Brodie & Burchill, Joiner Associates). Voice of the Customer is today's hot approach for improvement (with books still coming out in 2015). It replaced the business model as the way to improve. Most Continuous Process Improvement efforts which sprung up within businesses focused solely on responding to the ever-changing whims of the customer. It was reasoned that you must satisfy your customer to be successful. Even to the point that many businesses use the customers' input to help define their vision for the future.

Regulations/Policies

Yes, you do have to adhere to and comply with existing regulations. Especially ones dictated by the government — foreign when working with overseas organizations, as well as domestic regulations at home. While it is true that you can't afford to ignore these, you also can't afford to address only compliance requirements.

Leadership "Vision"

In the history of business, vision has long been king. And just like there were great kings there have also been great visions — however we also know there were some not-so-great kings declaring some outrageously short-sighted visions. This can be seen whenever the top person in an organization (whether a 15th century tavern or a late-19th century automaker) would announce an edict of where the organization was going to go regardless of any of the three business systems. The lack of alignment between the leader's vision and the organization's architecture, business model, or customer wishes warns of future failure.

No vision fulfills itself; significant work must be accomplished, sacrifices made. So in this regard, leadership vision is a key influencer on every organization — an influencer that can create excitement and engagement, or be seen (and treated) by the culture as a joke or fallacy.

APPLYING THE CONCEPTS

To completely design, analyze, or understand an organization you have to understand the systems and the relationships between them. An organization's long term success can be predicted by analyzing how well the organization understands and nourishes the relationships between the Business Architecture, Business Model, and the Key Influencers.

UNDERSTAND THE 3 SYSTEMS AS A WHOLE

"The right way to go" is to understand the three systems as a whole, and to embrace and nurture the relationships between them. Business Architecture supports all the what's the organization needs to know. The Business Model supports all the how's — not just how the Business Architecture will be spelled out, but how the company will interact with its staff, management, customers, shareholders, government agencies, etc. And Key Influencers (vision, culture, and external forces) are all monitored and understood. In essence, leadership is at all times keenly aware of the architecture, the model and the influencers. All major decisions are guided by this complete awareness, not by any reductionist or isolationist view of the business. When all three systems are aligned organizational development thrives.

EMBRACE AND NURTURE THE RELATIONSHIPS BETWEEN THEM

The relationships among the three systems are an often-overlooked area of improvement. Even when we find organizations that recognize the three they tend to focus on only one. If they tried to keep an eye on all three, they tended to ignore how they interrelated, missing critical relationships between them. To be better, it is important to look at the ecosystem as a whole, including how each of the systems interact and affect each other.

CONCLUSION

Around 400 BC the Greek philosopher-scientist Democritus put forth the concept that atoms were the smallest individual units of matter, that all matter was made up of atoms and space between atoms. A few thousand years later scientists discovered the sub-atomic particles of electrons, protons and neutrons. Decades later they decided protons were composed of quarks. A few years later, quarks were determined to be held together by gluons. Since then we struggle with such concepts as quantum dots and vibrating strings as the tiniest of the tiny. Why the history lesson? Precision comes with deeper and more complex layers of understanding.

What does this have to do with Business Architecture? Some business concepts are no more than fad phrases, lasting a year or two. We do not put Business Architecture in this category. On the contrary, Business Architecture provides a model and a method for exploring and understanding the critical components of functioning organizations. What a business does, how it does it, and how it generates value cannot be understood by simply looking at the org chart or the service catalog in isolation. Even the culture of an existing enterprise cannot be understood without conducting both an internal examination of staff, managers and leaders along with an external examination of customers, stakeholders and rules and regulations. Change is not optional; it's essential. And now, more than ever before, change comes at lightning speed. We embrace Business Architecture, not as a catch-phrase, but as a means of more precisely understanding the organization's complex nature.

RESOURCES:

For more information on the implementation and maturation of Business Architecture components, we recommend our first book, "Why Organizations Struggle So Hard To Improve So Little: Overcoming Organizational Immaturity" (ABC-Clio, 2009).

For more information on how to implement meaningful analytics see "Metrics: How to Improve Key Business Results," or "Planning & Designing Effective Metrics," both offered by Springer.

For more information on how to create professional development plans for every position in your organization, see "The Professional Development Toolbox" (2014) by Martin Klubeck.

How Business Architecture Enables Agility in a Dynamic Market

Dr. Michael Poulin, Clingstone Ltd., UK

WHAT HAPPENS IN A MARKET BUT NOT IN AN ENTERPRISE

About 30 years ago, the industry was concerned with delivering valuable products and services to the market (Porter1985), to the consumers. At that time enterprises operated on principles formed after WWII—vertical management lines of business based on either products or geographical locations. In a decade, complexity of products established a need for cross-functional processes (Rother 2003). As a result, an entire operational model of enterprises became process-centric.

A business process is an exceptionally robust organisation that when repeatedly run in the same execution context (Poulin 2013) delivers the same outcome. In a manufacturing business, in a prosperous time when many different outcomes are required more often, the process model is irreplaceable. However, when business processes grow, they form structures of interdependent entities with business interactivity and conditional logic, which make them complex—less observable or transparent. This also leads to a reduction of comprehensiveness and manageability of such structures. The complexity formed by the business process structure starts generating risks of its own.

Then, for the last 20 years, communication and informational capabilities allowed businesses, even small and medium enterprises (SME), to become international and global. As a consequence, more distant and less connected business processes around the globe have to face a significant increase in business complexity attributed to the compliance of regional, international, and local laws. This is amplified by the disproportionate evolution of economy between countries and regions and a need to consider quite different regulations, even in relationships between an enterprise's divisions. If we add a "no-latency" information exchange around the world and compare this to the time required to modify any business process, as well as all dependent super-processes, a conclusion becomes almost obvious, a process-based enterprise model (vertical and horizontal processes) cannot contend by itself with fast and massive market changes.

A business, if limiting itself to a process-centric mindset and operating model, acquires a real risk of losing agility to its environment, as shown in Figure 1. We need a new mechanism on the top of business processes that would add dynamics to the use of processes, i.e. would provide business flexibility. This is not a digitization or Cloud Computing; a flexibility of business solutions is based on minimal cost of adoption of a business change, minimal time to market of this adoption and minimal cost of maintenance and modification of this adoption over time (or adoption of the next related change (Poulin 2013). Business flexibility is not a trivial matter, but Business Architecture is the instrument for gaining and keeping it in the enterprise.

Figure 1.

Let us offer you a couple of quotes to set the spirit and direction of thoughts about the situation where many modern, new, and brick-n-mortar, businesses appear nowadays. A Legendary CEO of General Electric Jack Welch once said *"When the rate of change outside exceeds the rate of change inside – the end is in sight"* (Daft 2014). Another quote attributed to an unknown author states, *"You can't do today's job with yesterday's methods and be in business tomorrow"* (Dholakia). So, what can help businesses to survive, become agile and finally succeed in a highly dynamic global market?

Our answer is: An explicitly operating Business Architecture. Let's see what this actually means, and how it works.

A GENESIS OF BUSINESS ARCHITECTURE

Business Architecture is a natural and native organising element of the enterprise system. If properly defined and realized, it leads to sustainability and competitive advantage in the dynamic economic environment, via the strategically valuable business flexibility.

Business Architecture is the architecture of the system constituted by the enterprise business. Because of this, Business Architecture exists in any business, commercial or not-for-profit, matured or start-up. It is another matter whether Business Architecture is formally organized and operates as a team of dedicated professionals or is carried by the company executives among their duties. The former usually takes place in large enterprises, while the latter is typical for SME.

The first time an enterprise Business Architecture emerges is at the moment when a new company puts together its Enterprise Business Model (EBM) on media. The core business functionality or services of the future company and vocabulary of the EBM form a new Business Architecture. It includes the fundamental elements of the enterprise structure that are self-sufficient and cohesive. Other elements of the company only realize the Business Architecture, though some of them may also be fundamental, but derived from the Business Architecture.

A formal manifestation of Business Architecture takes place when the corporate executives feel that the development of a vision and strategy requires more effort, resources, and information than they can contribute, as well as when a translation of the strategy into reality needs even more work and specialization. At this moment, shown in Figure 2, executives simply delegate their architectural (design) responsibilities to the role known as Business Architect. As you can see, this has little in common with what Information technology (IT) departments and some

Technology Standards consider to be Business Architecture and a related, architectural role.

A thoughtful reader would notice that Business Architecture is not only for preparing materials for the executives and Board in order to help them make decisions about strategy. When Business Architecture formally appears, the company is usually at such maturity and complexity that it cannot be easily split into vertical Lines of Business (LOBs) without professional and creative, if not innovative, endeavors for making integral (efficient and consistent) solutions; the ones, which define what should be done in the company in order to transit and reach the strategic goals and objectives. Just a council of senior domain executives is not sufficient for such tasks at this level of complexity.

Figure 2.

It is logically expected that Business Architects inherit some executive's rights together with the architectural duties of defining what, why, where and when the company should enable its strategic movement. However, this is a hot-spot for discussions not only in companies, but also in the industry. Business Architecture, which is responsible for the translation of the strategy into functional and informational images of the company, then has to be materialized by the operational and delivery business functions, and if left without appropriate decision rights is helpless and useless for the company; it cannot assure any business value presupposed in the corporate strategy. In an ideal situation, the corporate business has to realize the principle of separation of concerns: executives define, decide, and protect the direction and strategy; Business Architects define, decide, and protect what the company should create (reuse, rebuild or construct); the business executives should define, decide, and protect the delivery of business changes.

THE GOALS AND PRINCIPLES OF BUSINESS ARCHITECTURE IN THE DYNAMIC MARKET

The goals and purposes of Business Architecture comprise three parts:
- Support and supply information for the strategic decisions conducted by the corporate executives and the Board
- Realize the first high-level translation of the strategic visions and directions into business functional and informational images of the corporate business; to bridge between strategy and its materialization
- Define and design sequential transition and transformation of the corporate business to the state defined by the strategic goals and objectives.

Goals of Business Architecture may vary depending on particular business needs, its markets and position in the markets, customer base, and surrounding business execution context. We will discuss all these aspects, but in any case the goals of Business Architecture have to meet requirements of:
- Sustainability in the dynamic market and general economic environment

- Orchestrating a creation and support for competitive advantage in the market for profit-oriented businesses
- Orchestrating an extending appealing of the not-for-profit business to the customers.

As a sub-goal, Business Architecture aims to create basic structures conveying its concept and operations. This structure should be transparent to the top corporate management and should be able to drive Activity Streams (Poulin 2015) of the business.

The concept of Activity Streams is close to the concept of Value Chain (Porter 1985), but wider. It contains activities not only for delivering values to the market and to the customers, but also incorporates a lot of other activities aimed to provide well-being of the corporate business. In contrast to Value Streams (Tapping 2002), Activity Streams may be expressed via Business Capabilities (M. Poulin 2015) and their combinations, not necessarily only via business processes or cases. An Activity Stream depicts a sequence and logic of exploitation of Business Capabilities and practically represents an orchestration of activities.

Figure 3.

The Business Architecture principles define directions and constraints for decisions, solutions, models, and activities that reflect corporate business strategy and meets needs of top executives, which is illustrated in Figure 3. These principles heavily impact enterprise principles for the entire organization, its Activity Streams, technology, marketing, and relationship management. There are 10 major principles we identify that sufficient and successful Business Architecture should follow; many of them are in practice already.

Principle 1. Forming the Enterprise Business. Business Architecture is about fundamental, self-sufficient and cohesive artefacts that form the core of the enterprise and that organize other business artefacts for delivering the enterprise's goals and welfares.

Principle 2. Separation of Business Concerns (Dijkstra 1982). In the complex environment or execution context a complex system has to address multiple concerns of quite a different nature in order to survive and evolve. One of the most proven styles of dealing with concerns is via constructing the system using small components and their combinations, where each component addresses only one concern. Every concern has to be analyzed and, if possible, decomposed in such a way, where different concerns may be addressed by different components. The described componentization allows building the most sustainable, robust, stable, scalable, and manageable system. The principle of Separation of Concerns corresponds with the principle of Composability (M. Poulin 2014) in a service-oriented ecosystem (SOE) (RAF 2012). That is, the business activities (or finer-grained services) can per se or in the combinations solve particular business problems.

For example, your insurance company receives information about written cases from a brokerage company, which actually sells policies to people on behalf of your company. Who is responsible for the quality of the information of each insured—your company or the broker? The same question relates to validating legal status of the insured. Your company is responsible for all mentioned concerns, but only after the contract with the to-be insured person is signed. However, your company does not deal with the to-be insured person. The separation of concerns in this case requires the broker to execute the data quality controls and legal verification on your behalf. The reason for this extra work for the broker should be addressed before the insurance is written; if a broker wants to get his fee for writing policies, he should do it properly, i.e. with needed controls. Otherwise, the work of the broker is unsatisfactory and it becomes a question as to why such broker is hired.

Principle 3. Transition orientation. Business Architecture's work and outcome forms the first step in the transition of the enterprise business to its strategic goals and objectives, i.e. to the realization of this strategy in a physical reality.

On the way to the strategic goals, the business solutions usually need to align with the changing environment. Because of that dynamic environment, not only might strategy plans require refinement, but also capability models and high-level solutions might expect to be adjusted. Business Architecture should work with a readiness to change. This can also affect the Business Transformation Plans (BTP) and change management processes (initiatives, projects, jobs, workflows, and applications).

Principle 4. Dependency on the Business Execution Context. The Business Execution Context comprises internal and external aspects. Internal aspects include strategy, directions of the Board and Executives, and needs of shareholders. External aspects include: consumer demand, partner's policies, supplier's policies, legislative regimes in all operational locations, and industry and logical government regulations. Changes in the execution context can impact the outcome of the Business Architecture work a great deal.

Any business organization operates in a chosen environment that dictates certain constraints, which affect that organization. These constraints can be driven by the nature, market, industry, geography, or governmental regulations. All delivery and operational activities, such as strategies, initiatives, projects, policies, decisions, and procedures, have to consider those constraints.

Principle 5. Authority. Business Architecture plays an authoritative role in the area of defining the business functionality and its change in the intermediary and final company outcomes. Business Architecture defines architectural principles and policies for architectural Governing. The latter applies to the usage, development, delivery and modification of functionality related to the business capabilities, and related products and external services. Business Architecture defines the metrics and controls the business design and realization.

Principle 6. Abstraction. Business Architecture works with tangible and intangible facts and produces intangible outcomes in the form of business capabilities, capability maps, Governing policies, some parts of Business Strategic Plan (BSP) and BTP, and to certain parts of blueprints, especially related to the transition milestone set in the future. These outcomes should be at a certain level of abstraction that defines what should be achieved while, simultaneously, does not place detailed restrictions on how defined artefacts are to be achieved.

During the realization of business strategy, the outcomes of Business Architecture become requirements for the rest of the corporate business, and, first and foremost, for its delivery and operational functions. For the defined artefacts like Business Capabilities, planned for later steps of the strategic transition, an abstraction of their functionality helps to overcome fluctuations of the economic environment and shift actual resource allocation as close to the usage moment as possible.

Principle 7. Prescriptiveness. Business Architecture is advisory to the corporate executives and the Board, while prescriptive at a high level to the rest of the corporate business. The Business Architecture conducts business solutions and leads the business strategic transition planning. The recommendations and outcome of the architectural work—Business Capabilities, Capability Maps, Blueprints and BTP—become the business requirements for the LOBs, business divisions and teams, as well as for Technology architecture, delivery/development and support teams. Business Architecture develops policies and ongoing architectural control over operations and delivery processes that are compliance mandatory.

Principle 8. Bi-directional communication. Business Architecture uses a bi-directional communication with the executives and with the rest of the corporate management and architectures. Business Architecture designs business capabilities jointly with the senior business and technology management of the company. Business Architecture contributes to communications and interactions with partners, suppliers, and even consumers.

Principle 9. Collaboration. Business Architecture works in collaboration with the management of all business domains of the enterprise and with the top corporate management. Collaboration of Business Architecture is based on the concept of collaboration, which can be explained as a style of joint work where the objectives and goals of this work become the objectives and goals of each participating party (M. Poulin 2013). The specific effect of collaboration is in that the participant of such work is ready to perform internal changes in its business (organization and operations) for the sake of this work.

Principle 10. Serviceability (RAF 2012). Business Architecture promotes and propagates orientation on service for internal and external consumers, as well as in the relationships with suppliers and partners. Service orientation is the fundamental element of any for-profit and not-for-profit business, because only via the services can it gain its revenue and profit. Business Architecture assumes that in each interaction between business capabilities, business services, business teams, people, and technology systems a servicing takes place. Orientation on service in business function, organization, and operations provide maximum business flexibility in the environment/market (Poulin 2013) and leads to the highest probability of gaining a competitive advantage in the dynamic market. Ability to provide or deliver service is the cornerstone of all work and outcomes of Business Architecture.

THE ISSUE OF OWNERSHIP IN THE EXECUTION CONTEXT

Business Architecture exists in every business organization of every industry, but may not be explicitly documented and practiced by dedicated people.

The power and value of a Business Architecture is in that it is quite stable, while particular realizations of the architecture may change along with the growth and maturity of the company. Nevertheless, Business Architecture periodically changes as well, in line with changes of the company's strategy. Thus, Business Architecture exists in a particular state each moment and transacts between its states. The direction of the transitions should be directed by the corporate strategy. However, in some cases, unforeseen situations like mistakes in market analysis, inadequate monitoring of market changes, or natural disasters can lead to deviations from the corporate strategy.

The major external factor influencing the work of Business Architecture is the business execution context. Though Business Architecture operates within the enterprise, it is responsible for the efficiency of the business in the outside world. An execution context comprises intangible artefacts such as:

- Internal governing policies
- Policies adopted by the enterprise from the industry regulations
- Policies adopted by the enterprise from the local law
- Policies adopted by the enterprise from the international unions and organizations that the countries where the enterprise exists and operates are participants
- Policies adopted by the enterprise from its contracts with partners and/or suppliers.

In general, the execution context is formed by any factors that can have a potential impact on the competencies and ability of Business Architecture to operate in accordance with the governing principles and policies.

An execution context includes a significant number of external factors, which are not under the enterprise's control. So, an execution context should be constantly monitored by the enterprise and reported to the Business Architecture. This monitoring may be performed by different enterprise's structural elements or even by external hired providers. Such monitoring is one of the most important means of agility to the dynamic market used by Business Architecture.

Since an external economic environment does not change sporadically and chaotically, the execution context may include both existing and emerging factors. For example, when Business Architecture considers outsourcing of the business data storage in the Cloud, the execution context of related business capability should consider emerging legislation related to data privacy and security. This is an important topic for EU Member countries. The EU's movement on data protection led by Germany and the UK's Data Privacy regulation put restrictions on the transfer of corporate and individual data across country borders. This means that a Cloud provider is curbed in its ability to store the data outside of the EU or even outside of particular country. If such legislation is finally in force, the Cloud providers will be in need for building data centers in some EU countries, which will increase the cost of Cloud services and make them less attractive to corporate businesses.

The policies and regulations of execution context impact separate divisions of the enterprise differently. This leads us to the concept of ownership in the business. Ownership is closely tied with corporate culture, motivation, and interpersonal relationships. Ownership is a strong incentive for many people, because it feeds self-esteem and can lead to financial benefits.

In essence, ownership is a set of rights and responsibilities in the enterprise that a role or a person has with regard to a resource, where the resource is an entity with some value and identity (M. Poulin 2014). The ownership has boundaries, which the owner tends to protect and which may result in serious problems for realization of business flexibility.

Ownership is usually associated with its influential realm within the ownership boundaries. There are three types of ownership boundaries that are important for Business Architecture:

- Administrative or management boundaries

- Leadership boundaries
- Individual interrelationship boundaries.

The administrative or management boundaries are defined via setting organizational and operational models, e.g. matrix management. Leadership boundaries may or may not match the administrative ones depending on whether the management and actual (informal) leadership in the group of people are the same. Individual interrelationship boundaries are formed by personal contacts and interpersonal trust. These boundaries can cross not only the other two types mentioned, but also the formal enterprise boundaries.

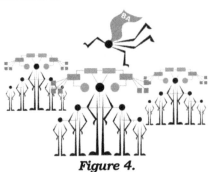

Figure 4.

One of the primary tasks of Business Architecture is to see the enterprise with and without existing internal ownership boundaries, as illustrated in Figure 4; to consider them in the architectural solutions and to replace them by functional and informational models that preserve only enterprise needs and boundaries. In other words, the Business Architecture's work and outcome primarily target the ownership boundaries that are naturally appearing in the consumer-provider relationships.

The Business Architecture should be able to design the solutions across internal administrative and leadership boundaries and has to help in defining and understanding the implications of such crossovers. Though this is one of the trickiest tasks, it is fundamental for providing any competitive advantage in a frequently changing external environment.

That is, one of the consequences of Business Architecture is making the ownership boundaries flexible and modifiable at the pace of changes in the execution context, while still preserving the principle of Separation of Concerns. In other words, any business capability combinations and architectural solutions require internal management boundaries to be dynamic as well. The current corporate strategy, expressed via business architectural models, recommendations and solutions, and changes in it, should drive the administrative management boundaries, not the other way around. The internal organizational and operational models have to be in the process of continuous adjustment, rather than appearing as constraints for the strategy implementation in the company. For example, if an international business has decided that competitive advantage may be reached via using centralized shared business services across all international locations, any resistance of the local business management should be seen as incompliance with the corporate policies and suppressed. At the time of writing this material, large financial institutions have started applying such solutions, at least, in the UK.

Business Capabilities as the Major Instrument of Business Architecture

As we mentioned before, a work of Business Architecture has two areas – a decision advisory for the top corporate management and a strategy implementation via the rest of the enterprise. In the latter, the first and the major technique of Business Architecture is defining and designing business capabilities. They may be categorized as:

- Fundamental—needed for the daily operation of the enterprise; the ones that are constantly re-designed in the part of resources, while the functional part stays practically the same
- Strategic—needed for reaching the objectives of the corporate strategy in the relatively distant future; the ones that can be adjusted along the way to the strategic goals
- Competitiveness—created for gaining competitive advantages in the market in a relatively tactical time-frame.

Individual LOB, division, departments, and business teams may have their business capabilities as well, but they relate to the architecture realization realm and are usually owned by lower level business management.

A new situation in the modern market identified as dynamism has put new requirements to the structure of business capabilities. Companies cannot rely on their internal resources and previous experience anymore, because the tempo of changes in the market and regulations worldwide now exceed the pace of changing internal resources. Business Architecture has no other choice but to review business capability notions and start seeing them as dynamic, abstract entities that should be easily and speedily modified and re-combined with other analogous entities (M. Poulin 2015). This may be done only in the case where the resource part of a capability becomes flexible, planned or reserved rather than actual. The major characteristic of a capability, beside its functionality, becomes its outcome.

Thus, a business capability turns out to be an ability of a business entity, a person or organization, to deliver certain Real World Effect (RWE) when the predefined business condition occurs. A RWE represents a measurable change to the shared state of pertinent entities, relevant to and experienced by specific stakeholders of an ecosystem (RAF 2012). A result of implementation and execution of a business capability is one of the forms of the RWE.

It is important to notice that the aforementioned understanding of business capability does not articulate how it works; instead it states only what will be delivered in the form of utilized functionality, and actual tangible or intangible outcomes, as shown in Figure 5. Also, it is evident that Business Architecture can define by itself what functionality should be in the business capability, but cannot design it without senior business management responsible for the resources (to be planned or reserved).

A relative abstraction of business capabilities permits modelling, composing, mapping, and alternative options, but with no resource planning. The resource part steps forward only after modelling, analysis, and revision have selected certain capabilities for going forward. This allows designers and planners to save a lot of effort.

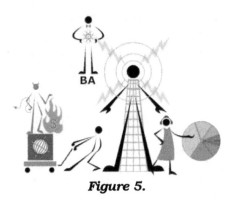

Figure 5.

The business capabilities described above form the basis for Strategic Business Plans (SBP) and Business Transformation Plans (BTP), especially in defining the business transformation roadmap leading to the strategic goals. Each step in this transition requires a blueprint for implementation. The Business Architecture solutions appear as the business requirements to the blueprints. The more distant a need in particular capability is, the more uncertainty a company experiences. This means that while the functional part of a capability becomes more and more based on analytical prognoses and identified industry trends, the resource part experiences fluctuations of the resource/methodology/technology environment. A loose coupling between the capability function and needed (adjustable) resources makes business capability a dynamic perspective instrument for the architecture of corporate business. However, a strong and wide monitoring of the market is a must-have. This relates to both availability, accessibility of the resources and market-financial-political risks.

A concept of business capability is closely linked with the concept of business service. The latter is defined as a means of accessing the capability or results of its execution. A business service encompasses the same business functionality as the capability; the service's body is nothing more than an implementation of the capability. A business service works only on invocation, which constitutes the predefined business condition, the consumer's need and willingness to invoke the business capability via the service. A business service exists as a wrapper of business capability that provides interfaces for the capability consumers.

Using business service concept, Business Architecture enters into the reality of SOE, which is covered by standards (RAF 2012). That is, the work of Business Architecture already has a solid formalized ground that can be easily managed, because its details and specifics are known upfront. This also includes several modelling patterns, such as business collaboration and cooperation. Business services may be simple and composed. A simple business service comprises manual and automated elements in any needed combination, which is dictated by the business functionality and resource availability. Composed business services consist of several simple and/or other composed services. The major advantage of business services is that due to their interfaces and special implementation they can be quickly and easily recomposed providing new flexible business solutions and competitive advantage over those who do not possess the capability of service technique. More details about business services and SOE are available in the literature in the references (Poulin 2013), (Poulin 2009).

Corporate Culture and Motivations

Corporate culture is the most liquid substance in an enterprise, and is also the most solid thing in an enterprise, especially if you want to change it. Business Architecture at a corporate level is not sustainable without cultural support. However, corporate culture in the majority of modern organizations was formed based on business principles defined about 50 years ago (Porter1985) and oriented on the reproductive function of business led by mostly vertical, hierarchical structures of management.

Corporate culture is one of the most powerful intangible values that attributes to both success and failure of Service-Oriented initiatives. When we talk about Business Architecture, we cannot abstract corporate culture from communication channels and functions. This is because the interaction between capability-service is a reflection of the culture of those who interact.

Peter Drucker warned: "Company cultures are like country cultures. Never try to change one. Try, instead, to work with what you've got" (BBQ 2014). However, culture is not a spiritual monolith, which if set once stays the same regardless of the environment. We think that each culture is formed and reformed by certain constraints and incentives that fit with the living conditions of some people better than others. While constraints belong to the business execution context and the position that the business occupies in it, the incentives are more under enterprise control.

Figure 6.

This means that the culture will resist reforming only if the incentives do not adequately match the living conditions, and that people who promote solutions constructed by the Business Architecture as 'modus operandi' have to demonstrate strong incentives that complement the current business situation in a company and its personnel.

Many would agree that organizations with a strong culture can be much more productive because their people are both motivated and also fulfilled. We use the term "strong culture" with regard to the culture where people similarly respond to an external stimulus; i.e. those people who share the same values and rules. There is no straight borderline between strong or weak corporate culture: different culture categories like "The Clan Culture", "The Adhocracy Culture", "The Hierarchy Culture", "The Market Culture" have their own pros and cons in different business situations.

A Business Architecture armed with a strategy, understands that tomorrow brings both expected and unforeseen changes, and with the capability-service vision of the world needs a particular type of corporate culture, as shown in Figure 6, to deliver the maximum business value. This culture has to be based on servicing each other, managers, departments, entire company, clients and consumers. A customer orientation is the main characteristic of such a culture where customers are recognized outside and inside the enterprise.

This is not an Adhocracy culture, which set the priority of self-protection even against internal and external consumers to the top. This is not a Market Culture either that focuses on the external environment and differentiation between it and the position of the company. If this environment changes too fast and frequently, the employees cannot handle overpressure of management to follow each change efficiently and on time. This culture crashes in the dynamic market.

Effective Business Architecture demands a corporate culture that combines elements of Adhocracy and Market Cultures. This fits with the service-centric organization concept. Such culture transforms boundaries of ownership and forms a special type of business behaviour: a business team owns only activities and resources it performs by itself, but reaches outside of its boundaries for the needed supplements provided by other teams. Some teams can play an assembly role realized via orchestration of business processes and cases. Business teams working in such a manner are accountable to their consumers for the outcome, though it may be a combined outcome from several other teams servicing the one; business teams are responsible for their own work and acquisition of all supplements needed for the team's outcome.

This approach requires a change in the corporate culture; a team can obtain supplements from anywhere including external resources and outsourcing. This creates a challenge for the business teams that used to supply that one team; now suppliers have to be not only competent, but also competitive against internal and external offers. This requires a high level of dedication and commitment from the people in the teams.

The way to win a business cultural change is to find something personally valuable (an incentive) to everyone. A notion of servicing naturally carries such values as: "if I am served well, I will serve well too". Corporate culture has to orient people on the service. This will convert capability realization and monitoring of the market changes in the proactive manner. All described aspects of culture transformation should stay on the grounds of clear vision and sharing of related values among people.

The cultural changes should be part of the strategic vision if not strategic planning. "…only cultures that can help organizations anticipate and adapt to environmental change will be associated with superior performance over the long time", James Kotter predicted two decades ago (Kotter 2011). Business Architecture needs all personnel to be involved emotionally, only in this case the outcome of the capability-services can be the best and the customer demand satisfaction the highest.

INPUTS, OUTCOMES AND IMPACTS OF BUSINESS ARCHITECTURE

Business Architecture enables business agility in a dynamic market not only via its outcomes, but due to its existence and function. The larger a company becomes, the more conservation of integrity and coordination it needs, because a mistake at the high level of architecture becomes more and more costly. Business Architecture appears as an engine of adoption of business changes in circulation that each enterprise element passes during its life-cycles.

If we take a "snapshot" of enterprise, we can find a variety of enterprise elements that constitute its 'body' and behaviour such as:
- Strategy and tactics
- High and low level planning
- Marketing and market demands
- Business network and CRM

- Business organizational structure
- Business operational structure
- Corporate financial structure
- Business performance model
- Revenue model
- Corporate governance
- Value proposition and Capabilities
- Value Streams and Activity Streams
- Business services, processes, and products
- External relationships with regulators, partners and suppliers.

This list is not extensive, and includes elements of corporate organization, management, relationships, and others. All of them exist in a certain structure, while Business Architecture is situated among them as illustrated in Figure 7.

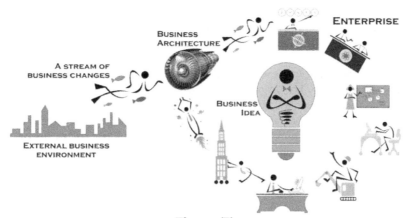

Figure 7[1].

Business Architecture receives inputs for its work from three major sources:
- Top corporate management: executives, Board, corporate strategy, and Enterprise Business Model
- Marketing and monitoring of external economic environment: including consumer demand, and industry regulations and laws
- Internal feedback and requests from the enterprise elements.

Every enterprise has its own system of triggers and priorities for initiating a work of Business Architecture, but the latter has to have a right and a mechanism for raising risk alerts and concerns based on integral analysis of information from all sources. An agility to the market is an ability of the business to react to market fluctuations with reasonable responses or do not react based on the calculated impact of the risk. So, having a view into trends and producing related strategy while acting with aligning tactics is the rule of thumb; if a company founds its capabilities only on previous experience, it leads to trouble in the modern market.

Business Architecture outcome consists of:
- Analytical and advisory materials from the executives and Board
- Options of possible responses to changes and related solutions

---

[1] http://www.123rf.com/license_summary.php

- Governing principles and policies that promote the executive vision and stimulate its realization
- Collections of business capabilities' definitions, capability models, capability maps and related solutions
- Contributions into SBP and BTP
- Core parts of blueprints for all transition steps and milestones
- Architectural controls throughout delivery and operational functions
- Directives and patterns for relationships with partners and suppliers.

Corporate management is assumed as delivery powers of the business where the outcomes of the Business Architecture work appear as business requirements. For example, the Business Architecture team has defined a couple of complex business capabilities that need strong cross-divisional governing. The best response from the management would be the creation of a new management structure for this purpose, instead of trying to divide the management among existing organizational elements.

A real world case of this nature has taken place in one of the biggest UK banks when it defined, designed and realized centralized shared business services in its Equity division. Operationally, this meant that management of regional units had to give up managerial power over several local business groups and those who were subordinates yesterday became independent service suppliers. When this process continued, regional management remained with only business units that customize the products for local customers; everything else was finally done via business services. However, if some of those services could not provide as needed, an outsourcing was always an option, which downgraded the service trust.

We differentiate between Business Architecture and its implementation. Different enterprise elements in different combinations can realize the same architecture. This is the same formation as we know from business processes: a business process realizes the particular business function, has certain inputs, and produces concrete outcomes. However, many different processes can realize this business function, use the same inputs, and produce analogous or the same outcomes.

Business Architecture accumulates and massages information from the aforementioned sources and comes up with solutions of what should be done in the given situation, in order to reach strategic goals. The solutions become the basis for financial investments for the future development and operational programs and projects. When enterprise EBP and BTP are set in line with those solutions, they reflect the business flexibility and agility to environmental changes. Business organizational and operational models with related value and Activity Streams, if adjusted to the architectural solutions, will automatically respond to the market changes with maximum efficiency. We can trace the impacts of Business Architecture outcomes practically everywhere in a company, including corporate culture.

Business Architecture is not everything that Business Architects touch. It addresses concerns related to "what", "why", "where", "when" and "for whom" an enterprise conducts the business; the rest of the company addresses an extremely complex concern, "how" to conduct this business in the best way. There is no a strict boundary between "why/what" and "how", which makes the work of Business Architecture challenging. In the circulation of activities, "how" becomes "why" and "what" becomes "how" (Poulin 2013). However, there is a logical dependency between what and how: we usually have to understand first what we are going to do and why, and only then how it may be done. Otherwise, we fulfil an image of a master with the solution looking for a problem.

FRUITS FOR THOUGHTS

Will McInnes, a famous business transformation visionary and facilitator, once said: "Business as usual is utterly screwed. It values the wrong things, rewards the wrong people and behaves in the wrong ways. Here we are in the 21st century and the world has changed so completely, so profoundly, yet if you took a CEO from the 1950s and parachuted him, and it would be a *him*, not a her, into 99% of our business organisations today, he'd know his way around" (McInnes 2012).

However, if the same CEO would be tasked with building a company nowadays, he will most likely fail. The world economy is changing with unprecedented pace.

To survive in such an environment and even prosper in the long-term, a corporate business needs a mechanism for adoption of external and internal business changes. There are many contributions to these changes; the recent financial crisis that demonstrated previously unknown limitations to the world financial system, digitization of our daily life, globalization of companies, informational revolution, and massive initiative of Governments in different countries to keep a business on a leash via flows or regulations. Modern structure of our enterprises appears incapable of handling such highly dynamic markets appropriately and needs a special mechanism oriented exclusively on dynamic changes and agility of business to these changes. This is what Business Architecture can and should deliver.

Business Architectural function existed, exists, and will exist in all companies until we have such systems as a business. However, only explicit execution of this function enables the sufficient growth of the company. The business Architecture concept is relatively simple, it is a mechanism that links changes in the dynamic market with corporate strategy and a means of realization of this strategy. Business Architecture work produces capability definitions/designs, their models, combinations and solutions, core elements of blueprints, analytics, proposals, governance, and contributes to the SBP and BTP. Business Architecture is compact, but influences all aspects of the enterprise and its behaviour.

Business Architecture accumulates feedback and reactions of the corporate business to the architectural solutions and uses them for the new solutions; it requires a certain corporate culture and facilitates its transition to this culture. Business Architecture arms the company with models, services, and solutions that reflect external changes in the most flexible manner, which allows a company to reach agility with the dynamics and even form competitive advantages in the market storm. Nowadays, the ability to change quickly is the key to success.

REFERENCES

(Porter1985) Michael E. Porter(1985), "Competitive Advantage: Creating and Sustaining Superior Performance"(1985). Simon and Schuster. Retrieved 9 Sep. 2013

(Rother 2003) Mike Rother, John Shook. "Learning to See: value-stream mapping to create value and eliminate muda." Brookline, MA: Lean Enterprise Institute. 2003 ISBN: 0-9667843-0-0

(Poulin 2013) Michael Poulin, "Architects Know What Managers Don't". BuTechCon-Troubador Publishing Ltd., 2013. ISBN: 978-0-9575199-0-9

(Daft 2014) Richard L. Daft, "The Leadership Experience". Delmar Cengage Learning; 6th Revised edition. Feb. 2014 ISBN: 978-1435462854

(Dholakia) Chintak Dholakia, "Inspiration- An ebook featuring 1001 inspiring quotes"

https://books.google.co.uk/books?id=5nCTO2CQ4qQC&printsec=frontco
ver#v=onepage&q&f=false

(Poulin 2015)   Michael Poulin, "What Business Architecture Needs: Value
Streams or Activity Streams?". BLOG, LinkedIn. Jan. 2015
https://www.linkedin.com/pulse/what-business-architecture-needs-
value-streams-michael?trk=prof-post

(Tapping 2002) Don Tapping, Tom Luyster, Tom Shuker, "Value Stream Management: Eight Steps to Planning, Mapping, and Sustaining Lean Improvements, Productivity Press; Pap/Cdr edition. May 2002 ISBN: 978-
1563272455

(M. Poulin 2015) Michael Poulin, "Business Capability for a Dynamic Market"
Clingstone-Trobadour Publishing Ltd. 2015. ISBN 978-0-9575199-0-7

(Dijkstra 1982) Edsger W Dijkstra, "On the role of scientific thought". Selected
writings on Computing: A Personal Perspective." 1982. Springer-Verlag.
pp. 60–66. ISBN: 0-387-90652-5

(M. Poulin 2014) Michael Poulin, "Updated Principles of Service Orientation".
InfoQ, 2014

(RAF 2012) "Reference Architecture Foundation for Service Oriented Architecture". Version 1.0. Committee Specification 01. Dec.2012

(M. Poulin 2013) Michael Poulin, "Multi-Party Business Service Cooperation".
White Paper, Orbus, 2013

(Poulin 2009)   Michael Poulin, "Ladder to SOE:". Troubador Publishing
Ltd. 2009 ISBN 978-1848761-629

(BBQ 2014) "Book of Business Quotations", edited by Bill Ridgers. Economist
Books. Jun 2012 ISBN: 978-1846685934

(Kotter 2011) John P. Kotter, "Corporate Culture and Performance". Free
Press, Reprint edition. May 2011 ISBN: 978-1451655322

(McInnes 2012) Will McInnes, "Time for a revolution: bold new business models for the 21st century". BLOG. Dec. 2012 http://willmcin-
nes.com/2012/12/16/time-for-a-revolution-bold-new-business-models-
for-the-21st-century/

Business and Dynamic Change:
The Arrival of Business Architecture

Part Two – Where the Rubber Meets the Road

Sometimes you need to get into the gritty details of the architecture work. This section introduces some specific uses and applications of business architecture concepts. Some are enterprise-wide and some are specific to certain aspects of the architecture. In each case there is value in applying the architecture concepts described, supported by the writers' rationale and drivers behind the efforts.

LINKING ARCHITECTURES FOR BUSINESS RESULTS

Jude Chagas Pereira, IYCON

Mr. Pereira shows the practical implementation of multiple architectures, or layers which surround a business process. Ensuring that these multiple architectures are linked and removing redundant components is an issue that needs to be urgently addressed in a holistic manner. These architectures need to be linked together, visualized and presented in a unified manner, will ensure that the different stakeholders are firstly, reading from the same page, and secondly, provided the right information to support better decision-making. This approach delivers strategy-aligned, efficient processes which satisfy the needs of the majority of the process stakeholders. He demonstrates by example how this is done in a client situation.

DATABASE REVERSE ENGINEERING FOR BUSINESS DUE DILIGENCE

Michael Blaha, Modelsoft Consulting Corp

Mr. Blaha recommends the practice reverse-engineering databases as an effective means to understand current business and information architecture implementations. It is the foundation for determining the current business architecture and the implications of transitioning to a future architecture, especially in Merger and Acquisition scenarios. He provides multiple examples of situations that this approach has given insights in terms of the compatibility of systems, architectures, cultures, and processes in the respective architecture efforts. Reverse engineering provides an opportunity to re-architect enterprise data and expand the scope to include emerging needs such as big data.

HEAT-MAPPED VALUE STREAMS AS THE TRANSLATION FROM STRATEGY TO ACTION

J. Bryan Lail, Stephanie Ramsay, Ralph Shaw, Raytheon, U.S.

Authors Lail, Ramsey and Shaw demonstrate how Raytheon is using business architecture methods as a powerful force for business dynamic change through the use of heat-mapped value streams. Using subjective evaluation on capability gaps by the team of experts in the business, a focus emerges for a future value stream that spans across the changes in roles, skills, processes, teaming, cost structures and other elements to provide the new revenue channels. They have used these tools to drive from mission strategies down to specific actions for cross-functional teams. They provide examples of these methods.

APPLYING ARCHITECTURE TO BUSINESS TRANSFORMATION AND DECISION MAKING:
CASE AALTO UNIVERSITY

Patrik Maltusch, Aalto University and Virpi Nieminen, QPR Software, Finland

Authors Maltusch and Nieminen applied architecture concepts to combine/merge/consolidate three universities. The motive for the change was externally driven by government legislation. This transformation would not have been possible without the transparency brought by EA, which paved the way to breaking old organizational boundaries. Synergies were created in the form of new shared service centers and common IT assets to best serve the new unified university structure – and above all, to bring Aalto University one step closer to its vision.

BUSINESS ARCHITECTURE FOR PROCESS-ORIENTED LEARNING IN PUBLIC ADMINISTRATION

Darius Silingas, No Magic Europe, Lithuania; Barbara Thönssen, FHNW, Switzerland; Alfonso Pierantonio, University of L'Aquila, Italy, Nesat Efendioglu, Robert Woitsch, BOC Asset Management, Austria

The authors, Silingas, Thönssen, Pierantonio, Efendioglu and Woitsch, point out that 'Civil servants are challenged to understand and put in action the latest procedures and rules within tight time constraints.' They maintain this is done through a combination of a business process orientation and business architecture. Aligning these provides public organizations the means to better leverage their knowledge assets and provide improved services to their constituencies. The key to effectively deploying an environment that fosters the use of knowledge is the Model-Based Social Learning for Public Administrations. This approach takes advantage of process driven learning and structuring knowledge using architecture models.

LEVERAGING ARCHITECTURE FEDERATION TO INCREASE THE VALUE AND USE OF ARCHITECTURE

David Rice, EA Frameworks, LLC, USA

Mr. Rice brings to us his experience in very large organizations and provides an architectural perspective of governance and architecture management that uses architecture federation. He explains how this is done through 'a federation of independently managed, heterogeneous architectures (hereafter referred to as "component architectures"). He maintains that a standard taxonomy and organizing the architectures into tiers brings order to the architecture material. Organizing the architectures in terms of components and tiers with a standard taxonomy provides the enterprise with a means of contrasting the federated architectures in terms of differences and similarities. This gives the architect and management insight into where to combine things or keep them separate.

BA PRACTICAL DATA GOVERNANCE

Michael S. Connor, American Family Insurance, U.S.A.

Mr. Connor explains how, for most organizations, Data Governance has generally focused on standard data management functions such as data policies, metadata, etc. In contrast, BA activities and related discussions have led a life very separate from DG; for obvious reasons, BA has been treated similarly to other kinds of high-level architecture. Now in an era of great change and the "need for speed," BA requires more of an implementation focus and the DG Engagement model can satisfy this pressing requirement solidifying strong, broad-based business partner consensus and commitment. While delivering a necessary service for the BA process, the model now evolves to the next level of value for the organization.

Linking Architectures for Business Results

Jude Chagas Pereira, IYCON

INTRODUCTION

Organizations today have adopted business process management as a must-have initiative to further their success. This is driven by many factors, the need to rationalize cost, the allure of promised results, and also the mounting peer pressure where "everyone is implementing BPM."

Irrespective of the motive that started an organization onto the BPM journey, every organization today finds itself in a juncture, where they have to measure the cost of the BPM initiative, and quantify the benefits to the stakeholders.

As part of this journey, organizations find that they now own multiple initiatives which are based around the BPM banner, but not truly linked or aligned.

In addition, business processes need to be linked with organizational strategy to ensure effective strategy execution.

Ensuring that these multiple architectures are linked and removing redundant components of the same, is an issue that needs to be urgently addressed in a holistic manner.

SETTING OUT

At the onset of the BPM journey it is important to understand the current landscape of the organization which is reflected in the business processes of the organization. In most cases, especially in mature businesses, such as banking, government, airlines etc. the core business processes are automated, with an ERP system such as Oracle or SAP, Core Banking System, or any suitable transaction system, depending on the industry.

While automated transactions form the backbone of the core business processes of the organization, these in reality represent just over half the business processes in any organization.

Let's take an example of a bank (Figure 1). The core banking system will cover all the main business processes, from Retail & Consumer Banking (such as account opening, cash management, online banking etc.) to Wholesale Banking and Wealth Management. Additionally, other systems will be utilized for back office transactions such as HR, Finance, and Strategy. However, there are multiple functions of the bank which may be only partially automated (hybrid) or completely manual.

As a result of this varied process landscape, there emerges a need to capture the entire set of organizational processes within a process repository. This is captured using a business process tool and helps the organization to understand the "as-is" process landscape of the organization.

As part of this exercise, gaps in the existing process, or potential improvements will be noticed and documented. The output of the "as-is" process mapping, forms a baseline of the processes of the organization.

The next step is to decide which processes need improvement based on the observations recorded during the "as-is" process mapping. This needs to be done based on a cost-benefit analysis. In addition, this may also involve changing or updating technology.

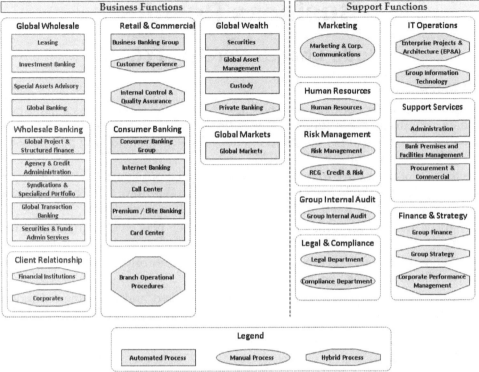

Figure 1: Example of a Banking Process Landscape

Here IT supports the business by modifying systems, or implementing new systems. However, managing the changes and understanding the impact on business process is a constant challenge. IT turns to frameworks such as Enterprise Architecture to enable them to document the enterprise landscape of the organization. In many cases, an Enterprise Architecture Tool, which is specifically built for this purpose is utilized.

Multiple Stakeholders

In some organizations, the business processes are owned by IT, under departments such as Enterprise Projects and Architecture. In other organizations, the business processes are owned by separate departments such as Organizational Development, or Process Improvement.

In addition, there are other stakeholders of the business processes who drive changes to the same. These could be the Quality Department, the Internal Audit Department, and the Risk and Compliance Department, which rely on the business processes to effectively carry out their functions.

Once of the biggest challenges faced, is that each of these stakeholders, utilize some dimensions of the business process, but not others. This creates a lack of ownership of the business process as a whole. In addition the department to which the business process belongs also has to deal with multiple stakeholder needs, and may maintain versions of the same process to satisfy the different stakeholder needs.

Let's take a look at the main stakeholders of a business process.

- *Process Owner:* This is the department whose business processes are documented. E.g. the Marketing Department or the Account Payable Department. They will raise change requests if the business process needs to be updated based on business requirements.
- *Business Process Department:* It is responsible for driving business process documentation, improvement and change management for the End to End business processes of the organization. They will raise change requests from the standpoint of business improvement or efficiency.
- *Internal Audit Department:* It uses the business process as a baseline to understand if documented processes are being followed and is tasked with uncovering fraud and other irregularities. They will raise change requests from the standpoint of plugging loopholes in the process.
- *Quality Department:* Owns the processes from a quality standpoint, and is responsible for ensuring compliance to a quality standard, such as ISO. They will raise change requests to ensure non-conformances observed in the process, or those related to the quality standard are addressed.
- *Enterprise Architecture & IT:* Tasked with supporting the Business Process Department and the Process Owners with appropriate technology that holistically integrates business processes, and enables an end to end business process, such as Order to Cash (O2C).
- *Risk and Compliance Department:* Looks at the business process from a regulatory standpoint. E.g. in a banking environment, the business processes need to comply with Central Bank regulations, or for listed organizations, the Sarbanes-Oxley Act (SOX).
- *Human Resources Department:* Looks at the resources who carry out these processes, and based on the process, define the competencies required for each resource.

PROCESS LAYERS

As a result of these sometimes conflicting needs of the different stakeholders, the Process Owners begin to adopt a silo based approach to process management, and maintain the business processes (or versions) separately for each stakeholder.

Let's take an example of an Accounts Payable process and decompose the process into its different layers.

Business Process Layer

The first layer is the Business Process Layer. This layer represents the basic business process, the interactions and the decision points.

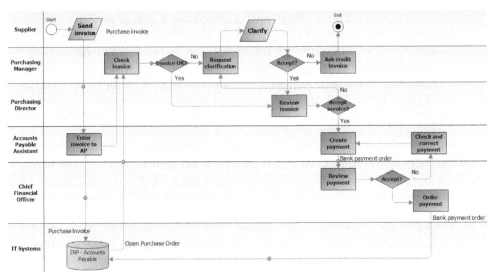

Figure 2: Accounts Payable – Business Process Layer

Compliance Layer

The compliance layer will consist of the risks and control points, incorporating the needs of Internal Audit, Risk and Compliance and the Quality Department.

The risk register will capture all risks related to the process as identified by the stakeholder departments.

Risk Register

Name	Type	Description	Risk Owner	Risk Category	Risk Sub Category
Diagram Hierarchy	Subprocess				
Processes	Subprocess				
Accounts Payable	Subprocess				
Improper payments to suppliers	Risk	The risk of improper payments to suppliers, due to errors or criminal intend will have a negative effect on Dentorexs' financial position.	Purchasing Director	Process risk	Financial Risk
Improper invoicing by suppliers	Risk	Suppliers sending improper invoices, e.g. for goods not ordered or at prices higher than initially agreed will have a negative effect on Dentorexs' financial results.	Purchasing Director	Process risk	Financial Risk
Purchasing Fraud	Risk	Purchasing fraud is the event where a purchaser's criminal behavior negatively affects Dentrorex's finances.	Purchasing Director	Process risk	Integrity Risk
Unauthorized Purchases	Risk	Unauthorized purchases by a purchaser are likely to have a negative effect on Dentorex operations and financial position.	Purchasing Director	Process risk	Integrity Risk

Figure 3: Accounts Payable – Risk Register Extract

The control points are also identified in relation to the risks. These are the areas which will be tested during the various process audits. This is maintained in the control register and appears on various audit checklists.

Control Register — Current View Filter: None

Name	Type	Description	Risks for Control	Control Owner	Control Test Date (Last)	Control Test Outcome
Diagram Hierarchy	Subprocess					
Processes	Subprocess					
Accounts Payable	Subprocess					
P14 - Ensure that the amount invoiced by a supplier is correct	Control	In order to ensure that the amount invoiced by a supplier is correct, the purchasing manager needs to provide and attach his/her approval prior to processing the invoice.	Improper Invoicing by suppliers	Purchasing Manager	8/4/2009	Passed
P15 - Approval by Purchase Director for Goods	Control	In order to avoid purchasing fraud by purchasers, the purchasing director need to review and approve every invoice for purchased goods prior to processing the invoice for payment.	Unauthorized Purchases	Purchasing Director	4/24/2009	Passed
P16 - CFO Approval for payments	Control	In order to avoid improper payments to suppliers, the CFO is required to review and approve every payment prior to processing it.	Improper payments to suppliers	CFO	4/30/2009	Failed
P2 - Approval over value of 5,000 by Purchase Director	Control	Purchase invoices with a value above 5000 are only approved and entered into accounts payable when purchase director approval is attached to the purchase invoice.	Purchasing Fraud	Purchasing Director	8/6/2008	Passed

Figure 4: Accounts Payable – Control Register Extract

In order to ensure that a proper relationship is maintained between the risks and controls, a Risk-Control Matrix is maintained. This clearly maps the risks with the related controls for each process level.

Figure 5: Accounts Payable – Risk/Control Matrix

Resources Layer

The Resources Layer defines the people, material, equipment and other resources required to successfully carry out the business process. In the Business Process Layer above (Figure 2), we can explore the details of the Role "Purchasing Manager".

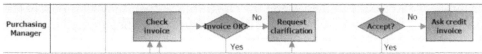

Figure 6: Extract of Business Process (Role: Purchasing Manager)

The role definition will include the process steps being carried out, along with their description, as well as the competencies required for the same. In addition a summary job description will also be included to enable the hiring process for the role.

Figure 7: Purchasing Manager Role Definition

Technology Layer

The Technology Layer reflects the underlying IT systems which enable this process and the system workflow required for the same. The details on this layer are highly technical in nature and usually follow the BPMN 2.0 notation for form and attributes.

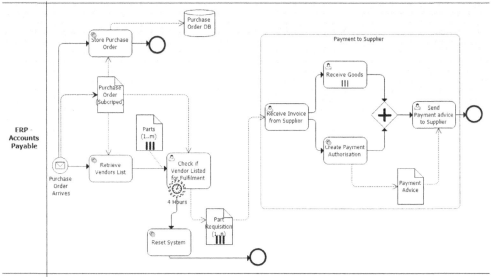

Figure 8: Accounts Payable – Technology Layer

ALIGNMENT

Alignment of these process layers is critical to provide a holistic view of the business process. Continuing the example above, we need to superimpose each of these layers onto the Business Process Layer as shown above. In order to do so, we need to represent each layer as a diagram.

Resources Layer

The Resources Layer is almost always built into the diagram as swim lanes or activity owners, making this the easiest layer to integrate. However, it is important to align the resources with activities and the Organization Hierarchy as shown in Figure 7 above, where the Purchasing Manager is shown reporting to the Purchasing Director, under the Purchasing Department.

Having the job description linked to the organizational unit allows easy verification of whether the tasks being performed by the position described is adequately reflected in the job description in terms of dimensions, accountabilities and skill sets.

Another detailed example of the competencies of an Assistant Manager, Events is shown in Figure 9 below.

Figure 9: Assistant Manager Events - Role

Compliance Layer

The Compliance Layer is the most critical layer to integrate into the business process, and this is the layer which is most often left running as a parallel system. This is done by adding the Risks and Controls along with their associations onto the Business Process Layer.

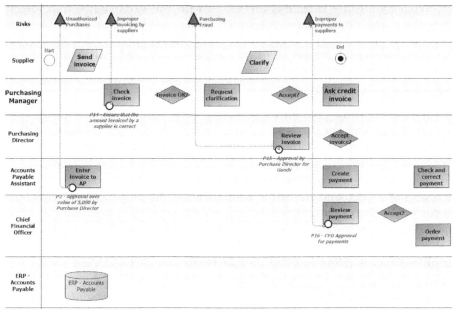

Figure 10: Risks and Controls Superimposed on Business Process

As we can see, all the compliance hierarchies, which were manually maintained, are now visualized onto the business process making the associations easy to communicate and manage.

The business process with the Compliance and Resources Layer integrated (Figure 11), now has all relevant information for the following stakeholders:

- Process Owner
- Business Process Department
- Internal Audit Department
- Quality Department
- Risk and Compliance Department
- Human Resources Department

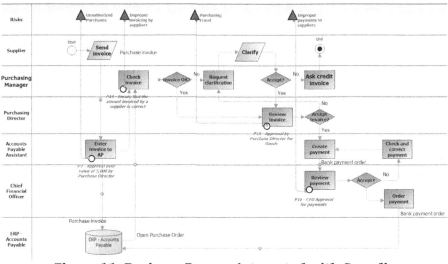

Figure 11: Business Process integrated with Compliance and Resources Layers

After consolidating the Business Processes with the Compliance and Resources Layers, the organization is now in a much better position to manage the business processes, and the changes to the same, while considering key stakeholder needs. This will provide a robust base for the organization to move forward on the roadmap towards delivering sustainable business results.

ALIGNING PROCESS WITH STRATEGY

Strategy is the driving force for every business. It determines the direction of the business and defines the medium to long term goals. Strategy is executed through implementation of strategic initiatives and via the business processes of the organization.

In many organizations, strategy and business process are owned by departments which do not report into the same structure (see Figure 1 above). This leads to disconnects in the execution of strategy, as the process improvements, and cost investments in the same, could have little or no impact on the desired strategic outcomes.

Example: Process Alignment to deliver Customer Satisfaction

Let's take an example. A bank has a strategic objective to be the "Preferred Bank for Retail Customers". The bank has selected "Customer Satisfaction" as one of its key measures. In order to benchmark their current ratings, the bank conducts a survey to understand the level of customer satisfaction and explore areas of improvement.

The results of the survey show that the customers have a high level of dissatisfaction with the bank's call center, which supports the internet banking process. This leads the bank to look closely at the call center process (Figure 12).

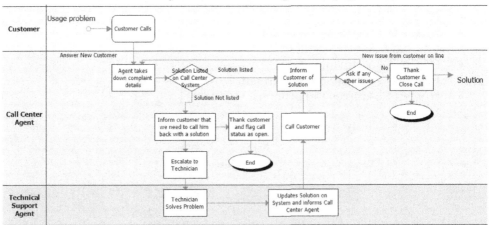

Figure 12: Call Center process

In order to monitor and improve the call center process, the bank defines the following Key Performance Indicators (KPI's), or process metrics, to monitor the process performance. Each of these process metrics needs to be aligned to the relevant process step, in order to closely monitor the process performance.

- Abandon rate of incoming phone calls – Linked to Step "Customer Calls"
- Average speed to answer phone call – Linked to Step "Agent takes down complaint details"
- Average talk time of phone calls - Linked to Step "Thank Customer & Close Call"
- First-call resolution rate - Linked to Step "Ask if any other issues"

The targets for these process KPI's are driven by the need of the process to deliver the stated strategy of the bank, as well as the industry benchmarks for the process.

If based on industry benchmarks, the average speed for banks to answer phone calls at a call center is seven seconds; then in order to perform better, the bank will set a target of five seconds or below to perform above industry average. This metric will be tracked over a period of time (Figure 13).

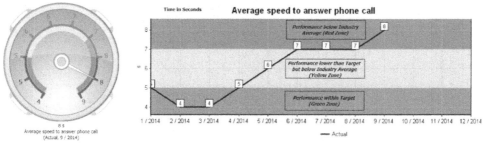

Figure 13: KPI - Average time to answer calls

The bank will then look at a detailed view of all the KPI's, and how, when consolidated, these measure the stated Objective "Customer Satisfaction with Call Center". This process could be carried out by the process owner, in conjunction with the Strategy Department.

However, the reporting of the KPI's and the ultimate objective performance is still being viewed by the bank as a parallel silo on the reporting, whereby the Strategy Department would send a Process KPI to the process owner, and the process owner would continue to view the process flowcharts and look for improvements on the same.

Now consider a more complex process, or an end to end process, such as an Order to Cash (O2C) process or a Procure to Pay (P2P) process. In such a scenario, the process map would run into a large number of steps, with multiple paths. Similarly the number of KPI's would be large, and related to different parts of the process. Therefore it becomes critical to visually integrate the KPI's onto the Process itself (Figure 14). In this way the process owner can clearly see the process bottlenecks, in order to improve the process performance.

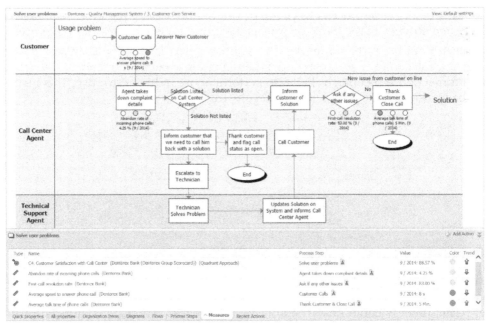

Figure 14: KPI's integrated onto the process

ALIGNING PROCESS WITH UNDERLYING TECHNOLOGY

As we have seen above, the Technology Layer is usually documented using BPMN 2.0 or other relevant notations. This helps to define the process flow as it should be carried out. In addition, we see that the Strategy provides indicators of where the process is performing below par.

However, in order to truly understand where the process is failing we need to look "under the hood" and align the process with the reality of the transactions that are flowing through the process.

We can achieve this by looking at the transaction logs of the ERP systems or workflow systems, using a technique called Process Mining. Process Mining (or Automated Business Process Discovery, ABPD) approaches process alignment from a completely new angle, the data.

The traditional way a process is analyzed, is time consuming, resource intensive and vulnerable to human interpretation. Process mining brings transparency and delivers fact-based information, in a fraction of the time compared to the traditional approach.

Unlike reporting and analytics solutions, process mining solutions use time stamps of the events read directly from the data. This enables automatic visualization of processes, delivering insight on processes and process specific KPIs.

Process mining presents the big picture of how the business processes are executed and what is the real status of the processes. It enables drilling down to all process variations and bottlenecks as well as benchmarking between any relevant dimensions such as factories or teams. Building the analysis based on event level data means that you are able to drill down to even individual process instances to see what is the root cause for poor performance.

The following are the benefits of process mining:
- Recreated Process Flowchart – an automatic visualization of the real end-to-end process based on the ERP transaction logs

- Duration Analysis - a visual analysis of the varying process lead times
- Influence Analysis - an overview of root causes for variations or bottle-necks
- Benchmarking - process comparisons per e.g. location, country, product depending on the dimensions of the data
- Variation Analysis - all process variations in one view
- Custom reports - information of process metrics specific to user needs on regular intervals
- Animation – a dynamic presentation of the real case execution
- Fact based – initiate process improvements based on real facts

CONCLUSIONS

In conclusion, we see that there are multiple architectures, or layers which surround a business process.

Ensuring that these architectures are linked together, visualized and presented in a unified manner, will ensure that the different stakeholders are firstly, reading from the same page, and secondly, provided the right information, to support better decision making.

This approach delivers strategy aligned, efficient processes, which satisfy the needs of the majority of the process stakeholders.

REFERENCES

IYCON PRISE© – A Roadmap to Strategy Execution – Process and Risk Integrated Strategy Execution. – www.iycon.com

QPR Software Plc. – www.qpr.com

Database Reverse Engineering for Business Due Diligence

Michael Blaha, Modelsoft Consulting Corp

Reverse engineering is the examination of something to discover its underlying concepts and to understand how it works. *Database reverse engineering (DBRE)* is the use of reverse engineering for a database. Database reverse engineering lets you reach into the databases of software, see their strengths and weaknesses, understand their technology, structure, content, and scope. At first glance, the topic of database reverse engineering might seem esoteric. But, it is highly relevant to business at the highest corporate levels as this article will explain.

Database reverse engineering can have a special impact on mergers and acquisitions (M&A). All too often, business plans falter because of difficulties with integrating the supporting information systems. Database reverse engineering can help this situation. With a modest amount of effort you can learn a great deal about software, see if there are incompatible data structures, or deep errors before committing to the terms of acquisition. You can prepare a better integration plan. This information is not only helpful to the business but also to system architects.

If you are doing M&A it behooves you to understand the other party's systems (as well as your own systems). This is part of business due diligence. Will systems from different organizations work together? Which systems are useful software? Which systems are obsolete? Which systems do you keep? Which systems do you discard? And how do you combine the data for the two organizations? Applications come and go but data endures. Data is the crown jewel of most organizations.

COMMENTARY FROM OTHER AUTHORS

Here are some comments from other authors about the importance of information systems integration for M&A.

- "In many sectors a large percentage of all merger synergies are dependent directly upon IT. In some, particularly financial services, it is the IT integration process that drives the merger timetable. There is a long list of merged organizations who've struggled, and in some cases failed to integrate their IT infrastructure effectively, resulting in a significant impact on the merger economics." [Mayes-2012]
- "The diligence phase is realistically the last chance to call off the M&A before both sides commit, and as such, a CIO should be looking for red and yellow flags that suggest the integration will be harder than expected (and budgeted for). Conversely, the CIO of the acquiring company can also be looking for positive reinforcement: systems or processes from the other company that remind everyone why the merger or acquisition seemed like a good idea in the first place." [Worthen-2002]
- "Companies that have merged, sometimes find that their information technology systems are not easily integrated, causing disruptions to

workflow or at the very least requiring additional time, expense and staff effort to make the systems work smoothly. If these clashes are disruptive enough, the merger could be judged to be a losing proposition." [Hill-2013]

WHAT IS DATABASE REVERSE ENGINEERING (DBRE)?

The following figure summarizes the database reverse engineering process. DBRE is driven by the available data and structures as well as the business purpose. For example, data conversion requires a thorough reverse engineering that examines every table and column. In contrast, for an assessment of database quality, a spot check of a portion of a schema can suffice.

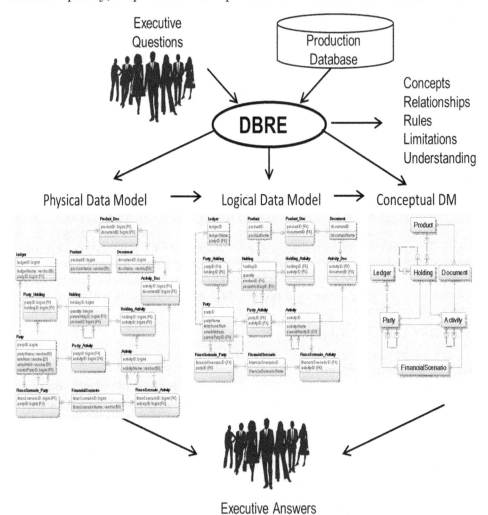

Figure 1: Elements of the Database Reengineering Process

After performing DBRE, the concepts in the database are apparent as well as relationships among the concepts. You can see the structural rules for data that can be stored. You can see the limitations that arise from the way that the database is architected. The bottom line is that you obtain a deep understanding of the database that you can exploit in different ways.

The initial product of DBRE is a physical data model that emphasizes physical constructs such as tables, keys, indexes, and constraints. The logical data model suppresses physical details and abstracts towards more meaningful concepts -- that is entities and attributes. The conceptual data model further suppresses detail and focuses only on the concepts and their relationships. DBRE has technical deliverables that include the various kinds of models as well as a deepened understanding of IT systems. The models, observations, and understanding give developers the wherewithal to answer the original executive questions.

Reverse engineering is an incidental effort, subordinate to some greater business purpose. In this article, the purpose of DBRE is to support the business activities of M&A. Therefore DBRE should have a limited effort. You are looking at the work of one high-skill individual or a small team of high-skill individuals. DBRE presupposes deep knowledge of data modeling, databases, and software engineering so you do need senior staff.

DATABASE GRADES

In communicating with business leaders, we have found it helpful to quantify a database evaluation with a grade. The grade reflects the consistency of the database and the extent of design and modeling errors.

The table below quantifies the grading scale. "A" is the best grade, and "F" is the worst, with "B," "C," and "D" denoting intermediate quality. An average database has about a "C" grade and the grades that we have found in practice do vary widely. Integration can flounder with flawed databases (grades of "D" and "F"). It can also flounder with quality databases where the structure and representations differ too much.

Grade	Explanation	Examples of Flaws
A	Clean	No major flaws. Uniform and reasonable style.
B	Structural flaws, but they do not affect the application	Inconsistent data types. Null constraints, unique keys, and enumerations are not defined. Cryptic column names.
C	Major flaws that affect the application (bugs, slow performance, lack of extensibility)	Inconsistent identity. Haphazard indexing. Foreign keys have mismatched data types.
D	Severe flaws that compromise the application	Primary keys are not readily apparent. Much unnecessary redundant data.
F	Appalling (the application does not run properly or runs only because of brute-force programming)	Deep conceptual errors in the underlying model, gross design errors, or both.

CASE STUDIES

We present six case studies, four of which are drawn from our own actual experience. We give a synopsis of the situation and look at the actual or potential benefits of DBRE.

Santander

The failed acquisition by Santander of RBS customers in 2012 is a costly mishap that could have been avoided by due diligence using DBRE. Problems with converting data from the RBS structure to Santander's structure caused the downfall of the deal.

- "Spain's Santander has pulled out of a deal worth $2.7bn (£1.63bn) to buy 316 branches of the Royal Bank of Scotland (RBS), leaving the British bank to hunt for other buyers. Santander UK pulled out of the deal citing delays in completing the transition including technology transfer and other separation issues. The bank would not expect the transition to be complete by the end of 2012. "[Santander-2012]
- "Santander entered into the deal to buy the branches and business of 1.8 million customers of the RBS in August 2010. It was initially expected to be completed by the end of 2011... Santander said according to an estimate by the consultancy, Accenture, the transfer of retail businesses would not be finished before 2014 and the transfer of corporate customers would not be completed until 2015." [Santander-2012]

The United-Continental Airlines Merger

The recent United – Continental airlines merger is another illustration of what can go wrong. Four years later the merged airline still has several major problems and IT integration is one of them. Airlines are known for being difficult to merge, but the United – Continental experience has been worse than the norm. The problems have led to poor customer service, high operating costs, and reduced profits. Here are some specific problems listed in a Wall Street Journal article. [WSJ-2014]

- "Its mechanics continue to operate under two separate information-technology systems for maintenance... [The systems] store complex data related to fixing the planes, keeping track of parts and generating the records needed by the airline, regulators and equipment vendors."
- "Last fall, the company's use of faulty information caused the airline to sell too many seats too cheaply, denting its revenue even after it made fixes."

A Leading Transportation Company

We consulted for a leading transportation company. A hedge fund acquired five precursor transportation companies, put them together, and then spun off the combination as a new company.

At the time we became involved, the new company was struggling to rationalize its information systems. They estimated that they had 3.5 different systems for each business function. They had the obvious costs of running redundant software. But a more serious problem was that the seams of the five original companies were apparent to its customers. Customers did not see a unified company but rather five different divisions with their own pricing, policies, and paperwork. The new company wanted to consolidate the separate systems so that they could build a single unified brand.

The board of directors initially approved a multi-million dollar project. But they became discouraged by the cost, time, and effort of combining systems. With the fragmented systems, the new business was not competitive. The eventual outcome was that the company was acquired by a competitor, who imposed their own systems as an integration solution.

If the hedge fund had looked at the systems of the companies it was acquiring, it would have seen the looming integration problem. A modest DBRE effort – less than a man-year of effort – could have given them such insight. It could have avoided the costly mess of acquiring the companies and spinning them out, only to have them acquired again.

Avelo

We worked with Avelo, a UK financial software vendor, prior to its acquisition by IRESS in 2013. Avelo was spun off by a hedge fund as the fusion of four financial software companies. Avelo started out with a strong portfolio of products, each one a leader or near leader in its market.

All the Avelo products were Microsoft based – coded in .NET and built on SQL Server. Reverse engineering revealed that the products had substantially different database modeling approaches that made it difficult for them to exchange data. For example, some applications were customer centric and others were account centric. The customer-centric software could look at the totality of customer activity. The account-centric software could only service its niche and could not consider customers more broadly. The differing data structures also made it difficult to cross sell, using the customers of one application as leads for another application. It also made it difficult to build a data warehouse to mine data.

To remedy this situation, management commissioned an effort to work towards integrating the applications. The applications were so dissimilar that it wasn't feasible to tightly integrate them. We had to settle for coarse integration. We devised a high-level model that transcended the applications and Avelo started evolving the applications towards the high-level model. We were making good progress at the time that Avelo was acquired by IRESS for business reasons unrelated to our project. Our consulting work ended and we were not privy to subsequent actions.

A Leading Engineering Firm

We consulted for a leading engineering firm (company A). One of A's business divisions was talking to another company (company B). Both had software products in the same business area. A was unsure if B was a potential competitor or collaborator. If B was a collaborator, A could freely exchange product information with them. However, if B was a competitor, A didn't want to be contaminated with information about B's products and risk legal complications.

Both parties agreed that we would prepare an outside, impartial evaluation of the database of B's product. Company A would receive a database grade for B's product but no other information. Company B would receive the database grade as well as the details of DBRE for their own internal consideration. This arrangement gave A insight into the quality of B's product while minimizing legal risk. Company A already had a rough understanding of B's product from public information.

So we performed the evaluation and assigned a favorable database grade. We informed both parties. Company B was satisfied with the details of the DBRE analysis which they alone received. Ultimately, the companies did not proceed with the joint business venture for other business reasons. But the independent DBRE analysis did shield them from the release of sensitive information. The independent assessment avoided the possibility of a legal dispute.

A Leading Chemical Company

We worked with a past client who wanted to sell an operating unit and could not separate out the data in time for the deal. Ironically they had reworked their systems a few years earlier (before our involvement) to more tightly integrate them as an IT goal. The tight integration worked out badly when they needed to separate out an operating unit for sale. The root problem was that the client had not tied their data management goals to strategic business goals. They had focused on optimizing at a tactical level and had missed the bigger picture.

Of course, the IT department should have talked to the business before starting the integration initiative. But these recriminations did not help at the time of divesture. Given the messy situation, DBRE could have been helpful for devising an approach to decoupling systems. Then they would better understand how to archive data, move the data to whoever was buying the products or operating units, update processes, re-align the data relationships to the processes and applications, and so forth. We did not get a chance to follow through with DBRE.

LESSONS LEARNED FROM THE CASE STUDIES

DBRE can contribute to M&A in two ways. DBRE can yield insights up front when you are evaluating the feasibility and economics of a merger. In addition DBRE can aid execution when you are following through on the details of effecting a merger. The case studies suggest several lessons.

- When merging businesses, you can avoid some surprises by using DBRE to understand the high-level structure and content of databases to be rationalized.
- DBRE can find gross errors in applications and data that will complicate system consolidation. About 50% of the time we find major database errors.
- It's important to have a vision or a target to drive towards integrated systems.
- Sometimes there can be a large, costly effort to integrate systems quickly. Other times systems integration must be incremental so as to minimize disruption to other activities.
- You may have to live with some information system chaos. DBRE can give you insights into how costly that will be.
- A third party can do the DBRE if you need to keep your distance from the software to avoid legal entanglements.

IN CONCLUSION

The skillful practice of database reverse engineering can deliver profound business benefits. The cost of database reverse engineering is tiny compared to the costs of M&A. Database reverse engineering can give you deep insights into the information systems of other organizations. These insights can give you forewarning about compatibility of systems, architectures, cultures, and processes. DBRE efforts should be coordinated with architecture efforts. Ultimately, you can increase your odds of business success.

REFERENCES

[Hill-2013] smallbusiness.chron.com/characteristics-corporate-winners-losers-mergers-67244.html

[Mayes-2012] www.computerweekly.com/opinion/How-to-get-IT-right-in-mergers-and-acquistions

[Santander-2012] www.ibtimes.co.uk/articles/393873/20121013/santander-pulls-out-rbs-deal-libor-direct.htm

[WSJ-2014] www.wsj.com/articles/united-continental-struggles-to-stabilize-1402263534)

[Worthen-2002] www.cio.com/article/2440630/mergers-acquisitions/success-factors-for-integrating-it-systems-after-a-merger.html

Heat-mapped Value Streams as the Translation from Strategy to Action

J. Bryan Lail, Stephanie Ramsay, Ralph Shaw
Raytheon, U.S.

INTRODUCTION

When a company makes a significant shift in a business model or product strategy, it should also assess the impact on how business is done internally, or gaps in business capabilities. In the language of business modeling, the company has chosen to pursue a new customer segment, is opening up new channels to those customers and related revenue streams, or is offering a new value proposition to those customers. The business architect works with business leaders to map those market-driven changes into a new plan for internal business operations. Capability mapping provides a toolset to analyze the market strategy, providing critical focus for the roles and processes that must change, how costs must be restructured, and how the right team is formed.

For a large market shift, the capability map provides a key means to describe all the aspects the business must perform, independent of current organization charts or specific processes as practiced currently. With an understanding of the heat map, or subjective evaluation on capability gaps by the team of experts in the business shift, a focus emerges for a future value stream that spans across the changes in roles, skills, processes, teaming, cost structures and other elements to provide the new revenue channels. A broad and strongly backed value stream cutting across organizations in the business provides a powerful means to address the key capability gaps. At Raytheon, we've used these tools to drive from mission strategies down to specific actions for cross-functional teams.

BUSINESS MODELING AND THE ARCHITECT

A key distinction between business models and business architecture relates to their scope and key stakeholders. The focus of a business model is on the creation, delivery and capture of value between the organization, its customers and its key partners (reference GUILD). That focus is, in turn, a subset of the business motivation, business environment, and infrastructure concerns required to formulate, deploy and sustain the business model. The role of the architect in using a business model framework might be as simple as helping business leaders build a common framework and language that aligns the team behind a clear strategy, providing structure and traceability that might otherwise be lacking. At the other extreme, the architect can use a business model framework to literally define and shape the future direction of the business. This doesn't mean that the architect owns strategy or makes leadership decisions, but rather provides the underlying methodology and framework to logically proceed all the way from market understanding, through business transformation, to the delivery of business results.

In its most basic form, the architect uses business models to create a clear depiction of a firm's business logic. If the enterprise is well-established (rather than a green-field start-up case), then the business leaders already have an inherent understanding of the elements that lie within the business model. They aren't necessarily aligned in their thinking of how each element affects other parts of the business, however, nor would they have a complete picture of the entire business model at readily at hand help them make decisions.

The methods and tools discussed in this paper can be used effectively at many levels of the organization. We will touch on three levels in use at Raytheon; defining the organization's focus for strategic execution, assessing critical capabilities for a specific market opportunity, and characterizing an internal value stream across business functions. In the latter case, we will provide specific examples on a current effort.

Our success at Raytheon in bringing together the strategy-level discussions around business models and the project-level (more conventional) use of business architecture is due to direct traceability to business value. As an example in Figure 1 at the strategy level, we use capability heat mapping to prioritize which value streams are most critical to executing the strategy. In this context, the gaps identified (red or dark grey for significant shift in capabilities, yellow or medium grey for some change) must have clear connection to business value and need, rather than just current pain points. The more strategic impact one needs for the new value stream, the more critical it is that the heat in the capability map is driven directly by strategic business goals. This connectivity has led to direct use of business capability mapping in the strategy development for parts of the Raytheon Company.

Figure 1. Relating heat maps to business value

CAPABILITY MAPS AND PRIORITIZATION

The business model captured in a proven framework can be equally useful to the creation of a new business enterprise and to adapting an existing business to new opportunities or challenges. Once a reasonable draft of the model has been developed and well understood, it is useful to assess the understanding of the current state against the prospective changes being contemplated.

In Raytheon, we are using business architecture methods including business capability maps tied to the global Aerospace & Defense industry. We are studying the impact on the business due to the changing nature of products and expanding geographic markets, factoring in changing dynamics between suppliers, intellectual property management, export restrictions and licensing, country-specific privacy laws, and other considerations.

Aspects of business architecture are being deployed in several units and at different levels of the organization within our company. We described earlier the use of heat maps, tied to business outcome, to understand strategic shifts in the business model. In this section, we will analyze a more specific competitive pursuit that requires a structured method of performing assessment of current business capabilities vs. future state, across organizational boundaries. Later in the paper, we will address an example that is more operational in nature, with a study on the end-to-end value stream for onboarding employees.

Business Capabilities are a high level way of conveying the component abilities of a system in a way that spans across organizations and allows the end-to-end workflow to be accomplished. Some capabilities may be unique to an industry, such as Banking or Aerospace & Defense, but some may be common to most businesses and organizational entities.

The approach we are taking is to start with a proven set of high level business capabilities, based on an abstraction of the Process Classification Framework created by the American Productivity & Quality Council (reference APQC). One important aspect of the capability map is that it is independent of the sub-group that implements that capability, or elements thereof. This allows the business-as-a-system view to be maintained, and sub-optimizations within a smaller group do not distract from the optimal business value being achieved.

Another benefit of business capabilities is the ability to perform assessments without an exhaustive list, such that it can be used to stimulate thought and dialog without becoming too time consuming to business participants. The intent is to keep the discussion at a high enough level to focus on the strategic elements, and avoid tactical issues that can be more effectively addressed elsewhere.

Structuring the business capabilities in a set order, then using that structure in a consistent manner to perform the assessments across organizations, produces a broadly useful capability map. These assessments can take many forms, and can involve a variety of participants. One example of such an assessment follows:

1. A diverse set of subject matter experts are gathered to level-set their understanding of the situation or business model that is being considered. This could be viewed as developing a concept of operations.
2. A business model framework is used to quickly convey the various aspects of the situation, including the revenue and expense side, key resources, and distribution channels as appropriate.
3. For each business capability in the list, the business architect guides the subject matter experts to assess the following:

   • Think through what their contribution would be in this new operating arena
   • Assess the ways they would accomplish that business value in their role, or across roles (stakeholders)
   • Be mindful of anticipated difficulty, thinking forward to capability gaps or areas for improvement

- Quickly capture the team assessment (good, needs improvement, bad) and relevant details that can be analyzed later
- Note what is known or unknown (scoping), with notes on lack of data around specific business parameters at the present time
- It is important to keep the discussions at a high enough level that the discussion does not dive into details, since breadth across the full spectrum of capabilities is more important at this stage

4. The architect and a small team should review the findings to aggregate themes around business capability gaps, creating a visual indicator (stoplight chart, heat map, etc. as shown in Figure 1)

5. This reduced list can be used to later prioritize the findings, and validate with the larger team to develop a plan of action

It may be necessary to iterate through this process a few times as the understanding of the situation increases, and as other foundational elements are worked out in the business model. Eventually, though, a set of recommendations should be developed to address those most challenging gaps in the business capabilities. This, along with the relevant business case for achieving improved business capability, would then be reviewed with the upper level management of the organization for further sponsorship and actions.

HEAT MAPS AND VALUE STREAMS

Heat Maps provide a view across business capability gaps and can often uncover cross-functional problems with value streams. Many times a business capability gap is found and indicated on the heat map in one functional area. As more analysis is done, it can lead to additional areas of concern across a value stream. The reason an initial finding is often found in one area is due to work being performed in silos. The silos occur when each functional area completes their tasks within the process independent of the entire chain of events. Functional silos serve a purpose in the organization because they tend to develop deep knowledge in their area of expertise. The trick is being able to execute critical value streams horizontally across the functions when most companies are organized vertically (reference SLONE). The heat map helps identify capability gaps agnostic to the current functions in the organization.

Value Stream mapping, derived from the Business Architecture Guild definition (reference BIZBOK), is an analysis linking together an end-to-end collection of activities that create a result for a customer. It is important to understand the current state when developing a future state value stream. Sources of waste in the current state like bottlenecks and delays in starting tasks are identified and eliminated in the future state. To maintain the gain, metrics should be deployed to measure cycle time improvements.

Employee onboarding is an example of a cross-functional value stream that was identified with business capability gaps at Raytheon. The purpose of the employee onboarding process is to provide new employees coming into the organization with the necessary tools and access to perform their job on the day they arrive. Problems with employees gaining the required system access on the first day of employment was initially identified as a capability gap; however, many of the steps are dependent on manual activities that require attention from other functional areas that have nothing to do with granting system access. The general value stream that requires improvement, focused on the employee onboarding case, might look something like Figure 2.

Figure 2. Top-level view of a value stream

For example, citizenship verification is performed by the Security Function. Once the verification is complete, the security personnel must note it in the system which has a nightly feed to the people file where the citizenship flag is set. If anything is held up or missed in this part of the process, it can delay system access. The delays are often perceived as an IT problem, because the ultimate goal is to gain system access and IT is responsible for granting system access. System access cannot be granted, however, until all of the steps are completed by other areas making this a value stream problem across all of the involved functions.

Figure 3 below shows the tasks each functional area performs to onboard an employee. Analysis of the process found that handoffs between the areas were disjointed with no clear owner of the entire process, end to end. Each time a task crosses over into another functional area, there was potential for a work stoppage along the way. However, the areas with the final deliverables, like system access, are where the capability gaps were originally identified.

The columns in figure 3 represent the functional groups owning the tasks performed when onboarding an employee. This figure further displays how a cross-functional value stream can move through several organizations and business systems instead of one platform that tracks the end to end process. For example, the tasks in the first column represents the input of data that flows into a Human

Resource system. Tasks in the second column represents data input that is recorded in a Facilities space management system. Security has some tasks that are performed to input data in the Human Resources system and others that are performed in their own system. IT has their own systems for identify management and service requests and Finance has their own system for timekeeping.

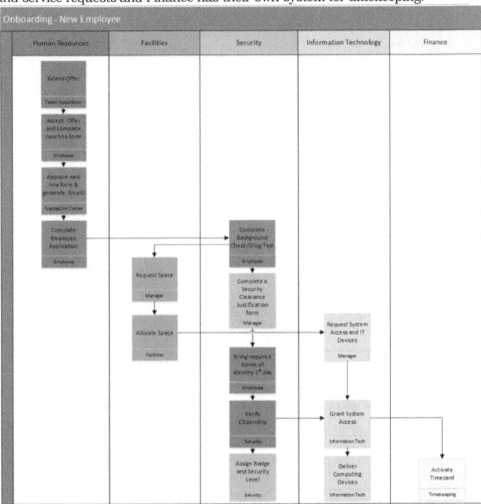

Figure 3. Decomposition of a value stream

Figure 4 shows the business capability gaps identified for the employee onboarding cross-functional process. As gaps are identified they are marked as red (significant gap/immediate risk) or yellow (change needed). Using the example of the system access delay being perceived as an IT problem, the initial heat map was scored red in the area of "service and solution support". This was based on delays in granting system access for new employees. Upon further analysis it was determined that there were several dependencies for granting system access in other functional areas. Many of the delays occurred during recruiting and citizenship verification. Because of these dependencies, "recruit and hire" and "compliance and regulation" were subsequently identified as significant gaps on the heat map. As the overall onboarding process was evaluated, some of the functional areas involved were deemed green in their own silo, but since there needed to be a change and more integration of the process, end-to-end they were marked yellow on the heat map.

Business Capability	Rationale for Change
Human Capital: Recruit and Hire (Red)	Recruiting Delays
Business Technology: Service & Solution Support (Red)	System Access Delays
Governance & Safety: Compliance & Regulation (Red)	Citizen Verification Delays
Property Management: Workplace Facility Mgmt. (Y)	Impacted by Change
Financial Management: Payroll Management (Y)	Impacted by Change

Figure 4. Gaps addressed by the future value stream

Gaps in business capabilities are derived by taking the company's strategic goals and identifying the missing pieces. One of Raytheon's key objectives is to expand their global footprint. The cross-functional business gaps found in the employee onboarding process, eventually led to an improvement project for onboarding international employees. The project vision was to accelerate global business through fast, agile and secure onboarding of new international employees. The "Key Value Stream and Execution" section describes how the International Employee Onboarding project gap analysis of the current and future desired state translated into roles, skills, processes, information and costs.

KEY VALUE STREAM AND EXECUTION

The International Onboarding End to End project was initiated for a couple of reasons. First, business capability gaps were identified in the employee onboarding process. Secondly, the international scenario of onboarding became the focus because of the strategic initiative to expand business globally. The timely onboarding of new international employees is a key activity for this initiative. Also, the international onboarding process is similar to domestic onboarding with only a few additional steps. So if international onboarding became the primary focus to start, then the new process could simply be applied to domestic onboarding.

An important rule of thumb, when evaluating value streams that go across functional groups, is to avoid jumping to technical solutions. This is the time to implement best practices before applying technologies. There are typically many areas for improving cycle times, where tasks get held up in a functional silo. Simply reorganizing tasks and roles across the cross-functional team can be an effective way to improve cycle times and eliminate bottlenecks. The focus of the international employee onboarding project was to evaluate the process prior to looking at technical solutions. The objective was to come up with a standard international employee onboarding process. The process needed to provide a common framework and language across the enterprise for providing new employees with the tools and access required to be functional and begin work on their first day.

To kick off the effort, representatives from each business unit and every functional area came together at an offsite to lay out the international employee onboarding process. Pre-work for the functional areas included identification of key tasks and the accountability for completing each task. All of the tasks identified were printed on post-it notes ahead of time, and then each functional area was asked to place only policy-driven tasks up on the wall. We intentionally studied the tasks in reverse order, starting from the end of the process (when the employee arrives) and working back to the beginning (when an offer is made). Starting from the end allowed the team to look for opportunities to move tasks up earlier in the process. By only putting up policy-driven tasks, the team was able to see the important areas that may need more attention and also the tasks that could not be eliminated from the process.

Eventually other tasks were added into the process, but they were evaluated case by case to see if they were really needed. During the exercise, there were many rich discussions between the functional areas about what was really needed in the process, when each task should occur and who should be accountable. Many tasks were eliminated or moved up in the process due to collaboration between all of the functional groups. The silos were starting to break down.

At the end of the two day workshop, the team was split up into four groups. Each group was asked to talk about the best way to organize to execute the international employee onboarding tasks to meet the goal of getting the basic tools in place for employees to be productive on day one of employment. All four of the teams had variations of the same type of organization. Their future organization would have liaisons that help managers and new employees through the process of onboarding from beginning to end. If there was a problem, they would be able to reach contacts within a functional area with deep process knowledge, for help in breaking down barriers. These liaisons would become familiar with the onboarding process and limitations and as a group perform ongoing continuous improvement. They could also track metrics that would help leadership understand where the ongoing improvements need to occur.

A couple of the teams also identified the need for a change control board where changes to the process are reviewed and approved by representatives in all of the functional areas. The change control board would also be responsible for communicating the changes to the process stakeholders. One of the teams identified another role that had been successful at one of the businesses. This role would be someone in the new employees department who would be their buddy. This buddy would be responsible for helping the new employee through their initial training and questions for the first thirty days.

Two new roles and a governance entity were identified to improve the value stream for international employee onboarding. First, the liaison role ensures the process moves from one functional area to the next, starting from the job offer acceptance to 90 days post start date (first day), with responsibility for continuous improvement. Second, the buddy role helps the new employee navigate training requirements and departmental procedures over the first 30 days. Finally, the change control board to provide governance and ensure concurrence across the functional areas of changes to the process and communication notifying the liaisons and key stakeholders.

Subsequently, a pilot was conducted with the new roles and governance. The intended value was improved cycle time for onboarding international employees. A key observation during the pilot was that there are many computer systems involved in the process, with many data feeds running from one system to another. The number of systems seems to be directly related to the number of functional areas involved. Another observation was that onboarding scenarios for contractors and business partners have similar tasks to new hires, but all use different methods and systems for tracking.

Figure 5 shows the tasks that are different and the tasks in common for employees, contractors and business partners. The next effort, continuing on the international employee onboarding improvement project, will be to complete a current state assessment of all onboarding scenarios for employees, contractors and business partners including the computer systems and information flows used by each. This assessment will help establish future improvement projects, using the international employee onboarding process as the template.

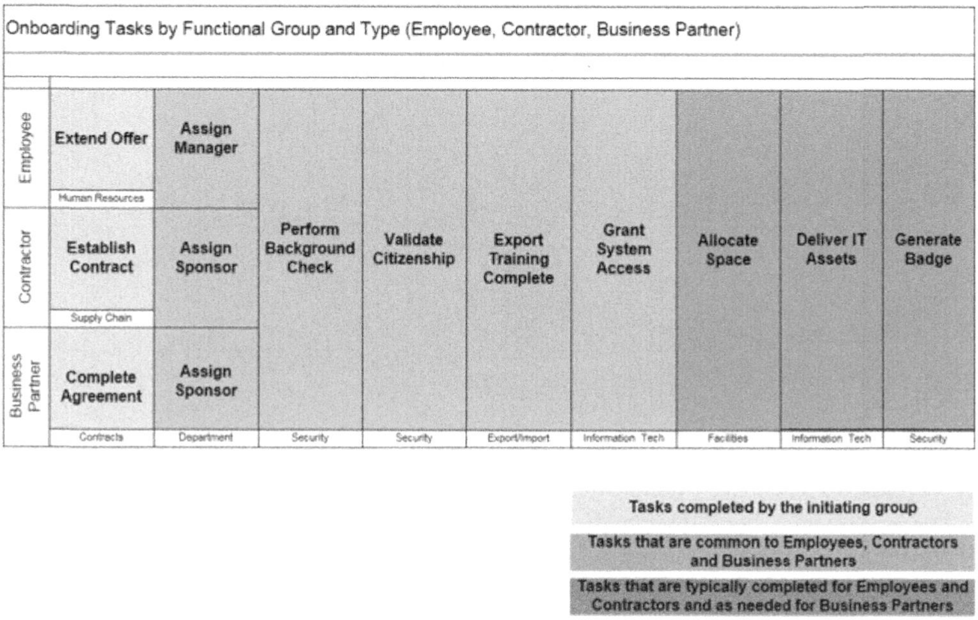

Onboarding Tasks by Functional Group and Type (Employee, Contractor, Business Partner)

Employee Extend Offer	Assign Manager								
Human Resources									
Contractor Establish Contract	Assign Sponsor	Perform Background Check	Validate Citizenship	Export Training Complete	Grant System Access	Allocate Space	Deliver IT Assets	Generate Badge
Supply Chain									
Business Partner Complete Agreement	Assign Sponsor								
Contracts	*Department*	*Security*	*Security*	*Export/Import*	*Information Tech*	*Facilities*	*Information Tech*	*Security*

Tasks completed by the initiating group

Tasks that are common to Employees, Contractors and Business Partners

Tasks that are typically completed for Employees and Contractors and as needed for Business Partners

Figure 5. Overview of the value stream

CONCLUSION

We see many benefits for translating strategic business needs into cross-business execution using methods from business modeling, capability mapping and value stream analysis. The journey can be long, through engagements with leaders at the strategy level, to analysis for specific market pursuits, to internal implementation of a better value stream across many business functions, but business architecture methods are a powerful force for business dynamic change.

REFERENCES

(GUILD) Business Architecture Guild whitepaper. Business Modeling and Architecture – A Powerful Combination, May 2015

(APQC) Process Classification Framework for Aerospace & Defense, http://www.apqc.org/knowledge-base/documents/apqc-process-classification-framework-pcf-aerospace-and-defense-pdf-version, 2010

(SLONE) Reuben E. Slone, J. P. The New Supply Chain Agenda. Boston : Harvard Business Press, 2010

(BIZBOK) Business Architecture Body of Knowledge v4.1, Business

Architecture Guild, http://www.businessarchitectureguild.org Nov 2014

Applying Architecture to Business Transformation and Decision-Making: Case Study

Patrik Maltusch, Aalto University, Finland
Virpi Nieminen, QPR Software, Finland

INTRODUCTION

The starting point for this case was the decision to merge three independent universities in Finland with the vision of forming one institution of higher education recognized internationally for its contribution to the academic communities of science, art, and learning (Mission, Vision and Values, 2015). When the Helsinki School of Economics, Helsinki University of Technology, and the University of Art and Design Helsinki became Aalto University, enterprise architecture (EA) was recognized as the best suited tool for simplifying the inherited complexity caused by the post-merger integration. The objective was to harmonize operational activities of the previously autonomous organizations and to align and optimize the university's use of IT assets in daily operations. The solution that followed resulted in an architecture-driven investment and project portfolio management system that ensures business-IT alignment of all development initiatives.

This case study is written from the perspective of Aalto IT management, focusing on the challenges it faced when strategic leaders decided to drastically change the course of business. This acid test on IT management paved the way for new ways of thinking, which required both agility and extensive involvement from a wide range of stakeholder groups to create an innovative solution in order to realign IT support with business needs. Based on IT's success in supporting business time after time using EA methods, EA was accepted as an official methodology for Aalto's organizational and operational development.

The case is structured as follows – first, it describes the relevant government initiatives and legislation impacting institutions of higher education in order to provide a sufficient understanding of the environment, in which the case takes place. The second section focuses on the target setting process that IT performed in order to realign its goals with the new University's strategy; followed by a section describing the organizational structure set in place to support IT in providing the best support for business. The fourth section describes the architecture-driven investment and project portfolio management system in detail with an emphasis on business value. Finally, the case is closed with an elaboration on further future developments under execution and the conclusion.

BACKGROUND

In the field of higher education in Finland, the concept of enterprise architecture was first introduced by the Ministry of Education and Culture in 2008 with the launch of the RAKETTI project. The goal of RAKETTI was to harness ICT to support the structural changes needed to create a common architecture for institutions of higher education. To address the lack of process automation and information system support, the focus of RAKETTI was set on developing semantic interoperability between information systems and creating a national data warehouse (IT Center for Science Ltd, 2014).

The RAKETTI project served as the first pilot case in Finland to test the use of EA in improving interoperability across organizational borders over a time span of six years. The project featured 200 specialists in 25 teams; and more than 150 subject area experts were consulted from different stakeholder groups in approximately 90 seminars, training sessions or workshops. When the project finished in 2014, some of the key deliverables included:

- common data models and definitions (http://tietomalli.csc.fi),
- new application services based on the above mentioned data models,
  - JUULI – Finnish research publications portal (www.juuli.fi)
  - Vipunen – Statistical service (www.vipunen.fi)
  - VIRTA – national data warehouse for student information and transcripts
- a cooperation framework for future collaboration initiatives, and
- Kartturi – national EA reference model recommendation for educational institutions.

Overall, the outputs produced by RAKETTI have facilitated daily operations and increased the interaction and cooperation between universities and other institutions of higher education (IT Center for Science Ltd, 2014).

Motivated by the positive results showcased already in the early phases of RAKETTI and the Finnish Government's goals for interoperability and cost-effectiveness, the Ministry of Finance drafted an Act promoting the use of EA. This Act, called the *Act on Information Management Governance in Public Administrations* (634/2011) was set into force in 2011 with the goal of improving interoperability across all public sector organizations by creating common EA definitions, such as glossaries, code sets, and data structure descriptions (Ministry of Justice Finland, 2011).

While this Act does not constitute a direct obligation on educational institutions, the Ministry of Education and Culture steering educational institutions does fall under the Act. EA as a change management tool brings transparency and predictability to long-term goals for all organizations operating under the Ministry's mandate.

In 2010, when the Aalto University was created to become one of the world's top institutions of higher education by fostering innovation and multi-disciplinary learning, Aalto was not and still is not obliged to use EA methods (History, 2015). However, it was clear that with the size of the University being close to 20,000 students and 5,000 staff members, the only way to achieve operational excellence, while reducing complexity in a systematic way, is through EA.

The Aalto University has been one of the forerunners of EA in Finland, which is reflected in the fact that Aalto is the founding member of the national Higher Education Enterprise Architecture Special Interest Group (KA SIG). Aalto was also the first university to implement and transfer data from its local data warehouse to the national data warehouse according to the Finnish national data model specifications (IT Center for Science Ltd, 2014).

TARGET SETTING

The objectives of Aalto's business leaders were clear and the need for EA was clear, but there was a dire need for IT management to understand what the overall Aalto University strategy meant for the long-term operational requirements of the University's post-merger IT services. To understand what was expected of IT, an extensive stakeholder requirements gathering process was started in early October 2012 with the commission that all relevant stakeholders are to be consulted in the creation of Aalto IT's future vision.

Tapping into stakeholder needs

The architecture team setup a plan for execution that included work shopping with all relevant customers, students, researchers, and other academic personnel. They scheduled interviews with University management, facilitated several IT personnel development days, and made sure that progress was communicated in line with internal communication guidelines.

The participation of stakeholders in the strategy planning process exceeded all expectations. The tremendous input received is summarized in the table below.

Activities	Quantity	Target	Stakeholders reached
Message and articles published internally	12	Aalto – Students and personnel	~15.000
Progress meetings held	8	Stakeholders	~150
Workshops (2 - 3 hours)	7	Customers, Researchers, Teachers, Students	~60
IT internal development days	3	Aalto IT & IT Board, IT personnel	~150
Internal interviews	10	Aalto Management & key persons	10
External interviews	5	External key persons	5
Ideas & proposals –inputs from workshops, interviews, development days	2200	Strategy	400

Formulation of strategic IT goals to meet business needs

Thanks to the valuable input received from stakeholders, IT management was able to formulate the strategic IT goals, summarized in the overview below.

In the short-term (2013-2014) – to ensure smooth IT operations and prepare to address mid-term objectives:

1. Ensuring stability and quality of basic services.
2. Gaining visibility and transparency to IT costs and IT operations at Aalto University.
3. Designing a common operating model, with a combination of distributed and centralized elements.
4. Defining integrated enterprise architecture as a basis for application transformation.
5. Strengthening key IT capabilities and competencies.

In the mid-term (2015-2016) – to increase cooperation between IT and other units in Aalto University and to optimize the operating model:

1. Optimizing the cost and quality of IT services to an agreed level and reaching the target level for overall IT costs.
2. Restructuring the IT service and project portfolio to meet the needs of the future.
3. Transforming the legacy application landscape into a modern customer centric application portfolio.
4. Reach highest level of EA competence maturity (maturity model introduced in next section "Preparing the Organization").

In the long-term (2016-2020) – to provide IT services efficiently and flexibly in order to address strategic IT needs in an agile and effective way. Aalto IT is a strategic partner for other service units in Aalto by becoming a renowned developer and provider of IT related services.

In a nutshell, the strategic direction of IT can be summarized as highlighting the importance of common practices, cost-effectiveness, and customer centricity in IT services and underlying structures. In order to execute strategy, the strategic goals needed to be broken down into development projects. IT management realized that in order to achieve the highest level of cost-effectiveness, management had to attain better visibility into the different development projects; and that these projects must be coordinated centrally to avoid duplication of effort. To address these key challenges, IT management set its first development initiative to building a common IT investment life-cycle management system with a supporting organizational structure and governance. The coherence of Aalto's future architecture could therefore be safeguarded by giving EA an important role in the investment decision making process.

PREPARING THE ORGANIZATION

Once the strategic direction of IT with clear goals was defined, the next step was to restructure the organization to embrace EA.

Positioning EA in the organization

To support strategy execution, EA's positioning at Aalto IT was described as follows "the mission of EA work is to reduce the complexity of business processes and IT, thereby increase the ability of our organization to improve our operational efficiency and to align the organizational structures with our strategy". The main drivers for EA work were identified as:

- Facilitating the transformation,
- Visualizing the essential,
- Providing a logical structure, and
- Aligning development initiatives.

EA was positioned not as a leadership process in itself; but as supporting the planning processes of leaders. In essence, principles of EA help determine to which extent organizational units should be allowed freedom to design their own processes, information structures, and infrastructure; and where collaboration is more beneficial for the common good.

Roles and responsibilities

To fix EA in the organization chart, an EA core team of three people was set up with the following work statements:

- We document and facilitate a professional dialogue between Aalto University and relevant external stakeholders to ensure interoperability between information, systems, and technology.
- This ensures cost efficiency and frees considerable staff time for departments to focus on their core functions and tasks.
- We manage the complexity inherited from legacy and simplify structures to enable interoperability.

The EA function is designed to provide two types of services for the rest of the Aalto organization: back-office related services and front-office related services. Back-office services relate to the development and maintenance of architecture (models, principles etc.) and the meta-model. Front-office services concern ensuring the success of ongoing projects while maintaining the overall alignment of the enterprise and providing status updates on the current and target states for development planning. In practice, enterprise architects at Aalto help development projects reach the common goal based on the agreed principles and targets. They cut costs by applying best practices and promoting the reuse of solution building blocks whenever possible.

The roles and responsibilities of the EA function are described in the table below.

Party / Unit	Roles and responsibilities in EA function
Provost's management team	The main sponsor of EA work and an important user of EA services. Promotes architecture-driven development and ensures adherence with the governance model.
Digital Transformation Steering Group (DTSG)	Governance body responsible for approving architectural principles and artifacts. Carries out architecture review board functions.
EA core team	Primus motor of architectural work. Responsible for day-to-day tasks and services related to both the development and utilization of EA.
Virtual EA working team and interest groups (e.g. master data interest group)	Important partner of the EA core team. Participates in architectural design and promotes compliance with EA in projects and operations.
Project teams	Important user of EA services. Responsible for ensuring compliance with EA.

EA development path

To guide Aalto in the EA adaption process, IT management decided to take inspiration from the EA competence maturity model as defined by Kartturi. As explained above in the Background section, the Kartturi maturity model was developed as part of the RAKETTI initiative to provide a framework for assessing architectural competence levels and to support in identifying EA development areas. The maturity model features five levels, each with a description of what the competence level entails. From the perspective of enterprise architecture, a competent organisation is well positioned to produce long-term, controlled solutions that support operations in a cost-effective manner. For an illustration of this model, refer to the figure below (IT Center for Science Ltd, 2013).

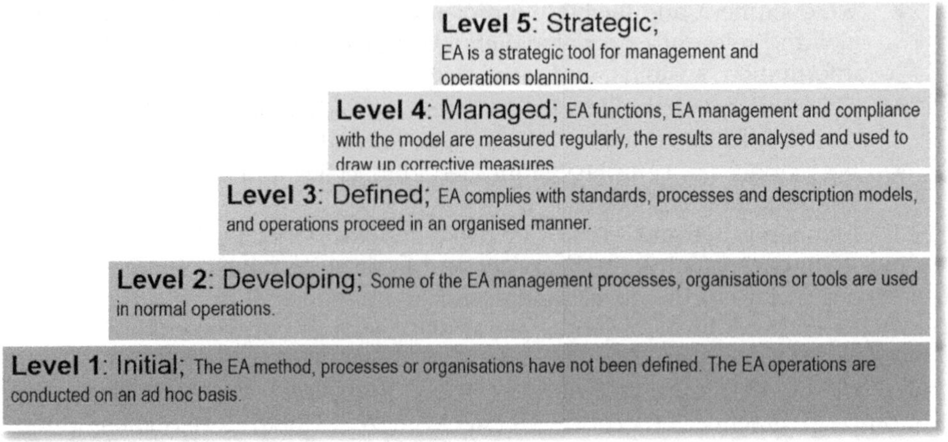

Level 5: Strategic;
EA is a strategic tool for management and
operations planning.

Level 4: Managed; EA functions, EA management and compliance
with the model are measured regularly, the results are analysed and used to
draw up corrective measures.

Level 3: Defined; EA complies with standards, processes and description models,
and operations proceed in an organised manner.

Level 2: Developing; Some of the EA management processes, organisations or tools are used
in normal operations.

Level 1: Initial; The EA method, processes or organisations have not been defined. The EA operations are
conducted on an ad hoc basis.

Figure 1: EA competence maturity model as defined by Kartturi

Aalto's objective with regards to EA maturity is to rise one competence level each year. The afore mentioned organizational restructuring to support EA and the IT investment life-cycle management system, explained in the next section, were initiatives to reach level two of the maturity model.

Today, Aalto is at competence level four, implementing an EA measurement framework.

SOLUTION DELIVERY

The design of the IT investment life-cycle management system started with an analysis of the requirements needed to be fulfilled before Aalto could see any significant improvements in its operations.

Requirements gathering

The goal of the IT investment life-cycle solution was to improve Aalto's cost-effectiveness by managing IT investment decisions centrally and by improving visibility into the different development projects. The requirements of the solution were as follows:

- New development cases are to be visually modeled, making it easy to identify potential project scope overlapping with other new, proposed or ongoing projects.
- To reach the target architecture, each development project must be aligned with the higher level strategic target. In other words, the contribution and value added to new projects or investments must be assessed in the light of desired business outcomes.
- EA is to be used in assessing a proposed investment's fit in the overall organization and interoperability with existing technology.
- Investment decisions must be facilitated with transparency into which stakeholder groups use such applications; and which applications are business critical for innovation.
- The interrelationship between projects and daily operations must be easily identifiable by their visualization to help project management officers execute projects in a way that do not interfere with the level of services provided to customers.

Fitting the solution in the current architecture

The new solution not only had to be designed, but it had to be fitted into existing architecture. Before starting the development of the IT investment life-cycle management system, Aalto had already started modeling and analyzing the current state of the university's architecture.

The QPR EnterpriseArchitect (QPR EA) tool and QPR's EA based Operational Development Methodology (ODM) template were used to systematically document and analyze dependencies and interrelationships between strategic objectives, processes, their information interfaces, application components and the supporting infrastructure. Once the architectural components were entered into the tool's centralized repository, the data was used to build four viewpoints to fulfil the needs of different stakeholders: architecture view, service view, business view, and the development process view. The figure below shows the QPR web portal cover page, through which different stakeholders can navigate to the architectural views applicable to their line of work.

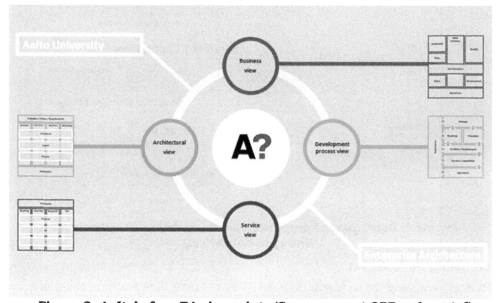

Figure 2: Aalto's four EA viewpoints (Cover page at QPR web portal)

Under the development process view, Aalto modeled the development process cycle. As can be seen in the figure below, each box represents a high level of business process, with the process interfaces - inputs and outputs - shown as arrows between the processes. Within each process are links to the outputs produced or to be maintained as part of the process. This type of a helicopter view of the whole Aalto University development process is important when designing new solutions, such as the IT investment life-cycle management system, in order to understand the impact and interdependencies of new solutions on the existing operations. The IT investment life-cycle process was positioned within the governance process with input (program portfolio) and output (project prioritization) interfaces with process "Development activities".

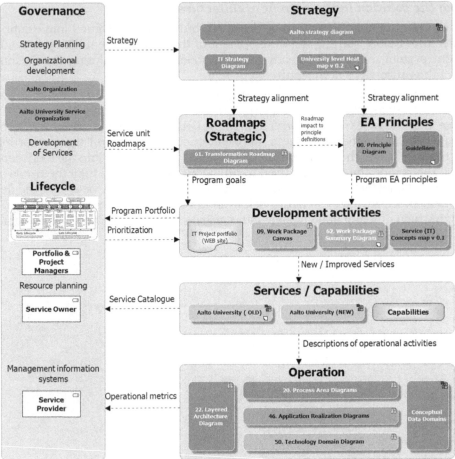

Figure 3: Development process view integrated with outputs (QPR EnterpriseArchitect)

Designing the solution

To start designing the new solution, the IT investment life-cycle process was modelled first with indication of the necessary roles and responsibilities. To assure compliance with the requirement of using EA in assessing a proposed investment's fit in the overall existing architecture, a feasibility check was embedded in the process at Gate 3 – refer to the figure below. In this step, the architectural fit and technical suitability must be assessed before senior management can make an investment decision.

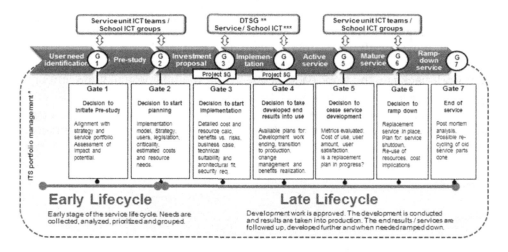

Figure 4: IT investment life-cycle model

Aalto's architectural development is solution-driven, which means that all common elements present within one or across multiple solutions must be identified and avoided. By collecting and structuring information about proposed development cases into a template of seven classification areas, it is possible to visually identify potential solution overlapping and to get an understanding of the interrelations between solutions. As can be seen in the figure below, the case classification areas are business actor, business service, process area, capabilities, requirements, application components and application realization.

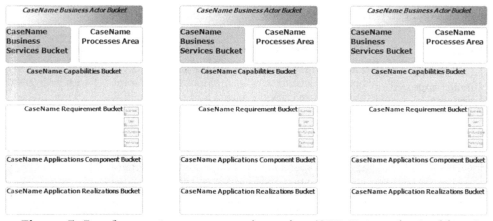

Figure 5: Development case comparison view (QPR EnterpriseArchitect)

Using a relation based architectural design tool, such as QPR EA, makes the generation of these case comparison views very fast and easy to produce; but it is not a must. The benefit of using such a tool is the ability to reuse elements and associations stored in the tool's repository. Each iteration builds on the previous understanding and shortens the learning curve considerably. The visualization of dependencies, redundancies, and interrelations greatly improve the decision making process by providing a common viewpoint that both business and IT can relate to.

As a final step in the IT investment life-cycle solution, the QPR EA tool was used to produce a solution transformation roadmap view. Moving from left to right, the figure below indicates the operating model being impacted by a new development work package, the application services and components impacted by new development work package, the work package itself, and the business requirement or target being addressed by the new work package.

This view fulfills the requirements of linking development initiatives with strategic targets, visualizing interrelationship between a development project and daily operations or services, and the need to identify relevant stakeholders through the operating model.

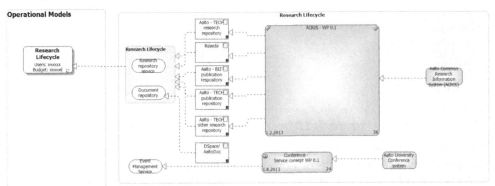

Figure 6: Solution transformation roadmap (QPR EnterpriseArchitect)

Measuring success

To continue on the path of success, Aalto University has identified the following key EA indicators to monitor EA implementation and efficiency gains in operations. If EA is integrated in an organization's operations, success can be measured with normal business performance metrics.

Metrics	Why and what do we want to achieve	Goal by 2017
Governance model approved and implemented	It is important for Aalto to have a governance model in place to be able to pinpoint ownership and prioritize critical projects and activities. It provides an escalation path for projects and guides interpretation of strategic intentions and goals. It is vital for projects of strategic importance to have good sponsorship and visibility at top management. Minor development activities also need to be regularly reviewed.	Model approved with acting bodies and assigned people in charge
EA principles approved and managed	Current IT principles (version 1.2) do not cover EA in detail. They need to be updated and adapted with the Aalto principles to include EA and to align them with strategy and functions' operation models. A revision of principles has to be performed on an annual basis to achieve the correct steering and business outcomes.	Approval of EA principles v2. (Replaces IT principles version 1.2)
EA involvement in development projects	The IT investment life-cycle model requires the Steering Group to analyze architectural fit before approving any investment projects (Gate 3).	80% of all projects to include EA involvement

(percent of projects in project portfolio)	Securing early EA involvement in development projects minimizes overlapping development effort, rationalizes incremental development, and reduces license costs by optimizing features based on realistic business needs.	already at Gate 0
Compliance (percent of projects in project portfolio compliant with prevailing principles and models)	Any exceptions in architectural designs increase complexity and cost of maintenance. Although a certain solution and vendor diversity is expected and required to secure academic independency, all exceptions have an impact and should therefore be carefully evaluated for approval by the Architecture Review Board represented by business owners. Maintaining a high level of architectural compliance minimizes the complexity that will unavoidably take place over time.	100% of all projects to be compliant at Gate 3
AS-IS and TO-BE architectures are up-to-date.	Keeping the EA repository up-to-date is crucial for staying agile and supporting business operations. With multi-vendor and multi-platform environments in a constant state of transformation, documenting changes in a structured and uniform way helps to keep track of change. Giving access to the repository for all staff and stakeholders ensures that information is never outdated, thus the general understanding of the environment increases.	AS-IS architecture is updated at a minimum of twice per year and publicly viewable by all stakeholders at any given time

Risk register and metrics

Aalto uses a standardized risk collection and security framework to ensure that risk levels are always up-to-date. Monitoring all activities is a challenging task, even with dedicated experts assigned to this. At Aalto, it has always been clear that EA needs to be aligned with quality and risk management activities. It has only been a question of time when the level of maturity at Aalto reaches a point where the use of the QPR portal can be extended to collect and report on risks in a more automated fashion. In 2015, Aalto launched the first version of the risk register and dashboard to be used by staff members. This will replace the Excel worksheet exercises of the past. Aalto expects the real-time risk dashboard to minimize administrative work, enable faster reaction times to risk occurrences, and result in new, agile ways of working.

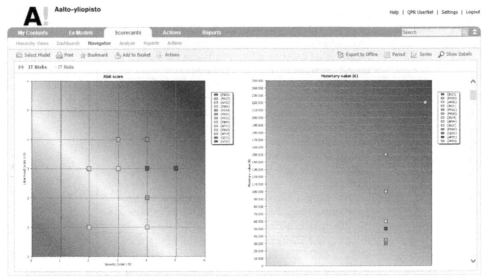

Figure 7: Risk heat map (QPR Metrics)

What influenced the way Aalto perceives EA

A more in-depth understanding of what really happened at Aalto can be achieved by looking at the forces of cultural change impacting service oriented ways of working. The underlying conceptual change provided the opportunity to challenge old ways of working and the legacy constraints resulting from decade old infrastructure based on administrative requirements. Breaking this pattern made room for innovative, business-driven outcomes, which promoted customer oriented solution designs without compromising compliance with legislative requirements.

There are a few factors that can be identified as having significantly influenced where Aalto stands today. None of these factors in isolation would have sufficiently created the momentum needed to shift old mindsets, but the combination of these events together affected the way the opportunity was born. These events, which took place between 2010 and 2014 are not listed in any particular order:

- Legislation to drive; however not to *oblige*, public sector towards EA thinking,
- Business challenge posed by the merge of three universities to create Aalto University,
- The window of opportunity and highly skilled people to drive change,
- Cultural shift to a service oriented way of working,
- Business problem that required to be solved involving major investment decisions,
- Economic distress from having to move from full state funding to partly self-funded operations,
- Business disruption caused by digitalization and technology-enhanced learning, and
- Technology disruption caused by cloud-based computing and mobile applications.

Aalto worked together with QPR's EA experts to design and implement the IT lifecycle management solution in the QPR EnterpriseArchitect tool using QPR's Operational Development Methodology (ODM) and the related, readily configured ODM template. The methodology implemented in the tool and template helped Aalto find pragmatic balance between EA theory and practice for best fit.

FUTURE DEVELOPMENT

As in many other organizations, the use of EA in Aalto University was initially limited to addressing tactical, technology oriented challenges. Aalto IT has been able to extract more value from EA by moving the focus of EA gradually towards the level of business and strategy, as was the case in the architecture-driven investment and project portfolio management system.

In March 2015, Aalto IT reached an important milestone in becoming a strategic partner for other Aalto service units and an important vehicle to achieving Aalto's vision - EA was accepted as an organization wide methodology for leading operations development. This decision was based on IT successfully serving the needs of business time after time through the use of EA. As a consequence, an EA charter was drafted and the development actions and projects defined within it will be monitored by Aalto's executive team responsible for organizational and operational development.

The following figures show the current focus of EA work with intended future focus.

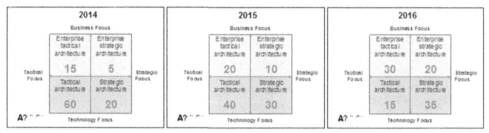

Figure 8: Focus of EA

CONCLUSIONS

Aalto improved operational efficiency and effectiveness by optimizing the university's use of resources and assets. This was achieved by making informed, educated decisions on IT investments, which in turn lead to IT budget cost savings worth €4,5 million within the first year of implementation - this figure represents a 12 percent cost saving from the annual IT budget.

This transformation would not have been possible without the transparency brought by EA, which paved the way to breaking old organizational boundaries. Synergies were created in the form of new shared service centers and common IT assets to best serve the new unified university structure – and above all, to bring Aalto University one step closer to its vision.

REFERENCES

History. (2015, April 20). Retrieved April 20, 2015, from Aalto University: http://www.aalto.fi/en/about/history/

IT Center for Science Ltd. (2013). *KARTTURI - korkeakoulujen kokonaisarkkitehtuurin menetelmäopas* (2 ed.). Helsinki: IT Center for Science Ltd.

IT Center for Science Ltd. (2014). *RAKETTI-hankkeen loppuraportti.* Espoo: Ministry of Education and Culture.

KA SIG. (n.d.). Retrieved April 5, 2015, from SIG: https://tt.eduuni.fi/sites/kity/SitePages/KASIGhome.aspx

Ministry of Justice Finland. (2011). *Laki julkisen hallinnon tietohallinnon ohjauksesta*. Helsinki.

Mission, Vision and Values. (2015, January 26). Retrieved April 9, 2015, from Aalto University: http://www.aalto.fi/en/about/strategy/

QPR EnterpriseArchitect. (n.d.). Retrieved from QPR Software: http://www.qpr.com/content/qpr-enterprisearchitect

QPR Metrics. (n.d.). Retrieved from QPR Software: http://www.qpr.com/content/qpr-metrics

Business Architecture for Process-Oriented Learning in Public Administration

Darius Silingas, No Magic Europe, Lithuania; Barbara Thönssen, FHNW, Switzerland; Alfonso Pierantonio, University of L'Aquila, Italy
Nesat Efendioglu, Robert Woitsch, BOC Asset Management, Austria

INTRODUCTION

In a modern society, public administrations (PAs) are undergoing a transformation of their perceived role from controllers to proactive service providers (Denhardt 2000, Vigoda 2002). They are under pressure to constantly improve their service quality while adapting to a quickly changing context (new laws and regulations, societal globalization, fast technology evolution, etc.) and decreasing budgets. Civil servants are challenged to understand and put in action the latest procedures and rules within tight time constraints. But this is not a *mission impossible* since there are a number of sources for improving public administration organizations so that they could perform faster, better, and cheaper (Boyne 2003, West 2015). Nowadays, public administration organizations face a need to innovate more often and more radically (Hartley 2005). Common approaches to innovating public administration service delivery include business process-orientation (Stremberger 2007, Fritzer 2010, Ahrend 2012) and enterprise architecture alignment (Peristeras 2000). Yet, probably the most important trend is towards transforming public administrations into learning organizations (Brown 2003), that collaboratively create and use their knowledge assets (Wiig 2002, Riege 2006, Boer 2010, Niehaves 2011, Dikota 2014). Business process and enterprise architecture models are seen as key artifacts that enable public administrations to capture, use, and govern their business knowledge (Becker 2006). Despite these clear trends, most public administrations struggle to become learning organizations through use of business process models as knowledge assets, as they lack a methodology and technology platform to enable such transformation. We will present conceptual ideas and a technical approach of a research project Learn PAd, which aims to fill this gap.

LEARN PAD: A PLATFORM FOR PROCESS-ORIENTED LEARNING IN PUBLIC ADMINISTRATIONS

In 2014, European Commission funded a specifically targeted research project Learn PAd – Model-Based Social Learning for Public Administrations (Learn PAd 2014), which aims to build an innovative, holistic e-learning platform that enables process-driven learning and fosters cooperation and knowledge sharing in public administrations (PA). The central Learn PAd idea is to use models for structuring the knowledge that is captured in textual laws, regulations and procedures, share them in an easily accessible format, encourage PA workers to use it as a knowledge base and enable them to contribute to refinements and enhancements of a knowledge base through Wiki technology. Learn PAd approach is visualized in Figure 1.

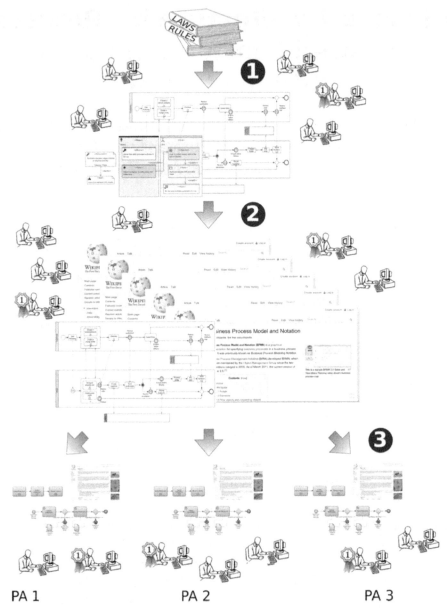

Figure 1. Illustration of Learn PAd approach

Learn PAd technical innovation is based on four pillars:

- A new concept of e-learning based on process-centric business architecture models and collaboratively managed knowledge assets;
- Open and collaborative knowledge content management combining modeling and Wiki technologies;
- Technological support for assessing quality of collaboratively created textual knowledge contents;
- A model-based simulation as a way to learn and assess learners.

Learn PAd considers learning and working strongly intertwined (learning while doing) and aims to provide an approach and technology for enabling public administrations to manage their business architecture as knowledge base, which enables organizational learning and performance improvement. Learn PAd is inspired by cooperative spirit and principles of open-source communities: the community produces the knowledge, and meritocracy is naturally promoted, with leaders emerging because of their skill, expertise, and contribution. There are five, main use cases how Learn PAd can be applied to enable business process oriented learning in public administrations:

- *Individual training* to support novices;
- *Organizational evolution* to support organizational change such as the introduction of a new business process, a redesign of a business process due to a new regulation, and ongoing process adjustments;
- *Support and reflection* to enable clear insights into actual process execution and performance;
- *Continuous process improvement* through process transparency, collaborative organizational learning and reflection;
- *Citizen transparency* to enable consumers of services to learn about their role in the public administration process and decision points.

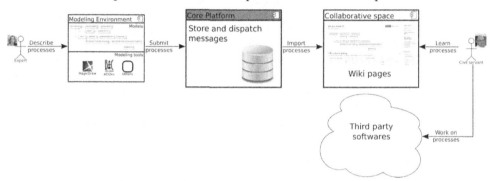

Figure 2. The main components of Learn PAd platform

The conceptual architecture of the Learn PAd platform is depicted in the Figure 2, which shows its main components (*modeling environment, core platform* and *collaborative space*), main actors (*expert* and *civil servant*) and a basic usage scenario. Learn PAd platform will also include additional components for: *model verification* (evaluating model completeness and correctness), *content analysis* (evaluating the quality of textual process descriptions contributed by civil servants via Wiki pages in a collaborative space), *ontology recommendations* (reasoning based on model semantics), *dashboard* (assessing performance of business processes and learning based on key performance indicators), and *simulation environment* (dynamic learning by executing business processes with predefined scenarios). While Learn PAd components and their technical capabilities are not the main focus of this article, it is important to understand that the platform is based on the *blackboard* architecture, where the *core platform* acts as a mediator, which provides unified data structure for use by specific components. This unified data structure is derived from Learn PAd metamodel, which defines elements that are necessary for capturing the business architecture of a public administration organization, including its knowledge and learning aspects. We will take a closer look at Learn PAd metamodel in the next chapter.

LEARN PAD METAMODEL FOR BUSINESS ARCHITECTURE OF PUBLIC ADMINISTRATION

Learn PAd sees business processes as the central knowledge asset, which enables delivering public administration services better, faster, and cheaper. However, business processes are not enough, since the public administrations also need to understand their motivation model, organization structure and roles, information objects/documents, performance measurements, etc. There are a number of modeling standards such as Business Motivation Model (BMM 2014), Business Process Model and Notation (BPMN 2013), Case Management Model and Notation (CMMN 2014), Unified Modeling Language (UML 2013), but they focus on isolated aspects of business architecture and lack an approach for integration with the other aspects. Thus, Lean PAd aims to provide an integrated and practical "just enough" metamodel, which can be used as a starting point for public administration business architecture (BA). Subsets of modeling standards are used in an integrated manner and additional custom meta-models are proposed for the aspects where *de facto* standards are not yet established, e.g. organization structure, measurements, competencies, documents and knowledge objects, etc.

Learn PAd metamodel was designed using OMiLab approach, which promotes an iterative process with workflows *Create, Design, Formalize, Develop* and *Deploy* (Visic 2014). The design process resulted in a metamodel in three abstraction levels as suggested by Model Driven Architecture (MDA 2014):

- *Learn PAd Conceptual Metamodel* (LCMM) identifies broad concerns that are important for PA business architecture;
- *Learn PAd Platform Independent Metamodel* (LPIMM) provides model kinds (sets of modeling elements) for each concept from LCMM and defines weaving model, which implements relationships from LCMM;
- *Learn PAd Platform Specific Metamodel* (LPSMM) defines implementation in a specific tool, e.g. UML profile in Cameo Business Modeler.

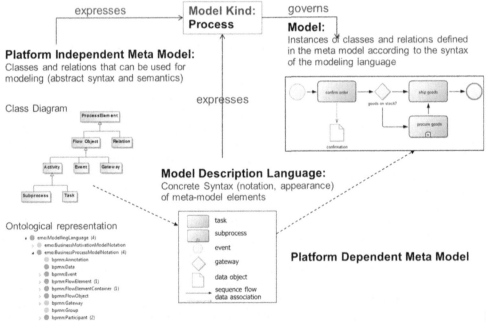

Figure 3. Explanation of models and model kinds

Figure 4 captures the major concerns of public administration business architecture and relationships between them. This is considered as Learn PAd Conceptual

Metamodel (LCMM). Each concept in LCMM represents a specific model kind. Model kinds are described in more detail in Table 1.

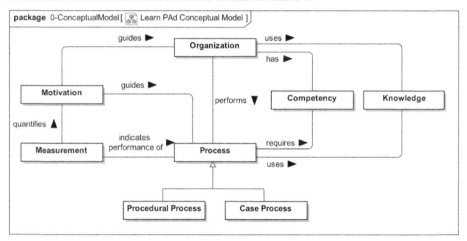

Figure 4. Learn PAd Conceptual Metamodel (LCMM)

Table 1. Description of Learn PAd concepts / model kinds

Model Kind	Description
Process	A general representation of work performed by an organization. Answers to "how" question in the enterprise architecture. However, process concept itself abstracts away from a specific way to perform the work such as procedural approach or case-based. Learn PAd offers a simple custom metamodel for identifying processes, specifying their attributes and value flow, which treats process as a black box and is independent from the way a process is performed.
Procedural Process	A specific representation of work, which is defined by a procedural step-by-step flow of activities. Learn PAd adopts a subset of Business Process Model and Notation (BPMN) for modeling procedural processes. As procedural process models will play a key role for enabling process-oriented learning in pubic administrations, this metamodel is the most complex and expressive compared to other model kinds.
Case Process	A specific representation of work that is performed using discretionary tasks rather than a predefined step-by-step flow of activities. Learn PAd uses a subset of Case Management Model and Notation (CMMN) for specifying case processes.
Organization	An entity, such as an institution or an association, which has a common goal and is linked to an external environment. The organization acts according to its motivation and performs processes to generate value for its stakeholders. Organization is decomposed into organization units, roles, people, and other types of resources. Organization has a number of competencies to perform specific processes and uses accessible knowledge while performing them. Learn PAd offers a custom metamodel for specifying organization elements.

Motivation	A representation of reasoning behind the business model of a specific organization. It guides organization in its business actions including business processes. Motivation model provides the answer to the question "why" in enterprise architecture framework. Learn PAd adopts a subset of Business Motivation Model (BMM) for modeling motivation elements.
Measurement	The assignment of numbers to objects such as business process or organization unit. Measurement is the basis for quantitative management. Any measurement can be expressed as a magnitude of measurement unit. The measurements that provide most important assessment of the business performance are specifically called Key Performance Indicators (KPI) and are typically assigned to business processes. Measurements are also used to quantify specific business motivation elements such as objectives. Learn PAd offers a custom metamodel for specifying measurements to be used as key performance indicators (KPI) for the processes.
Competency	The ability of an individual to do a job properly, which is a combination of practical and theoretical knowledge, cognitive skills, behavior and values. Organization must have competencies to perform its processes properly. Learn PAd offers a custom metamodel for specifying competencies.
Knowledge	A familiarity, awareness or understanding of facts, information, descriptions, or skills, which is acquired through experience or education by perceiving, discovering, or learning. Knowledge can be implicit (practical skill or expertise) or explicit (specification). Knowledge can be captured and transferred between knowledge sources in tangible knowledge objects. Organization uses knowledge while performing its processes. Learn PAd offers a custom metamodel for specifying knowledge elements.

In addition to the stack of metamodels, Learn PAd defines ontology in order to enable semantic lifting, reasoning and recommendations. For Learn PAd we use the Enterprise Ontology called ArchiMEO (Hinkelmann 2013), developed by FHNW. ArchiMEO is an ontological representation of the ArchiMate 2.1 standard (ArchiMate 2012). ArchiMate is an enterprise architecture modeling language that offers an integrated architectural approach for describing and visualizing different architecture domains and their underlying relations and dependencies. ArchiMEO represents all concepts and relations defined in ArchiMate 2.1 in Resource Description Framework Schema (RDFS) 3.0. For general concepts like location or time, ArchiMEO also includes a Top Level Ontology (TOL) following (Bertolazzi 2001). Use of ArchiMEO ontology provides the semantics needed in Learn PAd, e.g. for recommendations. Semantics were defined in ArchiMate 2.1, e.g., the concept of "*Business Process*" and its relations: "*Business processes or business functions are assigned to a single business role with certain responsibilities or skills [competencies]. A business actor that is assigned to a business role ultimately performs the corresponding behavior. In addition to the relation of a business role with behavior, a business role is also useful in a (structural) organizational sense; for instance, in the division of labor within an organization.*"

For Learn PAd, ArchiMEO is enhanced with respect to application independent concepts like the ones representing business motivation aspects. Furthermore, two application specific extensions are made: one for describing domain knowledge and another for representing metamodels used by modelers, e.g., BPMN 2.0 for modeling business processes. These two extensions were derived from Learn PAd Conceptual Meta Model (LCMM) and the Learn PAd Platform Independent Meta Model (LPIMM) as described above.

Learn PAd Ontology consists of two parts:

- *Learn PAd Conceptual Metamodel Ontology* (LCMO), which refines the LCMM comprising ArchiMEO and extension for domain specific concepts and relations made for Learn PAd;
- *Learn PAd Platform Independent Metamodel Ontology* (LPIMO), which is the other extension of ArchiMEO for the ontological representation of the metamodels of the various model kinds used in Learn PAd.

FROM MODELS TO WIKI

Learn PAd project defined LPSMMs for two different environments, ADOxx and Cameo Business Modeler (CBM), in order to demonstrate that Learn PAd approach can be implemented in different modeling environments. LPSMMs are implementations based on specific mechanisms of modeling environments, which is out of scope for this paper. We will rather explain how wiki pages are created from user models that are based on LPSMM.

The user interface in Learn PAd is a wiki. Therefore, the models created with the LPSMMs are transformed into wiki pages. In Learn PAd, we use XWiki. The general transformation approach is depicted in Figure 5. After a model is created in a modeling environment, it is exported to an XML file. Then the file is parsed in order to create XWiki pages and to create instances of the respective concepts in the Learn PAd ontology. The result is a transformation of model elements into XWiki pages and structures. For every activity of a business process, XWiki page is created. Note that models of all kinds are represented in the wiki, i.e. documents used in activity or roles assigned to a process are also represented in the wiki. In the XWiki page the worker can see a description of the task and has links to the information associated with the task, e.g. to a wiki page about the documents and another wiki page showing the organizational chart. Learn PAd wiki also provides a shallow workflow functionality i.e. sequence of a process flow is represented as links between "activity wiki pages," decisions (e.g. gateways) are represented as questions to be answered, and sentries of tasks (stemming from models represented in CMMN) are displayed as checkboxes.

The ontology is populated using the same approach as for creating the Wiki pages. For all object types and their attributes of the platform, specific meta-models needed to support learning instances are created in LPIMO. In the next step, the instances are automatically related to instances of LCMO concepts, in order to provide semantics to the models and hence allow for reasoning. Reasoning in Learn PAd is used for recommending resources and for "retrofitting" comments and suggestions to models. An example of ontology use is provided in the next section.

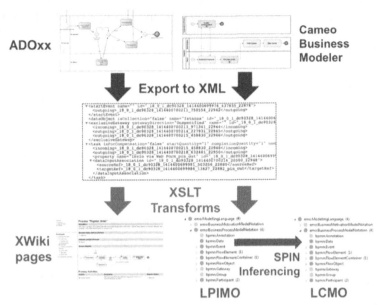

Figure 5. Generating XWiki pages & ontology from BA models

LEARN PAD BY EXAMPLE

A pilot partner in Learn PAd is the public administration of *Regione Marche* in Italy. One service they provide is to examine applications of entrepreneurs for setting up a new company. This process is called SUAP (*Sportello Unico Attività Produttive*). It is a highly complex process with many knowledge-intensive sub-processes and involving many parties. Knowledge-intensive processes are those that cannot be pre-defined as sequences of activities and gateways to direct the sequence along alternative paths, but instead depend on evolving circumstances and *ad hoc* decisions by knowledge workers regarding a particular situation (CMMN 2014). These knowledge-intensive sub-processes are of a particular interest for learning as they give the performer some freedom in taking decisions. We will describe how learning, both individual and organizational, will be managed with Learn PAd. For explanation purpose, we introduce two personas: *Barnaby Barnes* and *Susan Brown*. Barnaby is experienced in administration matters but newly hired at the Municipality of Monti Azzuri, which provides SUAP service. Together with his boss Susan they agreed on learning goals in order to close competency gaps. Figure 6 illustrates the models: (1) a person, in our example Barnaby, has acquired competencies he needs for the new job; (2) In his new job he has the role of a *SUAP Officer* belonging to an organizational unit within the Municipality. In order to fulfill this role he needs certain competencies that are described in a competency model. In addition, for certain activities specific competencies might be needed (3). The difference between acquired competencies and required competencies allows for identifying the knowledge gap (4) and depending on this to derive the learning goals (5).

When Barnaby starts work, Learn PAd offers him three ways of learning: 1) browsing a process, i.e. visiting the wiki pages representing a process and referenced objects (like the organizational chart showing which person has the role assigned to an activity or documents that are input or output of an activity); 2) simulating a process; and 3) learning by doing, i.e. using the wiki as a shallow workflow management system while working on a real case.

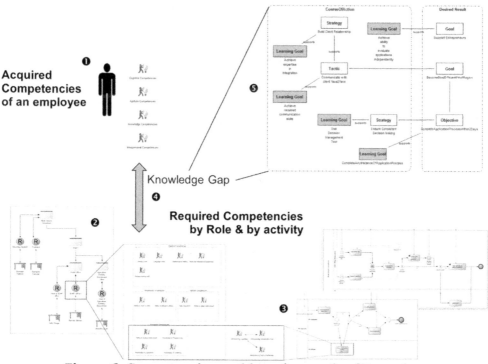

Figure 6. Competencies and learning goals of Barnaby

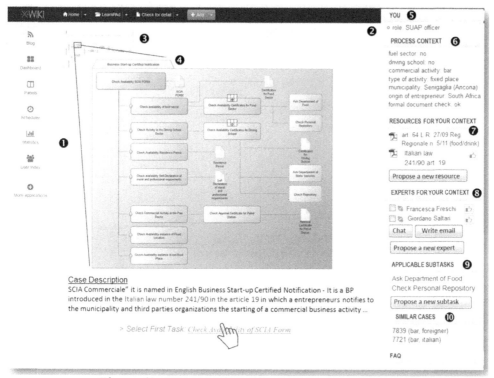

Figure 7. A screenshot of Learn PAd wiki page

Figure 7 provides a print screen of a wiki page. On the left, icons for general functions, e.g. a blog, are depicted. In the middle, (1) model object, describing information and a link to proceed to the next process step are provided. On the right, (2) the so-called context panel is shown. The (3) shows an icon of the main process, e.g. the SUAP, and (4) is a display of the knowledge-intensive sub-process the user is going to work on. In the context panel, firstly information on the user is provided (5). Here it is the role assigned to the user working on the process. The (6) represents process relevant application data, here: data from the application of an entrepreneur about opening a bar. We extract this data automatically from the application form. The data is represented in the ontology, which allows us to perform rules in order to infer, e.g., suggest relevant documents. Hence, (7) provides links to document resources related to the whole or to the sub-process, here: guidelines and law relevant for managing the application. The (8) displays contacts of experts in the field, either within the same organization or in another organization, in which the expert has the same role and responsibility. This information is also inferred from the ontology as we exploit background information on organization as well as on partners, the services they provide, the roles involved and the persons playing these roles. The (9) relates to applicable subtasks, i.e. to discretionary tasks that can or cannot be executed. Finally, (10) provides links to historical cases that can be consulted. Similarity is measured based on information that we keep about cases in the ontology.

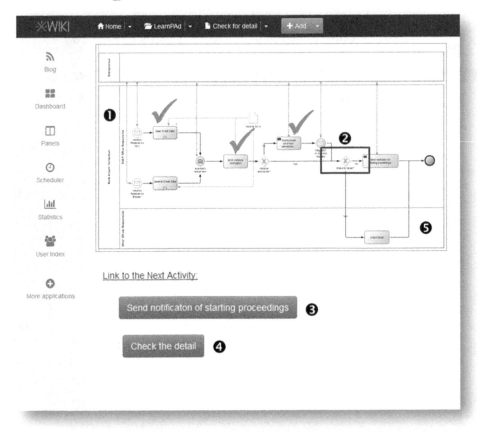

Figure 8. A screenshot of wiki representing a gateway

When all activities of the knowledge-intensive sub-process that are either required (if conditions for their execution are met) or selected (if they are discretionary tasks) process flow returns to the main process. Assume that some more activities were performed and a gateway is reached. As depicted in Figure 8, an enlarged process model (1) is shown and the already performed activities are marked, e.g. by a green tick. The gateway is highlighted by a red rectangle (2). Below the graphical representation of the process model the two paths possible after the gateway are represented by two links: (3) *Send notification of starting proceedings*, and (4) *Check the detail*. In case details are to be checked, the activity is to be performed by another role, which is indicated in the model as another lane (5). In case this decision is taken, e-mail will be automatically issued with a link to the respective wiki page and sent to employees performing this role. In our simplified example, Barnaby would be done with his work in the SUAP process.

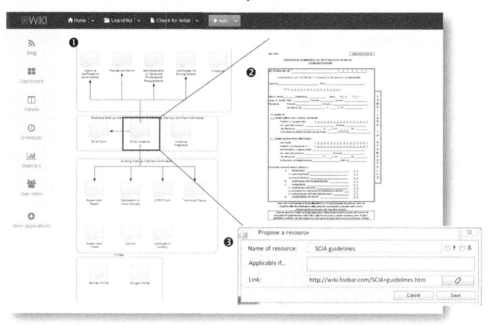

Figure 9. A screenshot of wiki representing a suggestion on documents

Since Learn PAd does also support organization learning, the users have a possibility to comment on all models represented in wiki and to make suggestions for improvements. Figure 9 shows an overview on all documents used in the SUAP process (1). Highlighted is the application form an entrepreneur has to provide to open a new business (2). The (3) shows an example of a suggestion of a new resource (SCIA guidelines) that should be added.

Comments and suggestions consist of two parts: structured information, e.g., the name of a new resource, and free text, e.g. the condition when the resource should be provided, respectively to which activity it should be related and in which way.

In order to reduce effort for manually gathering and analyzing comments and suggestions we developed mechanisms that semi-automatically create model updates. Therefore natural language processing techniques are applied for extracting information from free text, and reasoning is used for inferring background information from the ontology. Updated models, i.e. suggestions for changes, are indicated in the model registry (1) as depicted in Figure 10. When the respective model is opened, the suggestion (a new discretionary task) is already graphically represented (2). The comment (3) can be examined and lead to procedure of updating model if needed.

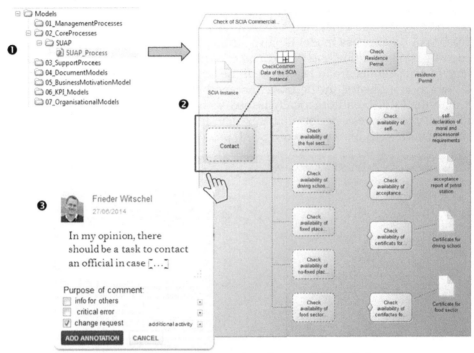

Figure 10. A suggestion for model update

If the process owner accepts the suggestion, the update can be enhanced, e.g. by adding planning items and input data. When the model is completed and ready for use the transfer procedure (see From Models to Wiki) will be performed and the new model can be used in new business process instances. Already running instances will be finished with the old model.

CONCLUSIONS AND FUTURE DIRECTIONS

In this paper, we presented a research work on establishing a metamodel for business architecture of public administrations and using it as a basis for e-learning platform Learn PAd, which combines model-based approach with collaborative knowledge management using Wiki technology, automated quality assessment of textual knowledge content, and model-based simulation for learning and assessing learners' knowledge. The metamodel was implemented in one open-use meta-modelling environment (ADOxx 2015) and in one commercial modelling environment (CBM 2015) and was validated by practical examples from Italian public administration case studies from *Regione Marche* and *University of Camerino*. At the time of this chapter editing, Learn PAd is still a technology under development. While the potential Learn PAd use cases and their business benefits are well defined, the technology needs to mature and the public administrations will need to go a long way to implement organizational changes in order to deploy Learn PAd, and benefit from the proposed approach. The partners involved in Learn PAd project are committed to making this happen and are open to collaboration through social networks and open source communities.

For those interested in the evolution of Learn PAd, we recommend to visit project website http://www.learnpad.eu, join LinkedIn discussions group *Public Administration as a Service* and follow *ProjectLearnPAd* on Twitter and SlideShare social networks.

ACKNOWLEDGEMENTS

This research was supported by the EU through the Model-Based Social Learning for Public Administrations (Learn Pad) FP7 project (619583).

We would like to thank all members of Learn PAd project, especially Antonia Bertolino, Guglielmo De Angelis, Daniele Gagliardi, Knut Hinkelmann, Andrea Polini, Barbara Re, Andrea Sergiacomi, Jean Simard, and Frieder Witschel for their contributions.

REFERENCES

(ADOxx 2015) ADOxx.org . ADOxx Meta Modelling Platform: http://www.adoxx.org/

(Ahrend 2012) Ahrend, N., Walser, K., & Leopold, H. Comparative Analysis of the Implementation of Business Process Management in Public Administration in Germany and Switzerland. PoEM 2012 Proceedings.

(ArchiMate 2012) The Open Group. ArchiMate® Version 2.0: https://www2.opengroup.org/ogsys/catalog/U132

(Becker 2006) Becker, J., Algermissen, L., Falk, T., Pfeiffer, D., Fuchs, P. Model Based Identification and Measurement of Reorganization Potential in Public Administrations-the PICTURE-Approach. PACIS 2006 Proceedings.

(Bertolazzi 2001) Bertolazzi, P., C. Krusich, C., and M. Missikoff. An approach to the definition of a core enterprise ontology: CEO. In OES-SEO 2001, International Workshop on Open Enterprise Solutions: Systems, Experiences, and Organizations, pp. 14-15.

(BMM 2014) Object Management Group. Business Motivation Model (BMM), version 1.2, 2014: http://www.omg.org/spec/BMM/1.2/

(Boer 2010) Boer, A., van Engers, T. Knowledge acquisition from sources of law in public administration. In Knowledge Engineering and Management by the Masses, 2010, pp. 44-58.

(Boyne 2003) Boyne, G. A. Sources of public service improvement: A critical review and research agenda. Journal of public administration research and theory, 13(3), 2003, pp. 367-394.

(BPMN 2013) Object Management Group. Business Process Model and Notation (BPMN), version 2.0.2, 2013: http://www.omg.org/spec/BPMN/2.0.2/

(Brown 2003) Brown, M. M., & Brudney, J. L. Learning organizations in the public sector? A study of police agencies employing information and technology to advance knowledge. Public administration review, 63(1), 2003, pp. 30-43.

(CBM 2015) No Magic. Cameo Business Modeler Analyst: http://www.cameobusinessanalyst.com

(CMMN 2014) Object Management Group. Case Management Model and Notation (CMMN), version 1.0, 2014: http://www.omg.org/spec/CMMN/1.0/

(Denhardt 2000) Denhardt, R. B., & Denhardt, J. V. The new public service: Serving rather than steering. Public administration review, 60(6), 2000, pp. 549-559.

(Dikota 2014) Dikotla, M. A., Mahlatji, M. R., Makgahlela, L. A. Knowledge management for the improvement of service delivery in South Africa's municipalities. Journal of Public Administration, 49(3), 2014, pp. 847-859.

(Hartley, 2005) Hartley, J. Innovation in governance and public services: Past and present. Public money and management, 25(1), 27-34.

(Hinkelmann 2013) Hinkelmann, K., M. Maise, and B. Thonssen. Connecting enterprise architecture and information objects using an enterprise ontology. Enterprise Systems Conference (ES), IEEE, 2013.

(Learn PAd 2014) Model-Based Social Learning for Public Administrations (Learn PAd). FP7 specifically targeted research project: http://www.learnpad.eu

(MDA 2014) Object Management Group. Model Driven Architecture (MDA) Guide rev. 2.0: http://www.omg.org/cgi-bin/doc?ormsc/14-06-01.pdf

(Niehaves 2011) Niehaves, B., Plattfaut, R. Collaborative business process management: status quo and quo vadis. Business Process Management Journal, 17(3), 2011, pp. 384-402.

(Peristeras 2000) Peristeras, V., & Tarabanis, K. Towards an enterprise architecture for public administration using a top-down approach. European Journal of Information Systems, 9(4), 2000, pp. 252-260.

(Riege 2006) Riege, A., & Lindsay, N. Knowledge management in the public sector: stake-holder partnerships in the public policy development. Journal of knowledge management, 10(3), 2006, pp. 24-39.

(Stremberger 2007) Stemberger, M. I., Jaklic, J. (2007). Towards e-government by business process change – a methodology for public sector. International Journal of Information Management, 27(4), 2007, pp. 221-232.

(UML 2013) Object Management Group. Unified Modeling Language (UML), version 2.5 Beta 2: http://www.omg.org/spec/UML/2.5/Beta2/

(Vigoda 2002) Vigoda, E. From Responsiveness to Collaboration: Governance, Citizens, and the Next Generation of Public Administration. Public Administration Review, 62 (5), 2002, pp. 527–540

(Visic 2014) Visic, N. and D. Karagiannis. Developing Conceptual Modeling Tools Using a DSL. Knowledge Science, Engineering and Management, Springer, 2014, pp. 162-173

(West 2015) West, D., Blackman, D. Performance Management in the Public Sector. Australian Journal of Public Administration, 74(1), 2015, pp. 73-81.

(Wiig 2002) Wiig, K. M. Knowledge management in public administration. Journal of knowledge management, 6(3), 2002, pp. 224-239.

(Zwicker 2010) Zwicker, J., Fettke, P., Loos, P. Business process maturity in public administrations. In Handbook on Business Process Management 2, 2010, pp. 369-396)

Leveraging Architecture Federation to Increase the Value and Use of Architecture

David Rice, EA Frameworks, LLC, USA

INTRODUCTION

The architecture of any large enterprise is too complex to be described within a single, integrated architecture. To fully describe an enterprise in an integrated architecture, architects must either abstract the content into simple constructs that do not lend themselves to supporting detailed decisions, or they must compile massive amounts of data taken out of context that make comprehension difficult and architecture data management (including change control and impact assessment) nearly impossible. To deal with this level of complexity in describing an enterprise via architecture, it is useful to adopt the concept and practice of architecture federation.

To achieve the benefits of architecture, and to do so in a way that provides the most value at the least cost of time and effort, and lowest risk of redundant work, it is best to develop and maintain the architecture as a federation of independently managed, heterogeneous architectures (hereafter referred to as "component architectures"). A brief discussion of federation and its benefits, and the component architectures it comprises, will be presented in subsequent sections; however it is worth mentioning up front that a primary benefit of architecture federation is enabling the controlled sharing and analysis of architecture data across the enterprise, without impact on the autonomy of any one component architecture within the federation.

One of the primary objectives of doing architecture is to describe various aspects of the enterprise in a structured way to allow informed decision making, unfortunately all too often the development of architecture takes place in such a way as to be valuable only to the team developing it and does not provide sufficient connection or value to the rest of the enterprise. Architecture federation will result in the development of a cohesive set of architecture data, enabling the alignment of architecture efforts, while affording the necessary flexibility to development of and/or reuse of existing individual component architecture making up the federation.

WHAT IS A FEDERATED ARCHITECTURE?

A Federated Architecture contains two or more component architectures that align along agreed to concepts such as capabilities, activities, services, systems, etc. The alignment of these concepts is done via the use of "semantic alignment", to ascribe a meaning to the association between architecture concepts. The mapping values have their roots in Aristotle's work on categories, as will be described later. For the purposes of this text, some specific structures will be used to highlight the federation practice, particularly along the lines of the use of a standard set of taxonomies within a defined hierarchy of architecture tiers, but the reader can modify this approach as needed for their own environment. Typically, in a federation, the architectures are arranged in tiers; tiers are used to help define the context and boundaries for the content of the component architectures. For the purposes of this discussion, a general structure is shown in the figure below. This structure is a derivative of actual structures used at many client locations. The specific definition of each segment and the scope and meaning of "Enterprise" is of course use-specific, but the concepts presented here apply. Also, it is important to note that "solution" can, but does not necessarily equate to, an IT solution. A speifically designed manual process that solves a capability need for a business area is just as viable a solution as a design for a software application.

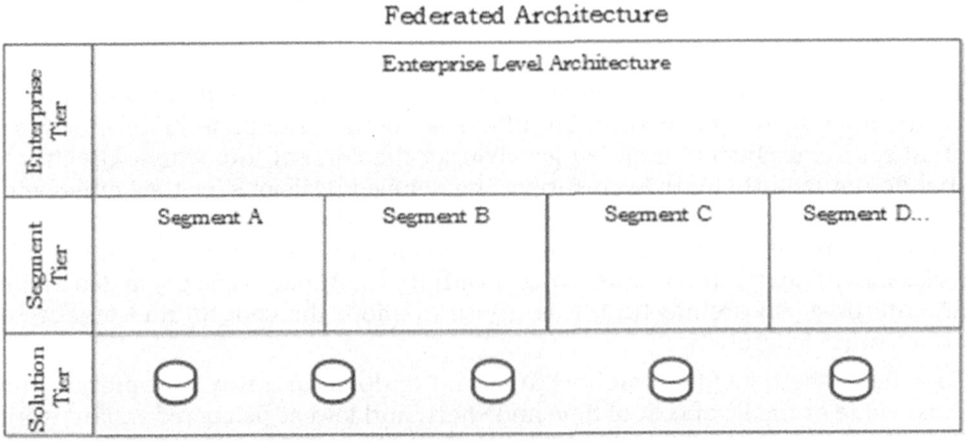

Federated Architecture

Figure 1: Federation Tiered Structure

WHAT IS ARCHITECTURE FEDERATION?

The activity of Architecture Federation is the process of relating two or more separate architectures in such a way as to allow the identification of both common and disparate concepts. The purpose of federation is to support the intended uses of each component architecture while also supporting decision making via use of the entire set of component architectures making up the federation. Federation may be used to (virtually) combine two or more architectures for a specific purpose. This federation is temporary and time specific to the task at hand. Other times, the federation may have a longer shelf-life and has the net effect of serving as a mechanism for building a larger architecture from two or more smaller ones.

Federation is carried out according to a set of guiding principles and rules, following a defined process. To federate architectures, the individual component architectures must either be built to be federated, or modified to be able to be federated—this concept is referred to as "fit for federation."

INTEGRATION VERSUS FEDERATION

While any true architecture effort is an ongoing activity that, to stay relevant and useful, is constantly updating data to reflect current reality and future plans, architecture efforts often have been characterized as overly complex and time consuming. One reason for this is that the size and scope of the architecture effort undertaken is often too broad and/or too deep. One reason for this is that for many, the focus is on building integrated, enterprise wide architectures. An integrated architecture is a single, large, integrated dataset that contains all the information about the enterprise. While there are some positive aspects to integrated architecture, in any complex enterprise, the rate of change will be such that to build a single, integrated architecture and keep it updated and accurate, will likely be cost and time prohibitive (if not simply impossible). As a result, integrated architecture efforts often result in very large, cumbersome sets of data that are difficult and time consuming to build, and even more so to maintain.

By contrast, federated architectures are characterized by smaller, multiple datasets that are purpose built and use the terms and definitions that are meaningful to the community of interest for which they are built. Federation is not a license to create architecture with no rules—quite the contrary: to be useful to the enterprise, each individual architecture must be built in such a way as to be internally integrated as well as "fit for federation," meaning it adheres to certain rules and principles and is built following required standards. Outside the constraints necessary to achieve federation, however, the architecture effort in a federated model is afforded far more flexibility than in an integrated model.

Another characteristic of architecture federation is that the effects of change do not have unintended ripple effects on the entire architecture. Because federation is accomplished through the use of defined interface points, the management of change across the enterprise is limited to changes that affect the defined interface points. This has a net effect of permitting more rapid change as well as less costly maintenance of the architecture. Some key differences between federated and integrated architectures are summarized in the table below.

Federated	Integrated
Requires agreed-to interface points	All artifacts are interface points
Allows different but complementary viewpoints	Requires common viewpoint
Allows different but compatible purposes	Requires common purpose
Allows architectures to be built and managed in multiple "places"	Requires all architectures to be built and managed as if in a single "place"
Allows different tools and methodologies	Requires common tool and single methodology

Table 1: Differences between Integrated and Federated Architecture

VALUE OF ARCHITECTURE FEDERATION

Architecture is a key information asset for managing change within an enterprise. A properly federated architecture affords an organization the opportunity to leverage architecture data assets to move toward the integration of cross-organization and cross-mission functions, and maximize the impact of the IT Investments, among other possibilities.

Architecture Federation brings value to an architecture effort in that it:

1. Provides a mechanism to demonstrate architecture conformance to overarching architectures, often a key compliance requirement for new or continued investments
2. Provides a way of determining commonality across the investments in the enterprise, often a key enabler of increased efficiencies in the enterprise
3. Provides a way of managing the complexity of architecture efforts, saving time and money
4. Provides a mechanism for collaboration and information sharing among architecture efforts without negative impact on the fidelity of each architecture effort in relation to its intent

Architecture Federation provides a means to size an architecture effort to be appropriate to its intended use, while allowing for its integration into the collective set of architectures that make up the enterprise.

BENEFITS

Implementation of a Federated Architecture is intended to provide useful analytical information to various stakeholders. These benefits accrue as the federation is progressively populated with widely sharable information and capabilities. Some of the key stakeholders and benefits are listed below.

Benefits to Decision Makers

Enables Rapid Access to Information for Strategic Decisions

Access to actionable, relevant, decision-quality architecture information will accelerate leadership's ability to make informed decisions that impact the movement of the enterprise toward their Strategic Goals.

Fosters Understanding of Interactions and Interdependencies

One of the primary uses of a federated architecture is to allow the enterprise to understand the interactions and interdependencies among its component parts. Decision makers need to understand the interactions among major capabilities and programs and the federation provides the means to govern and manage shared capabilities to realize the goals and objectives of the enterprise.

Supports Portfolio Management and Capital Planning and Investment Control

A federated architecture can be leveraged to describe the programs and IT investments for each capability within the enterprise. By evaluating the architecture data across the federation, an analyst and/or portfolio manager can gain an understanding of multiple uses of the same investment and identify where there may be multiple investments applied to support the same type of capabilities. Additionally, streamlining operations using the federated data will enable decision makers to better deal with growing pressures on resources and ensure the budget is optimally applied for long-term organizational effectiveness.

Benefits to Architects

Increases Architecture Development Speed, Reuse, and Accuracy

This benefit is the result of the use of common architecture concepts, reuse and leverage of existing architecture elements, and architecture federation practices. Use of existing architecture content to "seed" new architecture efforts can significantly reduce the time and cost for new architecture development, resulting in increased speed in fielding of a new or updated capability, and gaining improved interoperability. Architecture accuracy is increased through the use of previously defined and vetted architecture artifacts, and through incorporation of architecture development practices that result in architectures that are "fit for federation."

Provides Scoping Rules for Architecture Development

A common mistake made when developing architectures is exceeding the scope of the architecture purpose. Architecture federation provides "black box" content for solution-level architectures such that the boundaries of the solution are defined. Similarly, segment architectures are focused on management of the interfaces between solutions and defining common capabilities and services within the segment area, preventing the "deep dive" down to the detail to be addressed at the solution level.

Promotes Distributed Configuration Management

With a federated architecture, configuration management is reduced to maintenance of the federation and the configuration of artifacts owned at each level in the federation. Federation maintenance and artifact ownership at each Architecture Tier Level will be described in a subsequent section.

Benefits to Architectural Governance Bodies

Promotes Autonomy or Self-Governance

A federated architecture supports a governance structure that defines the responsibility and authority among components to achieve and support enterprise-wide goals. Once a component accepts its defined boundary, as depicted within the federated architecture framework, it enjoys autonomous control of the development and analysis of its architecture. The components determine the breadth and depth of detail relating to their individual architecture, and produce and archive the artifacts, as required, to meet or support the goals of the enterprise.

GUIDING PRINCIPLES

To maximize re-use of existing architecture and minimize the need for additional architecture development, the development of a federated architecture is guided by the principles below. The federated architecture will:

- Respect the diverse requirements of individual programs and investments while focusing on the associations that cut across organizational and program boundaries
- Focus on federating existing, disparate architecture artifacts regardless of structure and format—where possible—not re-building architectures
- Maximize the reuse of existing architectures at all tiers

FEDERATION GOALS

1. Support decision makers with access to a set of common architecture artifacts enabling shared common understanding of the enterprise to support decision making at the enterprise, segment and solution levels
2. Develop/Provide a means to identify internal and external interfaces to the enterprise
3. Improve information sharing of architectural content, ensuring that users find and use the right information at the right time, in the right context
4. Achieve increased agility that leverages existing architecture and/or artifacts to swiftly adjust or expand enterprise capabilities through architecture reuse and integration to meet organizational needs

ARCHITECTURE FEDERATION SCENARIO

Typically, in a federation structure, the architectures are arranged in tiers; each of the tier levels is defined as is appropriate for the organization upon completion of a review of elements of available architectures and identification of those architecture elements likely to work best within the given purpose of the architecture effort. A notional sample of one possible structure was presented above in Figure 1.

To communicate some of the structures, decisions and tasks involved in a federation effort, this section will discuss how component architectures can align around federation-standard taxonomies. This approach provides a number of benefits, including providing context of the component architecture as well as architecture development boundaries, architecture and design conformance traceability, and architecture data reuse opportunity.

CORE ARCHITECTURE ELEMENTS USED IN THE FEDERATION

The precise architecture elements at the core of the federation rules and processes that are part of the federation strategy will mature over time as the federation practice matures; however, in practice several core architecture elements, common across multiple methods and frameworks, have proven to be of special interest for federation. They are:

- Capability
- Activity
- Service

Some of the architecture elements often related to these core elements that are necessary to aid in identifying the proper semantic alignment (described later) are:

- Standard
- Guidance (e.g., Laws, Regulations, Policies, etc.)
- Performer (e.g., Role, System, etc.)
- Location
- Resource (including data and materiel)

These core artifact types can be found, in one form or another, by one name or another, in any commercially viable architecture framework such as the Department of Defense Architecture Framework (DoDAF) or The Open Group Architecture Framework (TOGAF) and in solution oriented methods such as UML and the Profiles available for its extension. Focusing on just these core elements, will help eliminate the barrier that sometimes prevents the implementation of a federated architecture; the requirement that a single framework or method (or even tool) be chosen. There is a necessity that these core elements have certain attributes to support the semantic alignment, and that will be discussed in a section to follow.

HIGH-LEVEL TAXONOMIES

In the context of a federated architecture, a high-level taxonomy is a structure or model that spans the contextual breadth and depth of the component architecture for a given core architecture element. At the enterprise tier, the Capability, Activity, and Service hierarchies establish the high-level taxonomy to be used by the segment architectures; setting the context for the alignment of the segments to the enterprise. The segment tiers expand on the taxonomies as appropriate to their focus area, and the resulting taxonomies are the structures used by the solution tiers for federation into the segments; ultimately resulting in a federated architecture.

DATA OWNERSHIP AND DATA MANAGEMENT IN THE ARCHITECTURE TIERS

The establishment of proper data ownership of the architecture elements within the federation is central to successful implementation of architecture federation. Establishing the proper ownership allows for the sharing of data across the federation as needed but delineates a clear line of responsibility for updates and maintenance of the individual elements. When using, building, or maintaining an architecture within a federation, it is critical to be able to trace the ownership of the individual elements to ensure that the context of the elements is known, as well as to have clearly established rights and responsibilities for handling and use of the architecture data.

The figure below shows conceptual elements for taxonomies within the architecture tiers. The Enterprise Tier has a taxonomy from which notional "Segment A" received a single, low-level element. The segment then expands on that element further, thereby adding more detail to the taxonomy of the combined set. Figure 2 shows conceptually how this tiered accountability across architecture tiers functions in more detail.

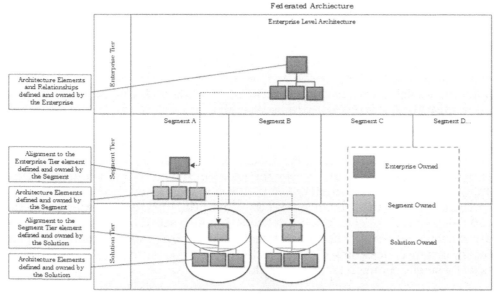

Figure 2: Data Ownership across Tiers

For this tiered approach of responsibility and function, ownership rules and processes must be established. One reason the establishment of ownership is important is that for federation to work, common elements must remain common. Elements that are "aligned to" by lower-level tiers must share a common definition that is known and consistent across all the lower-level tiers that have access to that element. Architecture elements defined by the tier are owned by that tier. The alignment and alignment value of the tier-owned items to unowned items is also owned by that tier. Also shown above are two solution architectures sharing the same segment owned architecture element. The ownership rules prevent the change of the segment architecture element by either solution, but both can elaborate further on that element to define how they provide solutions to the capability, service, or activity identified in the segment, and define their relationship to the segment element (via semantic alignment, discussed later).

CHANGE OF DATA OWNERSHIP WITHIN THE FEDERATION

As an architecture matures and existing solutions are documented or new ones developed or procured to address the defined elements in the architecture, the need will arise to promote lower-level tier elements to a higher tier. This concept allows, for example, the adoption of a capability delivered by a solution architecture as a standardized, shared element within a segment or across the enterprise. Promotion and demotion of architecture elements within the federation requires careful management and a complete understanding of the impacts. Additionally, the promotion of one element of a given component architecture does not necessitate the promotion of all artifacts in that architecture, as long as responsibilities are properly managed (as indicated above). The activity of architecture promotion is one of the architecture changes to be managed by the board or group responsible for the governance of the federation.

ARCHITECTURE CONTEXT

Architecture federation helps in setting the appropriate context for an architecture effort which defines the boundaries for the effort. Ideally, the context should be defined before the architecture effort is begun. The context is part of the architecture's metadata, which can be used for discovery, semantic alignment, and contextual comparison with other architecture efforts. Definition of context is a fundamental architecture development activity and setting the appropriate context is critical to determination of the appropriate federation for the architecture effort. The defined context of the architecture helps the architects determine the appropriate higher level tier that governs their efforts and what architecture data in that tier applies to and constrains their efforts.

Each architecture tier has specific goals, as well as responsibilities to the tiers above and/or below, that are used to determine the level of detail (or abstraction) necessary for the architecture. For instance, if the purpose of an architecture is to develop a specific but technology-independent reference architecture for Data Tagging then that context identifies the need to identify overarching Data Management services and guidance from the Enterprise Tier that are relevant to the capability area architecture being defined—but also sets a boundary condition to avoid diving too deeply into the architecture and moving into the solution space by, for instance, designing the architecture specifically according to the capabilities of a single, commercial product solution.

SEMANTIC ALIGNMENT

The workhorse of architecture federation is semantic alignment (also called value based mapping) of architecture elements from one tier of the federation to elements of another tier. Typically this alignment will be around the leaf level elements of the high-level taxonomies of the upper tier to the root elements of a lower tier. Semantic alignment refers to the relationship specified between the meanings of architecture elements. The semantic relationships specified between the architecture elements across tiers will be represented by one of four values:

- Same: lower-tier architecture is equivalent to the item in the higher-level architecture
- Similar/Type Of: lower-level elements meets some, but not all, of the criteria to be the "Same" as the overarching element
- Part Of: lower-level architecture item addresses part of the scope of the higher-level item
- Gap: specifically establishes the notion there is a gap between the higher and lower level tier architecture elements (this may be a summary notation once all other alignment is done)

These values (or the absence of them, indicating gaps) are critical to the use of the architecture in making assessments and recommendations for the enterprise. The root of these values and their meaning reach back to Aristotle's Categories – loosely aligned these are:

Aristotle	Federation Value
Not Said-Of and Not Present-In	Gap
Not Said-Of and Present-In	Part Of
Said-Of and Not Present-In	Type Of

Said-Of and Present-In	Same

Table 2: Aristotle's Categories and Federation Values

The assignment of specific values for the "mapping" of the architecture elements and the rules and criteria that govern the assignment of that value takes on a level of fidelity beyond that typically found in architecture federation. Most architecture federation activities merely "Map" one element to another, providing no meaning, context, or justification of that mapping. As such, it is not possible to deterministically use the mapping (and thus the federation derived from it) for any robust decision making. Absent a value-based map of say, several different solutions to a desired capability, it would be impossible to deterministically know just how much coverage the enterprise has for the desired capability, at least not without doing additional time consuming research or data calls.

One natural and easily understood way to establish and communicate the semantic alignment of the federation is via matrices. Clearly from the previous discussion, the tool used to establish the federation must be capable of traversing across multiple component architectures and to store the semantic alignment between them. By way of example of what a "federation matrix" can look like, a "Service to Service" federation matrix was constructed within IBM Rational System Architect®. For illustration to stakeholders, colors were used to portray Same (blue), Similar (Green), Part-of (Yellow) and Gap (Red). Each cell in the matrix contains (behind the scenes) further information about the justification for the assignment of that value, the audit trail of the alignment, etc. The services federated were from two different architectures at different tiers. This example is for illustration – but the data and federation values are real. The use of tools useful for federation will be discussed in a later section.

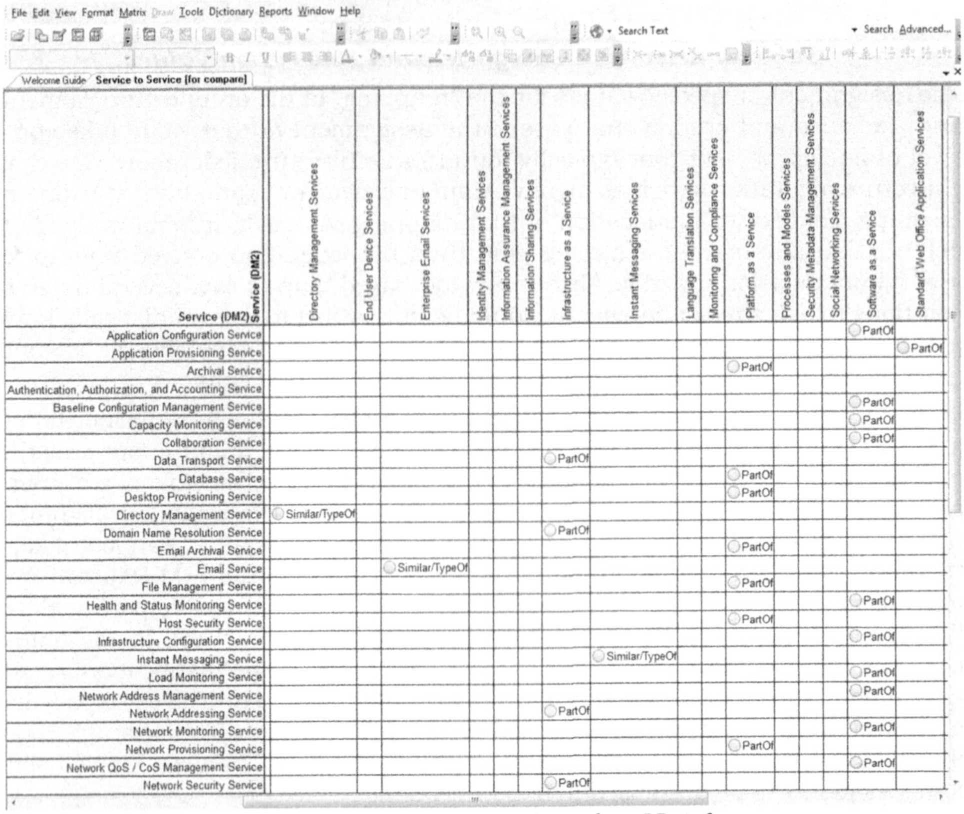

Service (DM2)	Directory Management Services	End User Device Services	Enterprise Email Services	Identity Management Services	Information Assurance Management Services	Information Sharing Services	Infrastructure as a Service	Instant Messaging Services	Language Translation Services	Monitoring and Compliance Services	Platform as a Service	Processes and Models Services	Security Metadata Management Services	Social Networking Services	Software as a Service	Standard Web Office Application Services
Application Configuration Service															PartOf	
Application Provisioning Service																PartOf
Archival Service											PartOf					
Authentication, Authorization, and Accounting Service																
Baseline Configuration Management Service															PartOf	
Capacity Monitoring Service															PartOf	
Collaboration Service															PartOf	
Data Transport Service							PartOf									
Database Service											PartOf					
Desktop Provisioning Service											PartOf					
Directory Management Service	Similar/TypeOf															
Domain Name Resolution Service							PartOf									
Email Archival Service											PartOf					
Email Service			Similar/TypeOf													
File Management Service											PartOf					
Health and Status Monitoring Service															PartOf	
Host Security Service											PartOf					
Infrastructure Configuration Service															PartOf	
Instant Messaging Service								Similar/TypeOf								
Load Monitoring Service															PartOf	
Network Address Management Service															PartOf	
Network Addressing Service							PartOf									
Network Monitoring Service															PartOf	
Network Provisioning Service											PartOf					
Network QoS / CoS Management Service															PartOf	
Network Security Service							PartOf									

Figure 3: Example Federation Matrix

It is important that any matrices used for semantic alignment have the following capabilities:

1. Have the ability to establish the alignment values defined for the semantic alignment
2. Support the semantic alignment of selected architecture elements between different component architectures in the federation (e.g., service to service, etc.)
3. The cells used to record the semantic alignment between component architecture are independent from the data owned by either component — as such they are neutral participants in the federation. The neutrality of this set of data is important to the federation. A key aspect of the federation is that the context of each component of the federation be maintained and the intrusion of other components be minimized to allow the greatest flexibility. The alignment mapping is not in context of either component architecture – but instead is an artifact used as a mechanism to enable federation – something not strictly owned by either component.

ARCHITECTURE DATA TAGGING

Perhaps the single most important activity that can be carried out in support of the federation approach is the tagging of the architecture data to signify the "owning" architecture (context). Central to the concept and practice of architecture federation is the ability for multiple, independently developed architectures (different perspectives and contexts) to coexist and be used together in a defined manner to address the desired uses of architecture. Federation and its ability to support multiple perspectives for an architecture element are in stark contrast to architecture integration, which presupposes a single context for an architecture element. The key to the federation performing properly; and the consumers of the federation being able to use the right architecture data, in the right way, for the intended purpose; is the assignment of the proper context to that architecture data.

The implementation of architecture federation will require the assignment of the owning context to each first order architecture element. Specifically, this means that each first order architecture element will be tagged (assigned) to an appropriate owning component architecture. Some of the attributes necessary to know about the component architecture include, but are not limited to: owner/sponsor, time-line, scope, purpose, vision, goals, objectives, measures, effects and desired outcomes.

> A first order architecture element is architecture data whose existence does not depend on the existence of another element. For instance, an "Activity" would be a first order element but an "Activity Flow", which depends on the existence of two activities to act as the "Source" and "Destination" for the element is not a first order element.

Tagging the architecture elements in this way facilitates the filtering of component architectures and their contents to the purpose or activity being addressed when using the federation. For instance, if a technical review is being conducted for a program to develop a solution to be fielded in 2017 to address data management, the owning architecture for the concept of "Data Management" provides the context for each architecture component within the federation to establish its relevance to the analysis timeframe and scope. Additionally, the context of the analysis (e.g., compliance, performance, compatibility, alignment with strategy, etc.) further refines the data within the federation to be used in the analysis. Having selected the appropriate set of federation component architectures applicable, the tagging in combination with the semantic alignment between the chosen component architecture elements then allows for the consolidation of the component architecture content into a "fit-for-purpose" dataset to use (in the case of this example) for the analysis. The analysis dataset retains context for each element and yet allows for the formation of a combined analysis view across the federation to address the desired outcomes of using the architecture. This is one example; but it is easy to conceive of many more.

FIT-FOR-FEDERATION RULES AND GUIDELINES

An architecture federation comprises multiple independent but related architectures. For the federation to work properly, it is necessary that all the component architectures of the federation contain sufficient detail to deterministically specify their place in the federation—for example, detail that makes it possible to determine in what tier the architecture belongs, the timeframe to which the architecture applies, and the purpose and viewpoint that must be applied to the architecture to provide proper context to its content. The rules and guidelines that are used to determine if an architecture is "fit for federation" are in addition to quality and conformance criteria that apply to architecture efforts that pertain to their internal consistency and compliance with standards and guidance.

The following factors must be balanced to come up with a specific set of rule and guidelines applicable to the particular enterprise:

1. Framework(s)/Modeling Method(s)/Data Structures for the architecture data to be used across the federation.
    a. Within each framework – of the available data-types which are those required to be used to build a fit architecture. While supporting multiple frameworks is possible, it is necessary to identify common elements in them for federation
    b. Within a single common framework/meta-model, of the available data-types, which are those required to be used to build a fit architecture.
2. What are the required attributes to be captured for each data type to be used in order to be fit-for-federation? Each data-type can have different attributes, so this is data-type specific.
3. What relationships are required to be present between data-types to support the use of the federation in its intended purpose?
4. How does one compare the attributes and relationships of given data-types across federated architectures, to establish the semantic alignment? E.g., what is the specific criteria for a defined value within the alignment? What specifically does it take to be Same, Type, Part, etc.? These are data type specific.
5. What is the intended analysis to be performed using the federation? For instance, if one of the analysis to be performed is intended to identify redundant IT investments – what specifically that means must be known and then exactly how that will be determined must also be known. Then, for the federation to be useful for that purpose, the proper attributes must be part of the fit-for-federation criteria.
6. Related to the above, is any analysis going to be performed, or is this federation mostly for "compliance" or to demonstrate a conceptual alignment? The more robust the expectations, the more criteria are required for a member of the federation to be "fit".
7. Governance and Authority: what authority does the organization sponsoring the federation have to demand/enforce compliance with the fit-for-federation criteria on any component architecture of the federation? Defining criteria with no ability to enforce compliance is pointless. In such a case, defining a minimal set may be the only option – limiting analysis and use of the federation for any specific purpose.

It is important to state that the overall federation is only as good as the least populated data-set (i.e., the weakest link). So if only minimal data, such as "name", is allowed as a completion criteria for any member architecture, then that lowers the maturity and usefulness of the entire federation, partly because any semantic alignment to those items is quite suspect.

FEDERATION ACTIVITIES AND RESPONSIBILITIES

The federated approach provides a great deal of flexibility in architecture development and maintenance; however, it also requires careful and complete architecture data management to realize the benefits architecture can deliver. Following are few key activities, and the tier that is responsible for them, that are necessary to support an architecture federation practice.

Enterprise Tier

*   Define the constraints on federated segments and solution architectures to achieve federation; also called the "fit-for-federation" criteria.

- Educate stakeholders, data owners, and architects about the use of the federation and constraints on architecture to be "fit-for-federation."
- Define scoping/context constraints on the segment architectures to achieve enterprise goals and support interoperability across the enterprise and with external stakeholders.
- Steward the entire federated architecture.
- Develop top-level taxonomies for the Enterprise Tier to ensure that segment architectures can align to the federation in a meaningful way.
- Establish a governance structure for the Federation.
- Develop and maintain the environment in which the federated architecture is maintained.
- Store, publish, and maintain semantic alignment "links" to enable traceability through each tier and across the enterprise.
- Provide configuration management to enterprise taxonomies.
- Manage interfaces and architecture information sharing across segment architectures.
- Facilitate capability to do enterprise-wide and solution-deep reporting across the enterprise.
- Define, build and manage the federated architecture to support the strategic plan of the enterprise.

Segment Tier

- Define constraints on the solution architectures to achieve segment goals and support interoperability between segment capability areas.
- Develop and maintain segment architectures.
- Maintain solution architecture alignment mappings.
- Provide configuration management to segment taxonomies.
- Provide segment specific content to taxonomies used for the federated architecture.
- Manage interfaces and architecture information sharing across solution architectures.
- Propose modifications to the Enterprise Tier to increase/improve alignment between and within tiers.
- Extend appropriate high-level taxonomies within each segment.
- Make the segment architecture and solution alignment results visible, accessible, and understandable.
- Adhere to the standards for federation and data sharing established by the enterprise.

Solution Tier

- Use the taxonomies and federation rules provided by the segment and enterprise tiers to map solution architectures to the federated architecture via the appropriate segment.
- Adhere to the standards for federation and data sharing established by the enterprise and segments.
- Maintain solution architecture element names and definitions, and other attributes as defined by the "fit-for-federation" rules and guidelines.
- Propose modifications to the segment architectures to which the solution aligns to increase/improve alignment between tiers and across solutions.

- Extend high-level taxonomies as appropriate to the solution being defined in the architecture.
- Semantically align to the taxonomies and categorization schemes provided by the segments as appropriate.
- Make the solution architecture and segment alignment results visible, accessible, and understandable.

THE RIGHT SET OF TOOLS MAKE FEDERATION POSSIBLE

The implementation mechanism of the federation (federation tools) must support data tagging and rights assignment to enforce and manage the data ownership rights and management responsibilities for each tier. The federation tool must also allow for data sharing across tiers, while enforcing the ownership rights and responsibilities to enable the assignment of alignment of lower tier elements to upper tier elements—a necessary process for the implementation of the federation Strategy. And of course a federation tool must support the ability to establish and maintain the semantic alignment between component architectures.

The architecture tool market is currently rife with tools claiming to be perfect for various types of architecture. Some of these tools have been around for years and by adding little or no additional functionality they claim to be capable of performing the tasks necessary to fulfill clients' needs when performing architecture data gathering, portrayal and analysis. Other tools are new on the scene and in only a short time claim to have somehow managed to capture years of knowledge and expertise. In some cases the claims are true, in some false, in most the truth lies somewhere in the middle.

For many, when they speak of procuring architecture tools they actually speak in the singular. While this approach might work for a single component architecture with a single tier scope, for architecture federation, multiple tools servicing different roles are required. The following classifications for tools should be considered for any serious architecture federation effort.

- Architecture Data Gathering Tools
  - Loosely Structured (Documents, Spreadsheets, etc.)
  - Highly Structured (Modeling Tools)
  - Current Infrastructure Query Tools
  - Natural Language Analysis and Processing
- Architecture Analysis Tools
  - Static (Activity Based Costing, etc.)
  - Dynamic (Simulation)
  - Comparison Tools
- Architecture Presentation Tools
- Architecture Storage Tools
- Architecture Version and Configuration Management Tools
- Architecture Testing Tools
- Architecture Implementation Tools

The resulting tool environment might look something like the figure below:

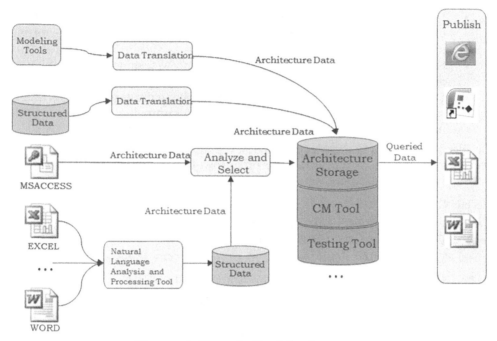

Figure 4: Sample Tool Environment

It is true that some tools will fit in more than one space, however, it is not true that any one tool will satisfy the needs in all spaces.

For example, the following configuration of tools has proven useful in several instances:

- Natural Language Analysis and Processing: JackalFish
  - o www.kbsi.com/products/jackalfish
  - o Used to process and mine loosely structured MS Office and PDF data
- Modeling Tool: IBM Rational System Architect
  - o www.ibm.com/software/products/en/ratisystarch
  - o Used to formally model discovered and mined data in the chosen framework(s) for each component architecture
- Storage/CM/Publishing Tool: Elements Repository
  - o http://enterprise-elements.com/products/what-is-it/
  - o Used to store (co-locate), CM, analyze, federate and publish the component architectures

SUMMARY

Federated architectures conform to common, shared architecture standards across autonomous component areas, enabling developing/owning entities to maintain diversity and uniqueness, while providing opportunity for the identification of shared services, common capabilities and capability needs, enterprise-wide assessment of impact of a solution change, and many other benefits generally associated with architecture. The primary, ultimate benefit of a federated approach to architecture versus an integrated approach is that in a federated model, the optimization of the whole (the enterprise) does not result in the potential suboptimization or misrepresentation of the parts.

Architecture is a key information asset for managing change within an enterprise. The benefits of maturing a federated architecture include (but are not limited to):

- Enhanced/effective production, management, exchange, and use of architecture information throughout the enterprise (internal and external stakeholders)
- Supporting the identification, definition, and assessment of capability gaps, overlaps, and sharing opportunities
- Forming the basis for maintaining and evolving existing business and IT capabilities, acquiring new capabilities and improving processes associated with internal capabilities, systems, and services

Developing a federated architecture offers a unique opportunity to leverage architecture data assets to move an enterprise towards its strategic objectives in a deterministic and inclusive way.

REFERENCES

a. Office of Management and Budget Circular No. A-130, Management of Federal Information Resources, 2003

b. Public Law 104-106: Clinger-Cohen Act of 1996, February 10, 1996

c. DoD Reference Architecture Description, June 2010

d. International Standards Organization (ISO) 704:2009

e. Studtmann, Paul, "Aristotle's Categories," The Stanford Encyclopedia of Philosophy (Summer 2014 Edition), Edward N. Zalta (ed.), URL = <http://plato.stanford.edu/archives/sum2014/entries/aristotle-categories/>.

BA Practical Data Governance

Michael S. Connor, American Family Insurance, U.S.A.

BA Practical DG Conclusion

Strategic business needs drive BA. BA drives all other architecture, whether application-, technical- or data-based. All architecture requires a practical approach to implementation. Many critical factors—such as the right people, plans, tools and technology—contribute to successful implementation. However, underpinning the success lie two important, practical, often underappreciated factors:

1. Necessary, agreed-upon, communicated *concepts* (terms) with clear definitions and actionable application.
2. BA appropriate, business-driven objectives with relevant *measures*, supported by repeatable process and based on practical follow-up.

Both factors rely on data to drive action enabled by practical data governance (DG). DG is based on a comprehensive framework encompassing standard policies, processes and detailed procedures, which are dependent on the requisite skills required to support the framework. Concepts are articulated—and communicated— through terms which represent a common language. This discussion makes up much of the upfront time and effort that provides the solid foundation for implementation. This shared language, in turn, gives context to the practical measures that focus the organization on what has been successful and what has not, based on expectations set by the transforming BA. Related to existing frameworks, factor one ties to the Business Knowledge View (from the Business Architecture Working Group of the Object Management Group/OMG)—this factor translates to DG policy and metadata. Factor two ties to the Organization View (from the Business Architecture Working Group of the OMG)—this factor translates to measure monitoring and action. Just as the absence of practical governance makes these two factors much more problematic, leveraging it fuels the most crucial success factor in the plan: people.

People Matter

People make or break the best plans, architectures, tools or technology. Even picking the best people does not ensure success—however, *engaging* with them does. At the heart of business challenges and issues, people provide the context, analysis, options, recommendations and practical actions for progress. While motivated senior management definitely helps to engage front-line management and staff in a personal way, providing executive-sponsored, enterprise-level structures for the open discussion and appropriate action related to how to implement and how to resolve disagreements increases an organization's odds for success.

Creating and managing ongoing DG provides a key forum and structure for balancing ongoing BA programs and supporting business functions with point-specific projects that deliver new and improved capabilities. DG does not take the place of other types of governance, such as portfolio management, but does help ensure the long-term considerations balance with short-term ones and enterprise considerations balance with unit ones. The origins of sustainability start with facilitated, structured discussions focused on balanced perspectives that drive practical action.

DON'T ASSUME CONCEPTS/TERMS: ARTICULATE THEM AND THEN AGREE TO THEM

Why Bother?

Real things, real actions always equate to concepts. If you don't believe that suggest changing sales compensation from the "concept" of Date Goods/Services Sold to Date Goods/Services Delivered or Paid in Full. If that doesn't start heated discussion then suggest changing the definition of "customer" or "new business." Different objectives or perspectives usually drive different concepts and their related definitions. The technique—metadata—coupled with DG drives the supporting process for concepts-definitions. Metadata provides context and communication for definitions and related factors (e.g., cross-references, aliases)—in fact, DG and metadata are so closely aligned, they should be treated as one integrated function. If the organization doesn't have a forum—or what could be considered a safety valve—for expressing these differences, standard operations can get gummed up, let alone an initiative as far-reaching as BA change.

While DG forums can potentially devolve into debating societies, focusing on practical applications and data analysis based on clear definitions provides senior management with the comfort level that informed discussion leads to better outcomes. In fact, well-run DG brings relevant stakeholders together on a regular basis to discuss and amiably resolve issues of approach, scope and key assumptions all in support of definitions relevant to implementing changes necessary for a new BA direction. Nothing endangers BA initiatives more than not clearly articulating concept definitions (e.g., "customer," "new business") and related assumptions. DG also provides the forum for a broad base of the business to consider and agree to necessary common processes, security, information life cycle management and data quality, among other factors.

Who Says So?

The first assumption of DG requires a plan for an ongoing process where all constituent units agree at the executive level that these are the rules and all units agree to follow these rules. In addition, for the second assumption, the executive level must sponsor time from middle management as well as frontline management-senior individual contributors to the work sessions required for success. If the executive level does not fully engage with these two assumptions—in the immortal words of the fictional character Tony Soprano—"fuggadaboudit."

While this advice may appear obvious to anyone who has attempted to clearly define and communicate terms—common language—this may be new advice for some in the middle of BA change. Because a new direction reflected in the BA may make great logical sense, that doesn't mean that everyone within the organization will explicitly support the direction, or more importantly, understand the implications for BA implementation.

People represent the greatest potential while at the same time representing the biggest challenge. Although it can be reasonably assumed that executives and related stakeholders (e.g., shareholders, board members, senior management) will focus on strategic goals and supporting BA change to one extent or another, implementation requires a greater level of commitment and engagement from the organization as a whole.

How Does the Organization Structure the DG?

After the BA is adopted and explicit, public endorsement given by executives, a sustainable, ongoing DG structure must be implemented or adapted to adequately support both terms/definitions and related measures. The most common structural model (see Figure 1) reflects three levels:

1. Executive Decision Making.
2. Operational Decision Making.
3. Operational Analysis and Recommendation.

The first level (top of the pyramid)—executive decision making (EDM)—consists of senior management typically including individuals with VP/SVP (Senior VP) titles. They take accountability for large organizations with cost centers directly below enterprise level organized around business functions such as revenue producing division or high level Financial function, The second level—operational decision making (ODM)—represents the middle management layer (s) immediately below the EDM level. They are responsible for the day-to-day operational implementation of the business objectives. The third and lowest level—operational analysis and recommendation (OAR)—represents the frontline management and senior individual contributors. Responsible lies with OAR for the details of data element definition, data analytics delivery, data usage practices, etc.

Data Governance Interaction

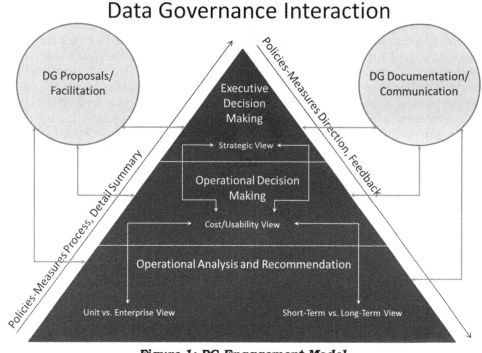

Figure 1: DG Engagement Model

How Does the Interaction Model Work for the Business View?

Figure 1 is divided into two main parts: inside the pyramid—the business view—and outside of it—the DG view. The pyramid represents the analysis, discussions and decisions made by business representatives, typically data stewards, managing data stewards, data executives. Data factors (definitions, usage, cost, etc.) drive these considerations required by the business representatives for BA implementation success. Clearly, this success directly correlates to transformation—including cultural and operational factors—as well as supporting processes, policies with related, detailed procedures and required skills. However, the reality landscape that data paints reflecting the success factors, depends on the reliability of the colors: the "red" of agreed-upon definitions, the "yellow" of common, standard measures and the "green" of implementation resting on the easel of the practical balance between strategy and operations; and finally, DG Interaction acting as the canvas that holds the portrait together.

The first level builds the BA shape and context of the portrait and supplies/communicates the strategic view through direction and feedback based on relevant policies and measures, reflected in the downward arrow on the right side of the pyramid. The EDM level also polishes operational decisions and recommendations with supporting analysis from the ODM and OAR levels. This process provides a key part of EDM deliberations which leads to appropriate, final decisions. Also recommended for the most effective results, pursue active interaction among the three levels via concurrent, face-to-face discussions—with or without DG facilitation. (However, DG facilitation does enable structural support for third party-led discussion along with other assumed supporting techniques such as reusable support tools/processes and standard communication methods.)

Level two—ODM—provides the patterns and color blends that build the core portrait finalizing operational decisions while leveraging OAR recommendations and supporting analysis which balances strategy and detail. While not exclusively considering cost of implementing and maintaining the recommendations and how usable/practical are the end solutions, they form a significant lens through which the portrait will be filtered. Level three—OAR—gives shading and context to the portrait by advocating opposing, critical questions such as how do we best maximize the unit's interest while maintaining the enterprise interests or how do we ensure short-term factors don't overwhelm long-term factors? OAR importantly also acts as the nexus of integrating threads from all aspects of the business at an actionable level. The combination of ODM and OAR communicate to the EDM level a useful, action-based summary of detail and implications for all affected business processes, as reflected in the upward arrow on the left-hand side of the pyramid.

How Does the Interaction Model Work for the DG View?

If the business deliberation and decision making part of the DG structural model provides the content of the BA data portrait, the DG part of the model provides the environment in which the artistic magic occurs—or perhaps more realistically, where the legislative "sausage" is made. Anyone who has experienced the DG process can vouch for its messiness, twists and turns as well as sometimes unexpected results. Human nature and the resultant interaction can easily trump plans, graphs and the best of intentions. This doesn't mean that the vast majority don't want to cooperate and move the organization forward, but it does mean that everyone reflects their own perspective and what they think best represents the interest of the whole.

This reality shouldn't prevent success, rather it should highlight the considerations required for driving plans and subsequent action. The fact remains that most organizations large enough to require BA change, inherently house complexity reflecting that size. Different perspectives are not only driven by size and complexity, they provide a coping mechanism for reflecting the vast landscape that drives the actions necessary for organizational success. And if all these perspectives miraculously align—such as Sales, Engineering, Manufacturing and Finance ending up on the same page—expect the Yankees and Red Sox to peacefully merge, Judge

Judy to join the Supreme Court and QVC to hire Lady Gaga as their new Fashion Hour host.

All perspectives emerging from your organization's culture can be accommodated leveraging four standard DG practices, as visualized in Figure 1:

1. Propose
2. Facilitate (Decide)
3. Document
4. Communicate.

Propose may sound like one of the last steps, not the first step in bringing different perspectives together; however, substitute suggest for propose, not dictate and it seamlessly starts discussions not ends them. Whether the sessions focus on concepts/definitions or measure/monitor, beginning with a blank piece of paper usually kills momentum. For example, proposing a draft of standard terms with concise, yet comprehensive definitions based on initial business input demonstrates planning, initiative, listening and context, all of which encourage productivity. When business participants feel their time productively spent, engagement and consensus rise, with a serious step taken toward accommodating different perspectives amiably.

However, to ensure that the first step toward incorporating various views leads to the next step, DG must lead by facilitating. Effective facilitation leads to practical, prioritized decisions, not just good, conceptual discussions—guiding the participants to a conclusion that satisfies a critical mass of stakeholders, must be a critical assumption for the deliberations. Successful facilitation starts with preparation, in this case by leveraging pre-work in the form of practical proposals. Since most people work better responding to concrete examples, root causes of disagreement are more easily articulated and then remediated through skillful conversation guidance—not direction. Guide better supports facilitation and represents the ability to lead through listening and diplomatic course correction; on the other hand, direct more likely represents pre-ordained points where discussion tends to sound more like a lecture than a question. To be clear, guiding does not imply a lack of discussion objectives or focus, only the flexibility to enable the conclusions emanate from the constituents, not the coordinator. At this point, good facilitation has enabled practical decisions.

Now that productive discussion has occurred, nothing will ensure a dead-end more than a lack of follow-up, especially a lack of documentation. While not necessarily the most exciting task, good documenting techniques—such as an easily updatable and accessible central repository for terms/definitions—drive more thoughtful discussion and more balancing of competing views. In addition, extending the usefulness of the metadata by integrating it with standard reports and other communication techniques helps ensure buy-in from all business functions and all organizational levels. On a related note, providing a standard method for accommodating different perspectives of a term and its related definition increases both consensus and potentially, adherence to standards. This method simply involves leveraging agreed-upon, core terms—such as cost of goods sold (COGS)—for both enterprise and "local" usage. For example, the various DG participants agree that the enterprise definition of COGS be set by Finance and named "Enterprise COGS." However this does not prevent numerous local—or division/unit specific variations of the term as long as the term employs a predicate to ensure clarity for use of the local term. For example, if Division A has a practical reason for a dedicated term for their use, simply agree to document in the repository "Division A COGS" as a standard term with a related definition. Now different perspectives are accommodated and the DG process leverages a practical metadata technique that straddles both facilitation and documentation.

To round out *propose, facilitate* and *document, communicate* propels the business constituents to consensus on usage, related change process and engagement. While communication always tops the "Duh-Obvious" list, execution can easily fall short. After we have spent so much time and energy bringing the various constituent groups to a decision beneficial to both individual units and the enterprise, not communicating the results to all parts and levels of the organization only ensures frustration. And the best approach to communication entails agreement before the start of the process for at least answering how communication will occur, what will be communicated, who will be responsible for communication, who will receive communication and when. The most optimal way of communication leverages current, successful methods integrated with the DG standard processes.

From Common Language to Practical Measures

Of all the techniques that contribute to successful BA implementation described in this chapter, taking inventory and defining terms clearly require little discussion. Most standard DG practices should incorporate them as part of the interaction process. However, setting priorities through understanding how to apply concepts/terms and ensuring a focus on necessary terms deserve some last comments. The DG engagement model sets up a forum with supporting policies and processes that enables applying the right term for the right constituents at the right time. Often a few, well-intentioned individuals take on this role of deciding when and how common language is applied, only to find out much later key constituents did not agree. In addition, these key constituents discover after the fact that precious time and attention was devoted to less important concepts, not the most critical ones. The framework of Propose, Facilitate, Document and Communicate solves focusing on optional activities instead of necessary ones.

A lack of common, agreed-upon language represents one of the most subtle traps for organizations undergoing the transition from one BA—implicitly built through organic activities over time—to another BA based on explicit plans directed by a need for change. This provides a preventable but common example of the organization doing the job right but not doing the right job. When everyone agrees on meaning before tasks start, it avoids re-doing tasks because of conflicting or misunderstood terms. Now measures can produce the necessary, practical actions based on relevant insight.

Relevant, Practical Measures

Just as the DG Engagement Model ensures the organization shares a common language it also ensures BA driven operational objectives are measured appropriately and supported by repeatable process and actionable follow-up. An example might help understand how measurement is supported by the model. As the Millennial generation replaces the Baby Boom generation as a primary economic force, many insurance carriers have switched from exclusively person-to-person (agent) sales channels to more of a balance between agent-driven and self-service, process-driven, indirect sales channels (e.g., web, mobile interaction, social media). This reality contributes to questions that arise from the origin of available data, what a new BA must measure and how it gets measured. In turn, other life-and-death questions arise such as: why was a particular policy purchased and what steps led to the sale? Details once assumed agents would provide now require automated data capture and more importantly, a new kind of context. This new context includes how various functions incorporate this new data into existing measures and what measures now make sense.

While projects deliver new capabilities and address specific application of data, a more holistic view—and integration of all the related disciplines—provides a bigger challenge. The DG Engagement model does not replace project-specific data delivery assuming incorporating standard disciplines such as metadata and data quality. However this model facilitates broader business involvement regarding key questions harder to address by a single project, such as data ownership, consistent application of data and security concerns (e.g., treatment of personally identifiable information). Individual projects may attempt to ensure involvement of the right stakeholders at the right time, normal business operations can drive conflicting priorities that make good intentions problematic.

On the other hand, the DG Engagement model—while far from perfect—provides a regularly-scheduled, structured forum where the various business stakeholders can step back and apply the missing holistic view representing the different perspectives. In the case of new sales channel data, this model promotes discussion and decision making related to what context is relevant for which business functions, what the data means, how the data is integrated with other initiatives. In addition the model enables understanding of the relationship between existing information delivery and how to leverage new data to existing so drive practical insights will drive profitable action. As the new BA spawns various projects to drive implementation, the DG model provides a repeatable, integrated process with standard artifacts ensuring decision making based on the widest possible audience with the broadest view balancing unit vs. enterprise views and short-term vs. long-term views.

Categories and Follow-up

A new BA—as well as other organizational influences—requires a balance between project based data delivery and ongoing data delivery. Subject areas (categories) act as that touchstone ensuring balance between both data forces, while ensuring a holistic perspective that reflects appropriate, consensus-based context as well as necessary, specific measurement. Subject Areas and their related subsets (de-composition) allow various measurements to be categorized in a way that supports practical use by all dependent stakeholders. Subject Areas should be considered as different kind of card catalog delivery—when a book (measure) is created, there is no issue of how to catalog, how to find it and how it relates to everything else in its category. Every data model, report, data feed, data discovery, etc. across every business function inform these Subject Areas by reflecting some organizational context, whether from a unit or corporate perspective. Since different perspectives drive different data usage through measures, these differences raise several related questions:

1. Does this particular context provide value for all stakeholders?
2. Does this particular context make sense for all stakeholders?
3. Was this context applied consistently?
4. If the context is wrong or distorted, what are the consequences?

These questions focus on category because how an organization uses data measures greatly influences decisions and related action plans. In turn, how data relates to Subject Areas influences how measures are perceived as well as how much impact they wield. Leveraging the DG Engagement Model—with supporting processes and artifacts—enables relevant, broad-based Subject Area deliberations and provides a convenient vehicle for productive follow-up.

Effective action is based on appropriate context that drives understanding of where you need to go, how you are doing related to objectives, who needs to be involved in next steps and what are the relevant, practical plans? Much of the literature focuses on methods for determining measurements, recommendations for content and the importance of measurement—however most of these discussions assume internal frameworks exist that will accomplish the required deliberations. The DG Engagement model again provides a standard, scheduled, supported forum for both discussion and decisions. The model doesn't represent the only way to get to follow-up regarding measures, but it does allow the organization to cost effectively extend current methods for a new purpose.

CONCLUSION

To date for most organizations, Data Governance has generally focused on standard data management functions such as data policies, metadata, etc. In contrast, BA activities and related discussions have led a life very separate from DG; for obvious reasons, BA has been treated similarly to other kinds of high-level architecture. Now in an era of great change and the "need for speed," BA requires more of an implementation focus and the DG Engagement model can satisfy this pressing requirement solidifying strong, broad-based business partner consensus and commitment. While delivering a necessary service for the BA process, the model now evolves to the next level of value for the organization.

REFERENCES

(Connor 2015) Michael S. Connor. "Constantly Making Mistakes and Beating My Hard Head Against the Wall from Over 30 Years Working in the Trenches." Cherry Valley, IL: The Imaginary Podunk Press, 2015.

Appendix

Author Appendix

MICHAEL BLAHA

Consultant, Modelsoft Consulting Corp

Michael Blaha is a consultant and trainer who specializes in conceiving, architecting, modeling, designing and tuning databases. He has worked with dozens of organizations around the world. Blaha has authored seven U.S. patents, seven books and many articles. His most recent publication is the Learning Data Modeling video course from O'Reilly Media. He received his doctorate from Washington University in St. Louis, and is an alumnus of GE Global Research in Schenectady, New York. You can find more information with his LinkedIn profile or at superdataguy.com. You can contact him at blaha@computer.org.

JUDE CHAGAS PEREIRA

CEO, IYCON

Jude Chagas-Pereira is an accomplished entrepreneur, with over 20 years experience in business and financial consulting. Jude is the CEO of IYCON, a company founded by him in 2002. IYCON is a transformational technology solutions company, whose mission is to serve businesses and governments, by delivering high quality strategic execution services, through world class technology tools, expertise, best practice methodologies and continued quality support.

IYCON is a leader in improvement & delivery of performance management execution, as well as a preferred performance execution partner for government & private corporations. Over the last twenty years, Jude has led over seventy enterprise projects, covering strategy execution and process optimization.

Under the IYCON banner, Jude has provided cutting edge technologies to his clients, to give them a competitive advantage in the market. He has also conceptualized the IYCON PRISE© methodology for Strategy Execution, which enables organisations to integrate, Strategy, Risks, Process, Initiatives and Quality Models.

Jude has enabled clients such as Dubai Airport Free Zone (DAFZ), Commercial Bank of Dubai, Al Tayer Group, National Bank of Abu Dhabi, Road and Transport Authority - Dubai, Department of Transport - Abu Dhabi, Emirates Global Aluminum, Abu Dhabi Food Control Authority, Camoplast Solideal, LOLC, Public Works Authority (Ash-ghal) Qatar, Du Telecom & Tata Teleservices among others, with IYCON PRISE©. Jude has been a speaker at the Strategy Leaders Summits held in the UAE and Qatar and presented on Risk Integrated Strategy Management, as well as Risk Integrated Process Management. He was recently featured by Forbes on the "Top Indian Leaders in the Arab World 2015: Owners" list.

MICHAEL CONNOR

Manager, Data Governance and Quality, American Family Insurance

Michael Connor is manager of Data Governance and Quality at American Family Insurance, headquartered in Madison, WI. He has over 30 years of management and consulting experience spanning several industries such as insurance, banking and healthcare. Mr. Connor's expertise includes major categories such as data management, application development, process re-engineering, sales/pre-sales and technical education.

MICHAEL POULIN

Head of Business Architecture, Clingstone Ltd.

Dr. Michael Poulin is a Head of Enterprise Architecture at Clingstone Ltd., the consulting firm focused on business change management, enterprise and solutions architecture. He has built up a wealth of experience in architecture in the UK and United States. His work focuses on bridging the gap between business architecture and modern technology. Michael participates in BAWG of WfMC and also contributes into OASIS SOA RM and RAF standards. Michael has also authored three books - Ladder to SOE, Architects Know What Managers Don't: Business Architecture for Dynamic Market and Business Capability in Dynamic

Market. He writes in LinkedIn, ebizQ and own (www.mpoulin.com) BLOGs, publishes White Papers (www.orbussoftware.com) and articles (www.InfoQ.com). He can be reached via michael.poulin@clingstone.co.uk.

NESAT EFENDIOGLU

IT-Project Manager and Researcher, BOC Asset Management GmbH

Mr Nesat Efendioglu holds a Dipl-Ing. degree in business Informatics, is currently working as researcher and IT-Project manager at the consulting company BOC (www.boc-group.com) in Vienna. He is involved in the development of knowledge processing out of conceptual and semantic modelling languages.

Nesat implemented processing algorithms on the ADOxx platform within the EU projects dealing with Knowledge Management in different domains such as FP7 projects; BIVEE, e-SAVE, Learn Pad, eHealthMonitor and currently in H2020 project Cloud Socket. Nesat has experience with development of algorithms for knowledge processing out of conceptual and semantic models. His professional interest includes the engineering and implementation of conceptual and semantic modelling methods and corresponding knowledge processing algorithms for fields Industry 4.0, technology enchanced learning, Big Data and Cloud.

LAYNA FISCHER

Front Matter, Layna Fischer

Ms Fischer is Editor-in-Chief and Publisher since 1993 at Future Strategies Inc., the official publishers to WfMC.org. In 2001-2006, she was additionally Executive Director of WfMC.org and BPMI.org (now merged with OMG) and continues to work closely with these organizations to promote industry awareness of BPM, BPME, BPMN, Knowledge Work, Case Management and more.

Future Strategies Inc. (FutStrat.com and BPM-Books.com) publishes unique books and papers focusing on BPM-based advanced technologies. As such, the company works closely with individual authors and corporations worldwide and also manages the renowned annual Global Awards for Excellence in BPM and the Awards for Excellence in Case Management.

Future Strategies Inc., is the publisher of the ground-breaking business book series New Tools for New Times, the annual Excellence in Practice series of award-winning case studies and the annual BPM Handbook series, published in collaboration with the WfMC. Ms. Fischer has been involved in international IT journalism and publishing for over 20 years.

MARTIN KLUBECK

Strategy & Planning Consultant, University of Notre Dame

Martin Klubeck is a Strategy and Planning Consultant at the University of Notre Dame, where he plays a significant role in strategic planning, metrics, and organi-zational improvement efforts within the Office of Information Technologies and across campus.

Martin is a recognized leader in organizational development, where he focuses on metrics vision setting, and professional development plan-ning. He has helped organizations design, create, and use meaningful metrics programs for more than 10 years. Mr. Klubeck's ability to take the complex and simplify it has made him a highly sought-after teacher, speaker, and consultant. Along with several publications and presentations, he is the e author of Why Organizations Struggle So Hard to Improve So Little: Overcoming Organizational Immaturity, Metrics: how to Improve Key Business Results, and, most recently, The Professional Development Toolbox: Unlocking Simple Truths. He is also the creator of MK Knowledge Builders, offering seminars, webinars, and consulting. Mr. Klubeck holds a master's degree in HR development from Webster University and a bachelor's degree in computer science from Chapman University. He can be reached at mklubeck@nd.edu

FRANK KOWALKOWSKI

President, Knowledge Consultants, Inc.

Frank Kowalkowski is President of Knowledge Consultants, Inc., a firm focusing on business performance, business/IT architecture and business analytical techniques. He has over 30 years of management and consulting experience in a wide variety of industries. He has been involved with many projects including business analysis, process management, business performance measurement, business and competitive intelligence and knowledge management. In addition to being a keynote speaker at international conferences as well as a conference chair, he has written numerous papers and spoken at conferences on a variety of subjects. He is the author of a 1996 book on Enterprise Analysis (Prentice – Hall, ISBN 0-13-282-3365) and numerous papers. Frank is currently working on a both a BPM book for managers and a new edition of the enterprise analysis book. He conducts frequent seminars nationally and internationally on a variety of business management and information technology topics. He is co-author of a quarterly column on architecture for the website TDAN.

WHYNDE KUEHN

Principal, S2E Consulting Inc.

Whynde Kuehn is Principal at S2E Consulting Inc., a consulting firm accelerating successful business transformations. She is a long-time business architecture practitioner, Business Architecture Practice leader, and played a key role in the largest business architecture-led transformation in the world. Based on her experience, Whynde's area of expertise is building and maturing business architecture practices, and using business architecture to achieve real business results.

Ms. Kuehn is a recognized thought-leader in business architecture, and has developed and taught comprehensive, large-scale business architecture training programs for clients and the business architecture community. She is a Co-Founder, Board Member and Editorial Board Member of the Business Architecture Guild.

As a result of her passion for social and environmental change, Whynde is on the Board of Directors of goods for good, an organization dedicated to community enterprise, and she has also founded Metanoia Global Inc. which helps social entrepreneurs start, scale and sustain successful businesses, with a focus in Africa. Through this work, her clients are demonstrating how business can focus on purpose as well as profit, and how enterprise can be a solution to poverty.

J. BRYAN LAIL

Business Architect Fellow, Raytheon Company, USA

J. Bryan Lail is a Business Architect Fellow at Raytheon Company. He works across market pursuits to assess capability gaps for the business from growth strategies and works with a cross-functional team to drive new ways of doing business to fill those gaps. Architecting the business includes rigorous methods for forming new business models, finding new value streams across organizational functions, and innovative use of information to increase probability of win in new markets. Previously Bryan spent three years as the Chief IT Architect driving business discipline into information architecture for Raytheon and teaching business architecture across the enterprise. He was a systems engineer for nineteen years between the Raytheon Company and before that working as a scientist for the Navy at China Lake. He has a Masters in Physics and is a Raytheon Certified Architect, accredited by The Open Group.

MICHAEL LANGTHORNE

Author, Administrator, University of Notre Dame

In addition to working in several administrative capacities at the University of Notre Dame since 1986, Michael Langthorne is the author of numerous articles for professional journals, along with several works of non-fiction and fiction. He is also co-author of "Why Organizations Struggle So Hard to Improve So Little: Overcoming Organizational Immaturity" and the forthcoming "Don't Manage, Coach!"

Gil Laware

President, Information By Design, Llc

Gil Laware is President of Information By Design (IBD), Inc. a professional services firm with practice areas in business performance management, business intelligence, business and enterprise architectures; application and systems development implementations. IBD also provides educational and training services worldwide for various companies. He has 30 years of management and consulting experience with Fortune 50 companies covering many industries: manufacturing, transportation, government, finance and banking services. He has been involved in projects including business analysis, business and IT strategic planning; business process management, redesign and improvement; data architecture and management; business and enterprise architecture; ERP; manufacturing systems; and CRM.

He previously work for Fijitsu Consulting, Whirlpool Corporation, Franklin Savings Bank, and held various managerial and consultative roles with the IBM Corporation. He was an Associate Professor in the College of Technology at Purdue University and adjunct faculty member at Iona College's Hagan School of Business. He has been a speaker at many business and educational conferences. As a co-author of a quarterly column on architecture for the website TDAN, Gil has authored over 40 papers other articles including a NIST chapter discussing the gaps that exist in the software development process that support manufacturing systems. He has also served on the Board of Directors of DAMA International and the DAMA Education and Research Foundation.

Patrik Maltusch

Head of EA Architecture Team, Aalto University

Patrik Maltusch is heading the EA architecture team at Aalto University. He is also acting member of the Finnish national enterprise architecture special interest group and one of the lead educators who have coached administration staff in the national wide Higher Education EA schooling program. Past experience include working as a customer service instructor for nearly ten years and a further fifteen years as network architect and business owner for internal infrastructure design in a global Telco company.

Patrik is also a distinguished and accredited security professional, risk manager, system auditor and a certified Higher Education Enterprise Architect. As entrepreneur and start up facilitator Patrik understands what staying practical means for business.

For Patrik, interoperability is the key to success in an ever growing and more complex ecosystem landscape. Something that can be achieved using EA methodology in a more visualized way.

Michael Miller

Global Information Architect, HSBC

Michael G. Miller is a member of the HSBC Global Finance IT Architecture and Strategy team acting as a Global Information Architect. He has responsibilities for enterprise architecture guidance of Global Finance projects.

Mr. Miller has over 35 years of IT experience in banking, securities and insurance starting in his career computer operations, programming and systems design, and then moving on to consulting roles in enterprise architecture and business intelligence. Michael's previous consulting roles include National Director of Enterprise Architecture and Business Intelligence, Executive Consultant CRM COE, and Principal - Management Consultant. He also teaches classes in Strategic Business Intelligence Implementation and Data Governance in Dubai, UAE.

He holds a BBA and four master degrees (MBA, MPM, MTM, & MISM) and has done over two years of doctoral work in Knowledge Management. He is a board member of the Data Management Association – Chicago Chapter, a Certified LEAN Six Sigma Yellow Belt (ISCEA), a Certified Business Process Management Professional (ABPMP) and a Certified TOGAF Enterprise Architect.

VIRPI NIEMINEN

EA Business Development Manager, QPR Software

Virpi Nieminen is the Business Development Manager at QPR Software in charge of growing QPR's global network of local reselling partners. Supporting partners globally is a natural extension to her consulting experience in operational excellence through the different roles she has held in the past in project management, internal control compliance, and enterprise architecture as a business analyst. Her past projects have involved private sector initiatives, as well as public sector initiatives on both EU member state level and on the supranational level at the European Commission.

Virpi is certified in TOGAF, PRINCE2, and ITIL; and in her consulting days, she frequently participated in the workshops organized by the European Committee for Standardization (CEN). Consequently, Virpi has an appreciation for common specifications, yet an understanding of the need for their customization in practical implementations to fit different business needs and governance models. Virpi holds a Master's degree in Management Science from Solvay Business School. Before her post-graduate studies in Belgium, she studied business management in Germany, Finland, and the USA.

QPR Software Plc is a publicly listed (NASDAQ OMX) software vendor providing world-class solutions for strategy execution, performance management, and process excellence with over 20-years of experience. QPR's comprehensive software offering is highly recognized by distinguished technology analysts, such as Gartner. QPR's products have 1,500+ customers from over 50 countries with more than a million licenses sold to date.

DON PADGETT

University of Notre Dame

Don Padgett has been co-authoring books, articles and hosting workshops and seminars focused on organizational development for nearly two decades.

In 1996, Don intermixed 15 years of IT sales and marketing management experience in corporate America with academic IT support when he accepted a position with the Information Technologies department at the University of Notre Dame. Three years later, he was presenting at conferences, in 2006 he co-hosted his first full day pre-conference workshop on metrics which spurred the relationship and basis of the book, "Why Organizations Struggle so Hard to Achieve so Little: Organizational Immaturity." In March, 2012 he co-lead a presentation titled "Measuring the Present: The Answer Key," which featured a section from the book. Since then he's been a regular presenter at regional and international conventions covering a variety of organizational development topics.

In addition to his work at the University he co-owns and operates Play Like A Champion Today, Inc. http://www.plact.com which offers a variety of ways for individuals, management and leadership to promote "champion" level performance.

Don is a charter Board Member of The Consortium for the Establishment of Information Technology Performance Standards (CEITPS). CEITPS was established to create standards for IT performance to fill the void that currently exists. Don continues to work at his passion for helping others achieve professional excellence and for promoting value-add recognition at home and work. You can reach him at don@plact.com.

ALFONSO PIERANTONIO

Associate Professor in Computer Science, University of L'Aquila

Alfonso Pierantonio is Associate Professor in Computer Science at the University of L'Aquila (Italy). His current research interests include Model-Driven Engineering with a specific emphasis on coupled evolution and bidirectionality. Alfonso has been involved in several national and international projects including FP7 Learn PAd, EU-FP7 Ossmeter, EU-FP7 Mancoosi (workpackage leader, 2008-2011). He has been on the program, steering, or organization committees of many international conferences. Alfonso is a member of the editorial boards of Systems and Software Modeling (Springer) and Special Issue Editor of the Journal of Object Technology. He published more than 100 papers in international scientific conferences and journals. He is currently director of the Master in Web Technology degree program.

STEPHANIE RAMSAY

Services Architect, Raytheon Company, USA

Stephanie Ramsay is an Information Technology (IT) professional with thirty+ years of experience in three industries (Retail, Healthcare and Defense). She has extensive experience in the areas of Service Delivery and Application Development. In recent positions at Raytheon, she has been responsible for implementing portfolio processes to manage the lifecycle of services. She has also been involved in architecting end to end services to integrate processes that have dependencies across several functional organizations. She holds a Bachelor of Science in Business Administration from the University of Phoenix and a Masters degree in Supply Chain Management from Penn State.

DAVID RICE

EA Frameworks, LLC

David Rice has over 25 years of experience in Enterprise Architecture, Data Architecture, Business Process Engineering and related consulting, training, mentoring and software product development. David has worked with clients across a range of industries and with clients at the national, state and local government levels. Mr. Rice has utilized many commercial modeling tools across a range of disciplines to aid his clients in the areas of Enterprise Architecture, Business Process Reengineering, Data Architecture, and the development of architecture based decision support systems. As an accomplished software engineer, Mr. Rice has also managed product development of several commercial modeling tools implementing the Zachman Enterprise Architecture Framework, the DoD Architecture Framework (DoDAF) and the Federal Architecture Framework (FEAF).

BRIAN SEITZ

Principle Enterprise Architect, Intellectual Arbitrage Group

Brian Seitz is a Principal Enterprise Architect specializing in IT Business Strategy, Design and Operations within Microsoft. With a broad base of knowledge and experience, Brian spends the majority of his time assisting others in developing and applying insights to increase the value and controllability of Information Technology.

His current focus is on R&D of the Next Generation of IT. This includes Business Model Design and Reengineering, IT Finance and Economics, IT Service Management, Business Continuity/Disaster Recovery, and Change Management. Brian has been in Architecture and Design fields for over four decades as a thought leader, initially starting in with residential design, migrating to mechanical and aerospace engineering and finally to Enterprise Architecture. Additionally he has established and deployed formal practices for major corporations around the world in Strategy, Marketing Planning, Economic Justification, and Enterprise Architecture and provided guidance and oversight for various technology standards in use today.

Prior to rejoining Microsoft, Brian was on a two year engagement establishing a shared services organization for a Federal Legal Department. During that time he implemented a Service Catalog and Order Management system using SharePoint that is in use today. Leading the ITIL Practice for the firm as well as mentoring five consultants (Senior and Junior). Simultaneously, he had been an Industry Analyst in the CAD, AEC and EDA industries writing and presenting at various conferences and consulting to Fortune 500 corporations. Within the MSIT organization Brian is best known for his voracious appetite for reading, learning and sharing knowledge.

RALPH SHAW

IT Chief Architect, Raytheon Company, USA

Ralph Shaw is the IT Chief Architect within Raytheon Integrated Defense Systems, and a member of the Strategy and Architecture group within Information Technology. In his 35 years with Raytheon, he had been a member of Software Engineering technical staff, led the

IT Infrastructure organization, led/participated in numerous strategic initiatives, technology innovation projects, and mergers and acquisition assessments. Over the past 15 years, he has represented the Business to the Raytheon Enterprise Architecture committees, increased IT adoption and awareness of architectural concepts and practices, and has most recently been leading efforts within IDS to apply Business Architecture to new business growth opportunities

DARIUS SILINGAS

Head of Solutions Department, No Magic Europe

Darius Silingas is a Head of Solutions Department at No Magic Europe, a vendor of a famous modeling platform MagicDraw. He focuses on helping No Magic customers to establish effective business architecture modeling solutions based on MagicDraw. Darius delivered hundreds training & consulting sessions worldwide, spoke at numerous conferences and wrote a number of articles on business and systems modeling. Recently, he acts as a dissemination and technology transfer leader in a research project Learn PAd (http://www.learnpad.eu), which aims to implement an innovative approach enabling public administrations to become process-oriented learning organizations. Darius has got Ph.D. in Informatics and is OMG Certified Expert in BPM.

KEITH SWENSON

VP of Research & Development, Fujitsu America, USA, Chair WfMC

Keith Swenson is Vice President of Research and Development at Fujitsu North America and also the Chairman of the Workflow Management Coalition. As a speaker, author, and contributor to many workflow and BPM standards, he is known for having been a pioneer in collaboration software and web services. He has led agile software development teams at MS2, Netscape, Ashton Tate & Fujitsu. He won the 2004 *Marvin L. Manheim Award* for outstanding contributions in the field of workflow. Co-author on more than 10 books. His latest book, "When Thinking Matters in the Workplace," explains how to avoid stifling creativity and enhance innovation through the appropriate use of process technology. His 2010 book "Mastering the Unpredictable" introduced and defined the field of adaptive case management and established him as a Top Influencer in the field of case management. He blogs at http://social-biz.org/.

BARBARA THÖNSSEN

Dean of Master of Science in Business Information Systems, University of Applied Sciences and Arts Northwestern Switzerland

Barbara Thönssen is a full professor and senior researcher with the Business Information Systems Department at the University of Applied Sciences and Arts - Northwestern Switzerland (FHNW). She did her PhD at the University of Camerino in the Dipartmento di Matematica e Informatica, where her thesis focused on automatic, format-independent generation of metadata for documents based on semantically enriched context information. She started her professional work in the field of natural language processing, developing electronic dictionaries to be used for spelling checking and automatic indexing. She was leading projects in electronic archiving, document management and workflow management for a number of large Swiss banks. She was responsible for E¬-Government and electronic archiving solutions for the Zurich City Council. In 2004, she joined FHNW where she lectures on Business Information Systems and is responsible for their Certificate of Advanced Studies for Information and Records Management. She is currently engaged in several national and international research projects like Learn PAd. Her current research focuses on bringing semantic technologies into practice.

WILLIAM ULRICH

President, TSG, Inc.

William Ulrich is President of TSG, Inc., a management consulting firm that delivers strategic transformation planning services to businesses worldwide. He is a thought leader on business architecture and leading authority on strategic business / IT transformation. Mr.

Ulrich is also President and Co-founder of the Business Architecture Guild, a mutual benefit member organization dedicated to standardizing and promoting business architecture worldwide. Mr. Ulrich has been a driving force behind the evolution of *A Guide to the Business Architecture Body of Knowledge*™ (BIZBOK® Guide) and the Certified Business Architect (CBA)® global certification program.

Mr. Ulrich is co-author of *Business Architecture: The Art and Practice of Business Transformation* (MK Press) and *Information Systems Transformation: Architecture-Driven Modernization Case Studies* (Morgan Kaufmann Elsevier). He serves as Co-chair of the OMG Architecture-Driven Modernization Task Force and Business Architecture SIG. In addition, Mr. Ulrich is a Senior Consultant and major content contributor with the Cutter Consortium. Prior to founding TSG, Mr. Ulrich served in a senior management capacity at KPMG, serving as KPMG's Director, Reengineering Strategies prior to leaving and forming TSG, Inc. in 1990.

ROBERT WOITSCH

Managing Director for Innovation Management, BOC Asset Management

Robert Woitsch holds a PhD in business informatics and is currently responsible as managing director for innovation management via European and National research projects at the consulting company BOC (www.boc-group.com) in Vienna. He deals with concept modelling and knowledge management -projects since 2000 starting with the EU-funded projects ADVISOR, PROMOTE and EKMF and has recently been working within the EU-projects like Akogrimo, LD-Cast, Brein, AsIsKnown, MATURE and coordinated plugIT and coordinates CloudSocket. Currently he deals with the EU-projects Learn PAd and ITSME4SMEs in the domain of technology enhanced learning. Dr. Woitsch is involved in commercial KM projects for skill management and knowledge balances and was a member of the Austrian Standardization Institute. Beside his engagement at BOC he teaches at the Department of Knowledge and Business Engineering at the Faculty of Computer Science at the University of Vienna. He published about 40 papers and is involved as reviewer and member of programme committees in KM-conferences.

WfMC Structure and Membership Information

WHAT IS THE WORKFLOW MANAGEMENT COALITION?

The Workflow Management Coalition (WfMC), founded in August 1993, is a non-profit, international organization of BPM and workflow vendors, users, analysts and university/research groups.

The Coalition's mission is to promote and develop the use of collaborative technologies such as workflow, BPM and case management through the establishment of standards for software terminology, interoperability and connectivity among products and to publicize successful use cases.

WORKFLOW STANDARDS FRAMEWORK

The Coalition has developed a framework for the establishment of workflow standards. This framework includes five categories of interoperability and communication standards that will allow multiple collaboration products to coexist and interoperate within a user's environment. Technical details are included in the white paper entitled, "The Work of the Coalition," available at www.wfmc.org.

ACHIEVEMENTS

The initial work of the Coalition focused on publishing the Reference Model and Glossary, defining a common architecture and terminology for the industry. A major milestone was achieved with the publication of the first versions of the Workflow API (WAPI) specification, covering the Workflow Client Application Interface, and the Workflow Interoperability specification.

In addition to a series of successful tutorials industry wide, the WfMC invested many person-years over the past 20 years helping to drive awareness, understanding and adoption of XPDL, now the standard means for business process definition in over 80 BPM products. As a result, it has been cited as the most deployed BPM standard by a number of industry analysts, and continues to receive a growing amount of media attention.

Workflow Reference Model

The Workflow Reference Model was published first in 1995 and still forms the basis of most BPM and workflow software systems in use today. It was developed from the generic workflow application structure by identifying the interfaces which enable products to interoperate at a variety of levels.

All workflow systems contain a number of generic components which interact in a defined set of ways; different products will typically exhibit different levels of capability within each of these generic components. To achieve interoperability between workflow products a standardized set of interfaces and data interchange formats between such components is necessary.

A number of distinct interoperability scenarios can then be constructed by reference to such interfaces, identifying different levels of functional conformance as appropriate to the range of products in the market.

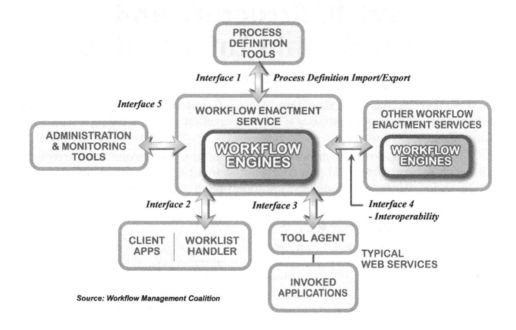

WORKFLOW REFERENCE MODEL DIAGRAM

XPDL (XML Process Definition Language)

An XML based language for describing a process definition, developed by the WfMC. Version 1.0 was released in 2002. Version 2.0 was released in Oct 2005. The goal of XPDL is to store and exchange the process diagram, to allow one tool to model a process diagram, and another to read the diagram and edit, another to "run" the process model on an XPDL-compliant BPM engine, and so on.

For this reason, XPDL is not an executable programming language like BPEL, but specifically a process design format that literally represents the "drawing" of the process definition. Thus it has 'XY' or vector coordinates, including lines and points that define process flows. This allows an XPDL to store a one-to-one representation of a BPMN process diagram.

For this reason, XPDL is effectively the file format or "serialization" of BPMN, as well as any non-BPMN design method or process model which use in their underlying definition the XPDL meta-model (there are presently about 60 tools which use XPDL for storing process models.)

In spring 2012, the WfMC completed XPDL 2.2 as the *fifth* revision of this specification. XPDL 2.2 builds on version 2.1 by introducing support for the process modeling extensions added to BPMN 2.0.

BPSim

The Business Process Simulation (BPSim) framework is a standardized specification that allows business process models captured in either BPMN or XPDL to be augmented with information in support of rigorous methods of analysis. It defines the parameterization and interchange of process analysis data allowing structural and capacity analysis of process models.

BPSim is meant to support both pre-execution and post-execution optimization of said process models. The BPSim specification consists of an underlying computer-interpretable representation (meta-model) and an accompanying electronic file format to ease the safeguard and transfer of this data between different tools (interchange format).

Wf-XML

Wf-XML is designed and implemented as an extension to the OASIS Asynchronous Service Access Protocol (ASAP). ASAP provides a standardized way that a program can start and monitor a program that might take a long time to complete. It provides the capability to monitor the running service, and be informed of changes in its status.

Wf-XML extends this by providing additional standard web service operations that allow sending and retrieving the "program" or definition of the service which is provided. A process engine has this behavior of providing a service that lasts a long time, and also being programmable by being able to install process definitions.

Awards

The Workflow Management Coalition sponsors three annual award programs.

1. The **Global Awards for Excellence in BPM & Workflow**[1] recognizes organizations that have implemented particularly innovative workflow solutions. Every year between 10 and 15 BPM and workflow solutions are recognized in this manner.
   WfMC publishes the case studies in the annual Excellence in Practice [2] series.

2. WfMC inaugurated a Global Awards program in 2011 for **Excellence in Case Management**[3] case studies to recognize and focus upon successful use cases for coordinating unpredictable work patterns. Awards are given in the category of Production Case Management and in Adaptive Case Management which are both new technological approaches to supporting knowledge work in today's leading edge organizations. These awards are designed to highlight the best examples of technology to support knowledge workers.
   Several books[4] have been published recognizing the winning teams. In 2013, WfMC updated the program to "WfMC Awards for Excellence in Case Management" to recognize the growing deployment of Production Case Management.

3. The **Marvin L. Manheim Award For Significant Contributions** in the Field of Workflow is given to one person every year in recognition of individual contributions to workflow and BPM standards. This award commemorates Marvin Manheim who played a key motivational role in the founding of the WfMC.

---

[1] BPM Awards: www.BPMF.org

[2] *Delivering BPM Excellence:* Published 2013 by Future Strategies Inc. http://futstrat.com/books/Delivering_BPM.php

[3] Case Management Awards: www.adaptivecasemanagement.org

[4] *Empowering Knowledge Workers:* Published 2013 by Future Strategies Inc. http://futstrat.com/books/EmpoweringKnowledgeWorkers.php

How Knowledge Workers Get Things Done. Published 2012 by Future Strategies Inc. http://www.futstrat.com/books/HowKnowledgeWorkers.php

Taming the Unpredictable: Published 2011 by Future Strategies Inc .http://futstrat.com/books/eip11.php

The Workflow Management Coalition gives you the unique opportunity to participate in the creation of standards for the workflow industry as they are developing.

Your contributions to our community ensure that progress continues in the adoption of royalty-free workflow and process standards.

THE SECRETARIAT

Workflow Management Coalition (WfMC)

www.WfMC.org

Index

Additional Reading and Resources

NEW E-BOOK SERIES

Download PDF immediately and start reading. ***Only $9.97 each***

- Introduction to BPM and Workflow
  http://bpm-books.com/products/ebook-series-introduction-to-bpm-and-workflow

- Financial Services
  http://bpm-books.com/products/ebook-series-financial-services

- Healthcare
  http://bpm-books.com/products/ebook-series-bpm-in-healthcare

- Utilities and Telecommunications
  http://bpm-books.com/products/ebook-series-utilities-and-telecommunications

NON-PROFIT ASSOCIATIONS AND RELATED STANDARDS RESEARCH ONLINE

- AIIM (Association for Information and Image Management)
  http://www.aiim.org
- BPM and Workflow online news, research, forums
  http://bpm.com
- BPM Research at Stevens Institute of Technology
  http://www.bpm-research.com
- Business Process Management Initiative
  http://www.bpmi.org *see* Object Management Group
- IEEE (Electrical and Electronics Engineers, Inc.)
  http://www.ieee.org
- Institute for Information Management (IIM)
  http://www.iim.org
- ISO (International Organization for Standardization)
  http://www.iso.ch
- Object Management Group
  http://www.omg.org
- Open Document Management Association
  http://nfocentrale.net/dmware
- Organization for the Advancement of Structured Information Standards
  http://www.oasis-open.org
- Society for Human Resource Management
  http://www.shrm.org
- Society for Information Management
  http://www.simnet.org
- Wesley J. Howe School of Technology Management
  http://howe.stevens.edu/research/research-centers/business-process-innovation
- Workflow And Reengineering International Association (WARIA)
  http://www.waria.com
- Workflow Management Coalition (WfMC)
  http://www.wfmc.org
- Workflow Portal
  http://www.e-workflow.org

THRIVING ON ADAPTABILITY: BEST PRACTICES FOR KNOWLEDGE WORKERS

http://futstrat.com/books/ThrivingOnAdaptability.php

ACM helps organizations focus on improving or optimizing the line of interaction where our people and systems come into direct contact with customers. It's a whole different thing; a new way of doing business that enables organizations to literally become one living-breathing entity via collaboration and adaptive data-driven biological-like operating systems. ACM is not just another acronym or business fad. ACM is the process, strategy, framework, and set of tools that enables this evolution and maturity: *Surendra Reddy, Foreword*

EMPOWERING KNOWLEDGE WORKERS: *NEW WAYS TO LEVERAGE CASE MANAGEMENT*

http://futstrat.com/books/EmpoweringKnowledgeWorkers.php

Empowering Knowledge Workers describes the work of managers, decision makers, executives, doctors, lawyers, campaign managers, emergency responders, strategists, and many others who have to think for a living.

These are people who figure out what needs to be done, at the same time that they do it, and there is a new approach to support this presents the logical starting point for understanding how to take advantage of ACM

Retail #49.95 (see discount on website)

TAMING THE UNPREDICTABLE

http://futstrat.com/books/eip11.php

The core element of Adaptive Case Management (ACM) is the support for real-time decision-making by knowledge workers.

Taming the Unpredictable presents the logical starting point for understanding how to take advantage of ACM. This book goes beyond talking about concepts, and delivers actionable advice for embarking on your own journey of ACM-driven transformation.

Retail #49.95 (see discount on website)

HOW KNOWLEDGE WORKERS GET THINGS DONE

http://www.futstrat.com/books/HowKnowledgeWorkers.php

How Knowledge Workers Get Things Done describes the work of managers, decision makers, executives, doctors, lawyers, campaign managers, emergency responders, strategist, and many others who have to think for a living. These are people who figure out what needs to be done, at the same time that they do it, and there is a new approach to support this presents the logical starting point for understanding how to take advantage of ACM.

Retail $49.95 (see discount offer on website)

DELIVERING BPM EXCELLENCE

http://futstrat.com/books/Delivering_BPM.php

Business Process Management in Practice

The companies whose case studies are featured in this book have proven excellence in their creative and successful deployment of advanced BPM concepts. These companies focused on excelling in *innovation, implementation* and *impact* when installing BPM and workflow technologies. The positive impact includes increased revenues, more productive and satisfied employees, product enhancements, better customer service and quality improvements.
$39.95 (see discount on website)

DELIVERING THE CUSTOMER-CENTRIC ORGANIZATION

http://futstrat.com/books/Customer-Centric.php
The ability to successfully manage the customer value chain across the life cycle of a customer is the key to the survival of any company today. Business processes must react to changing and diverse customer needs and interactions to ensure efficient and effective outcomes.

This important book looks at the shifting nature of consumers and the workplace, and how BPM and associated emergent technologies will play a part in shaping the companies of the future. **Retail $39.95**

BPMN 2.0 Handbook SECOND EDITION
(see two-BPM book bundle offer on website: get BPMN Reference Guide Free)

http://futstrat.com/books/bpmnhandbook2.php

Updated and expanded with exciting new content!

Authored by members of WfMC, OMG and other key participants in the development of BPMN 2.0, the BPMN 2.0 Handbook brings together worldwide thought-leaders and experts in this space. Exclusive and unique contributions examine a variety of aspects that start with an introduction of what's new in BPMN 2.0, and look closely at interchange, analytics, conformance, optimization, simulation and more. **Retail $75.00**

BPMN MODELING AND REFERENCE GUIDE

(see two-BPM book bundle offer on website: get BPMN Reference Guide Free)

http://www.futstrat.com/books/BPMN-Guide.php

Understanding and Using BPMN
How to develop rigorous yet understandable graphical representations of business processes.

Business Process Modeling Notation (BPMN) is a standard, graphical modeling representation for business processes. It provides an easy to use, flow-charting notation that is independent of the implementation environment.
Retail $39.95

iBPMS - INTELLIGENT BPM SYSTEMS

http://www.futstrat.com/books/iBPMS_Handbook.php

"The need for Intelligent Business Operations (IBO) supported by intelligent processes is driving the need for a new convergence of process technologies lead by the iBPMS. The iBPMS changes the way processes help organizations keep up with business change," notes Gartner Emeritus Jim Sinur in his Foreword.

The co-authors of this important book describe various aspects and approaches of iBPMS with regard to impact and opportunity. **Retail $59.95 (see discount on website)**

Social BPM

http://futstrat.com/books/handbook11.php

Work, Planning, and Collaboration Under the Impact of Social Technology

Today we see the transformation of both the look and feel of BPM technologies along the lines of social media, as well as the increasing adoption of social tools and techniques democratizing process development and design. It is along these two trend lines; the evolution of system interfaces and the increased engagement of stakeholders in process improvement, that Social BPM has taken shape.

Retail $59.95 (see discount offer on website)

BPM EVERYWHERE

Internet of Things, Process of Everything

http://www.BPMEverywhere.com

We are entering an entirely new phase of BPM – the era of "*BPM Everywhere*" or **BPME**.

This book discusses critical issues currently facing BPM adopters and practitioners, such as the key roles played by process mining uncovering engagement patterns and the need for process management platforms to coordinate interaction and control of smart devices.

BPME represents the strategy for leveraging, not simply surviving but fully exploiting the wave of disruption facing every business over the next 5 years and beyond.

Get 25% Discount on ALL Books in our Store.

Please use the discount code **SPEC25** to get **25% discount** on ALL books in our store; both Print and Digital Editions (two discount codes cannot be used together).
www.FutStrat.com

http://bpm-books.com